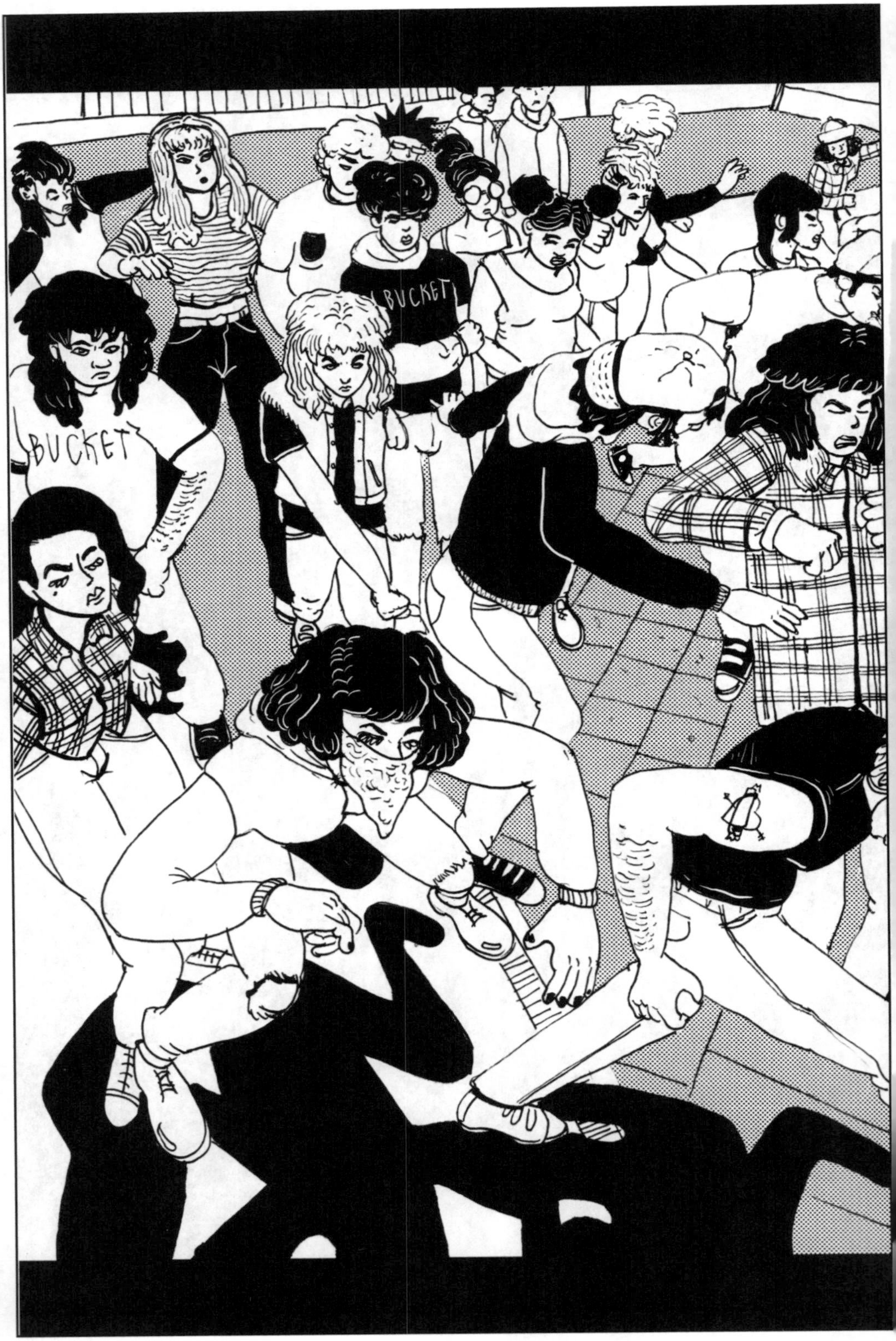
BUCKET
BUCKET

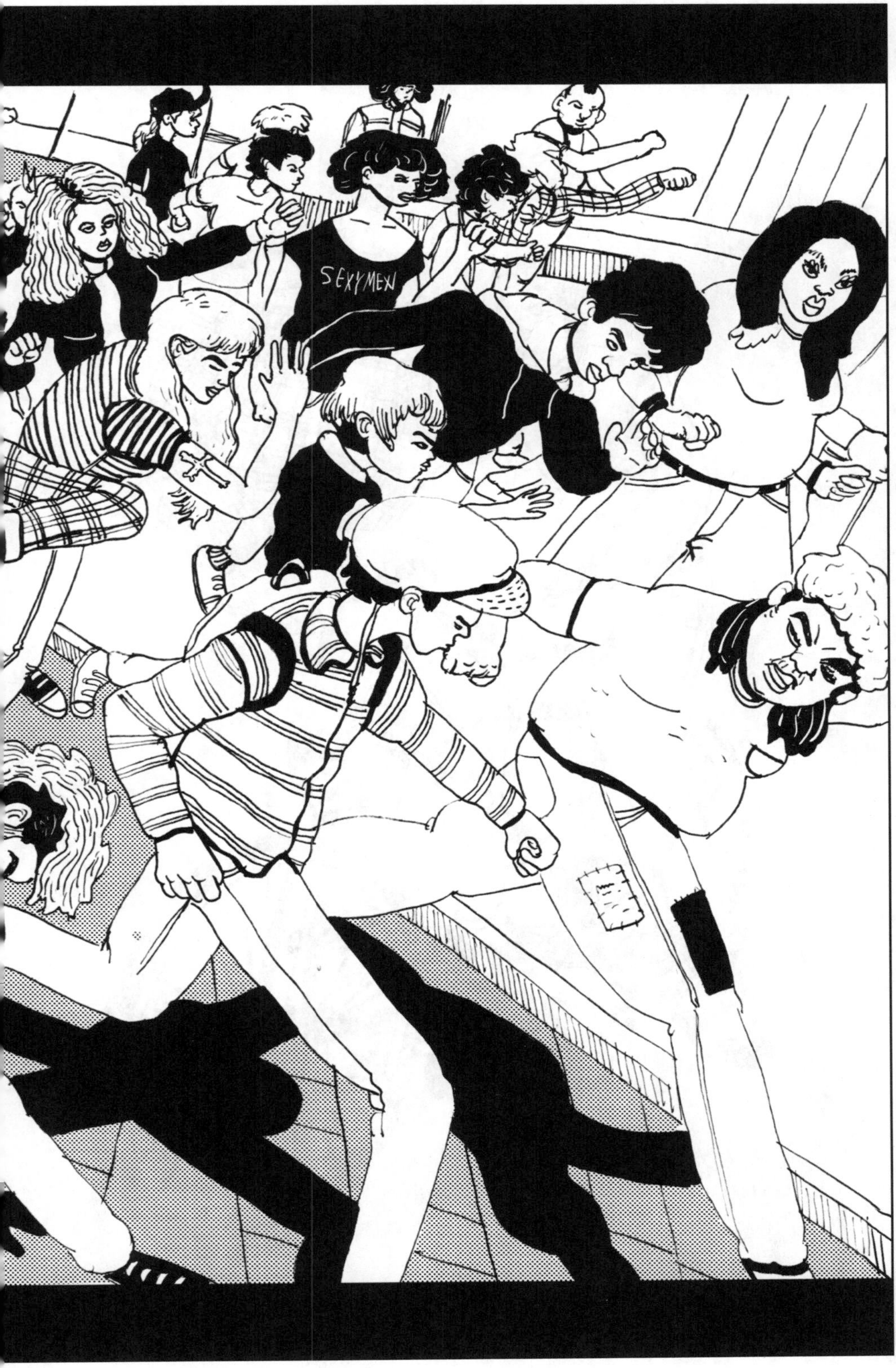
SEXYMEN

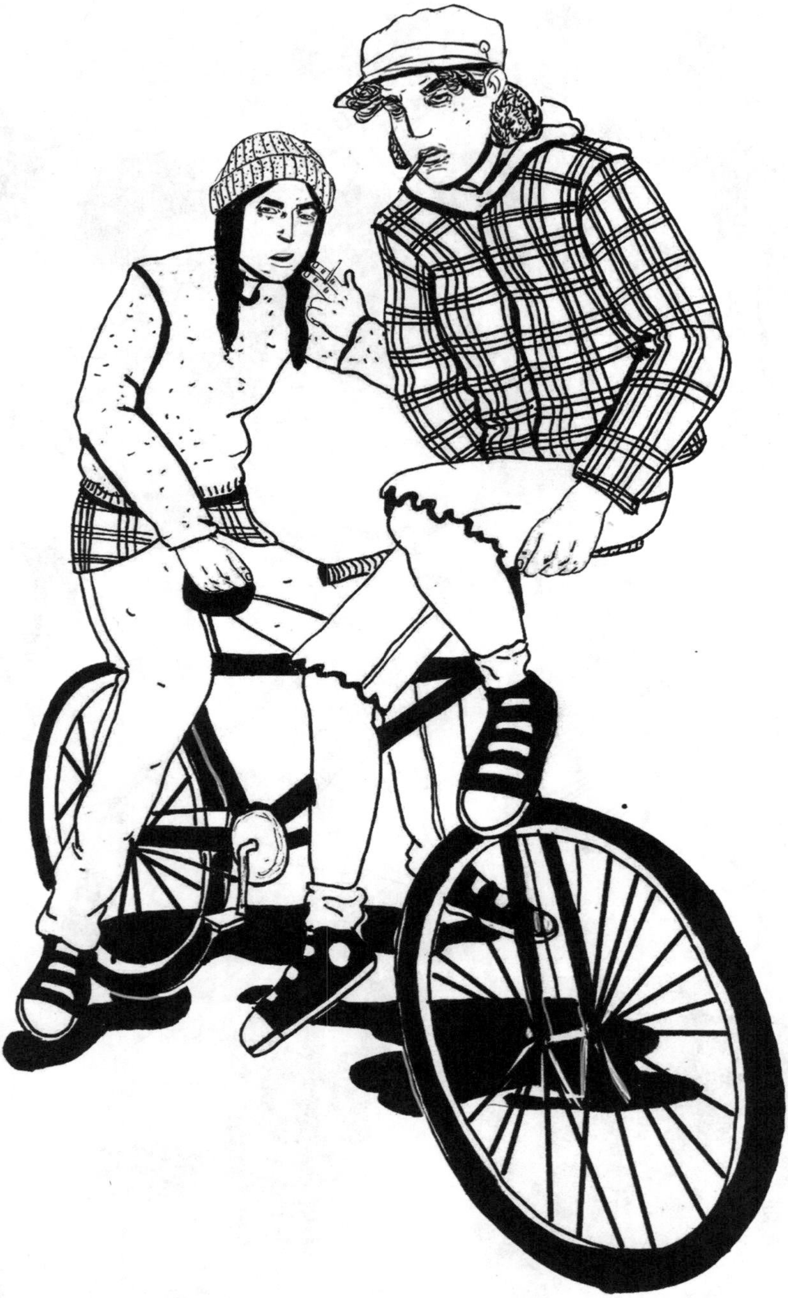

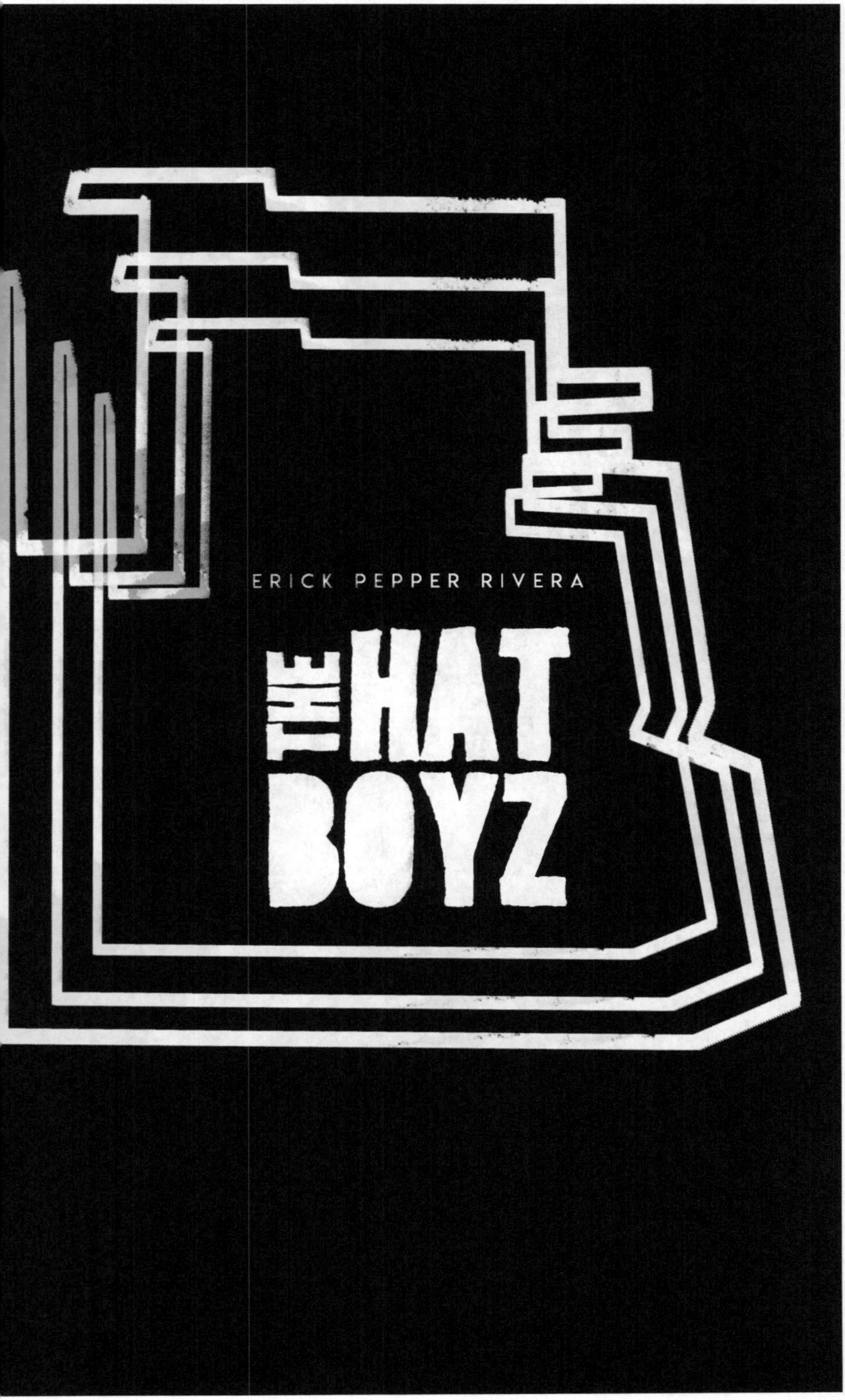
ERICK PEPPER RIVERA
THE HAT
BOYZ

The Hat Boyz
Text and Images © Erick Pepper Rivera 2019

ISBN: 978-1-64273-037-1

Written and illustrated by Erick Pepper Rivera
Cover design by Richard Rodriguez
Published by One Peace Books 2019

Printed in Canada
1 2 3 4 5 6 7 8 9 10

One Peace Books
43-32 22nd Street STE 204 Long Island City New York 11101
www.onepeacebooks.com

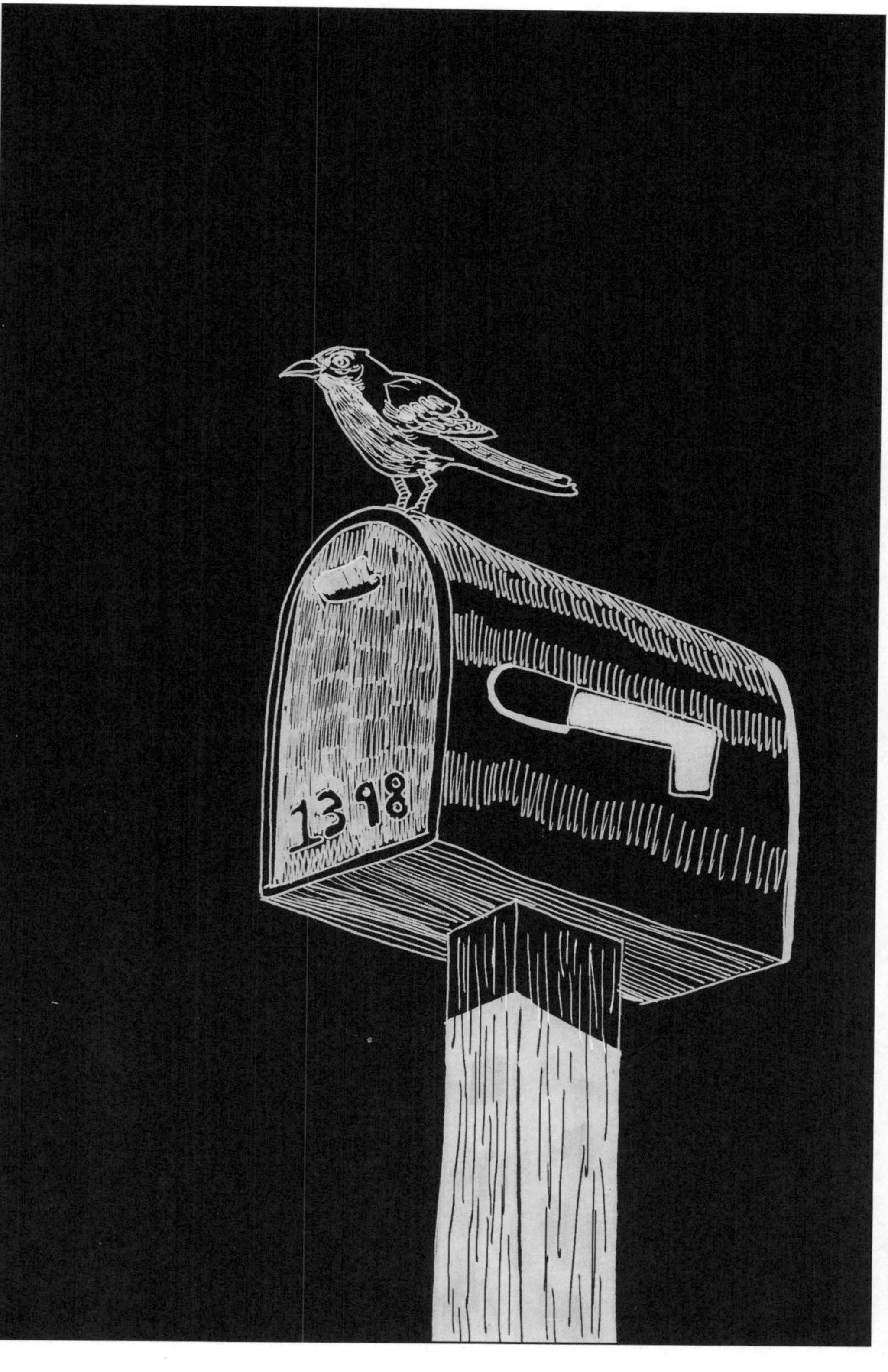
1398

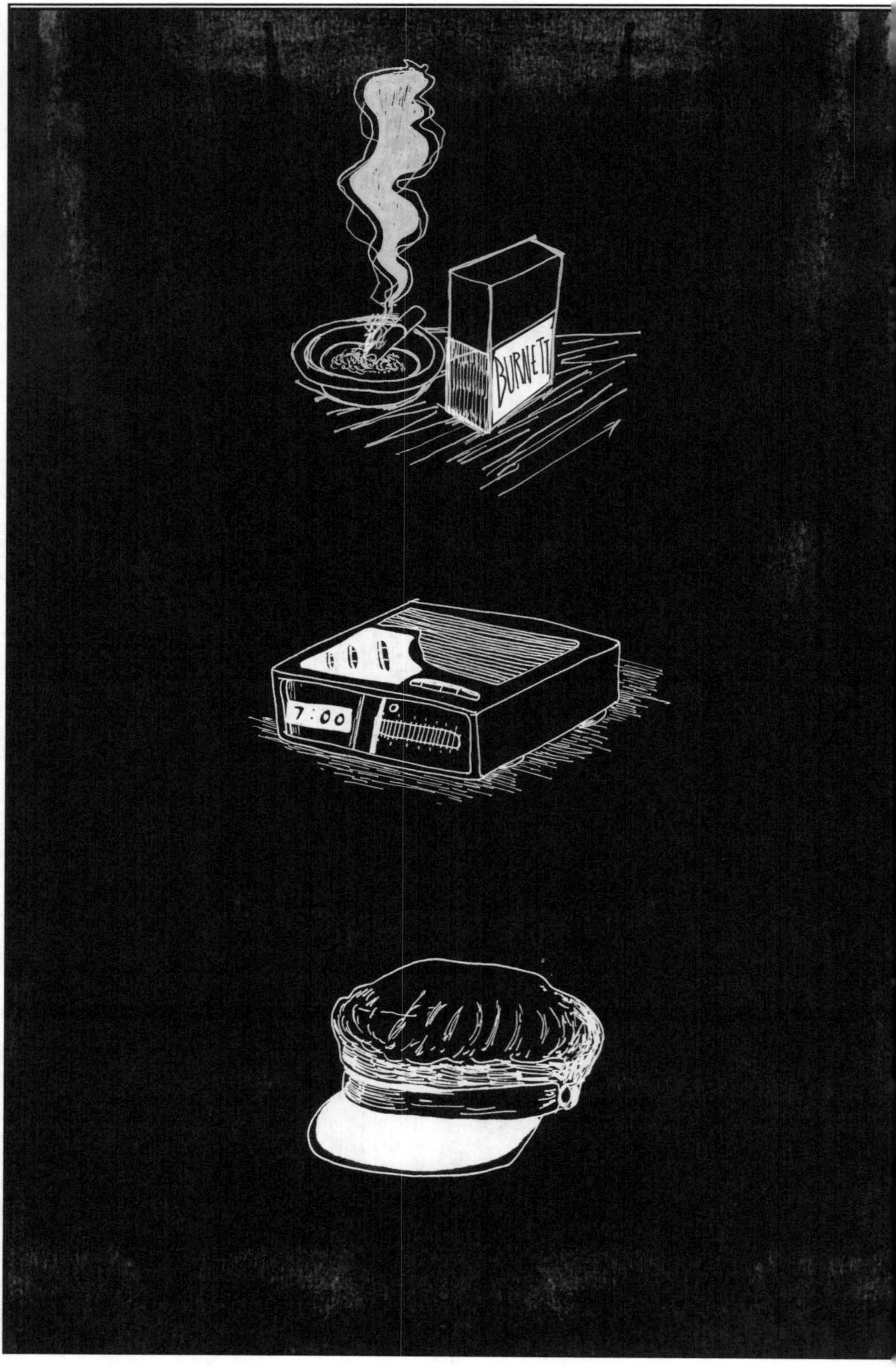
BURNETT
7:00

1398 E. 109th Street

WATTS, CALIFORNIA. MONDAY MORNING

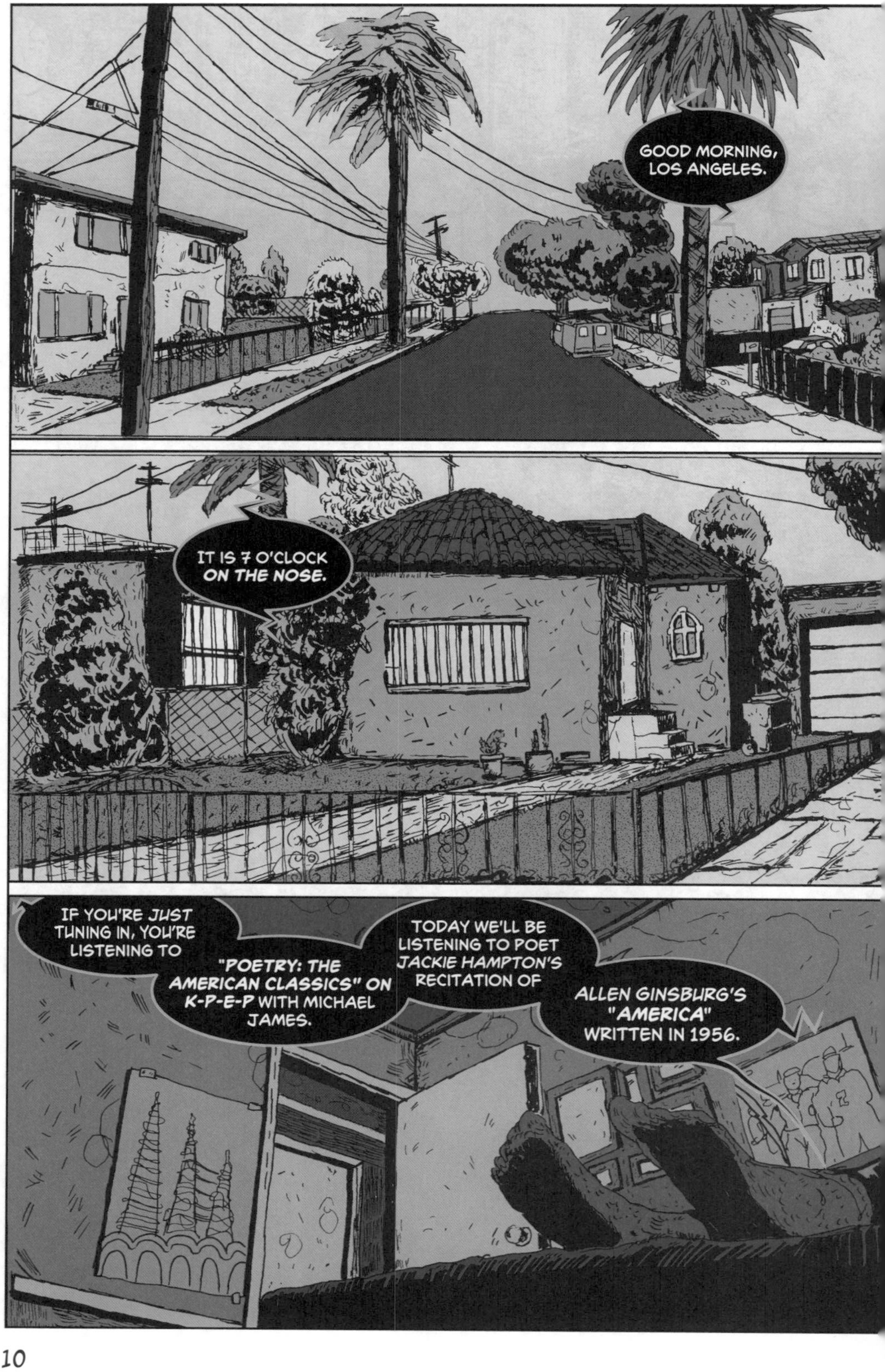
GOOD MORNING, LOS ANGELES.
IT IS 7 O'CLOCK ON THE NOSE.
IF YOU'RE JUST TUNING IN, YOU'RE LISTENING TO
"POETRY: THE AMERICAN CLASSICS" ON K-P-E-P WITH MICHAEL JAMES.
TODAY WE'LL BE LISTENING TO POET JACKIE HAMPTON'S RECITATION OF
ALLEN GINSBURG'S "AMERICA" WRITTEN IN 1956.

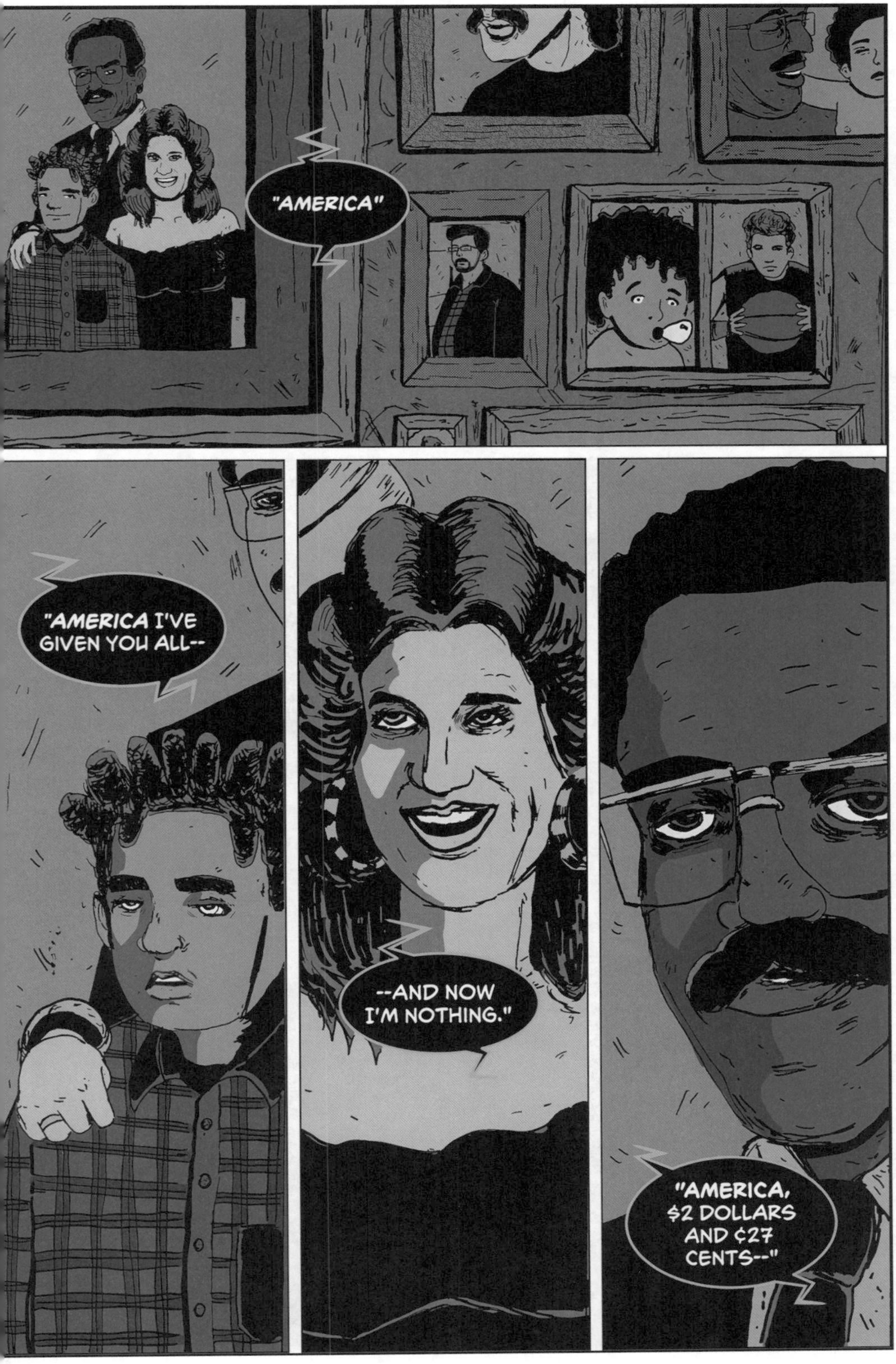
"AMERICA"
"AMERICA I'VE GIVEN YOU ALL--
--AND NOW I'M NOTHING."
"AMERICA, $2 DOLLARS AND ¢27 CENTS--"

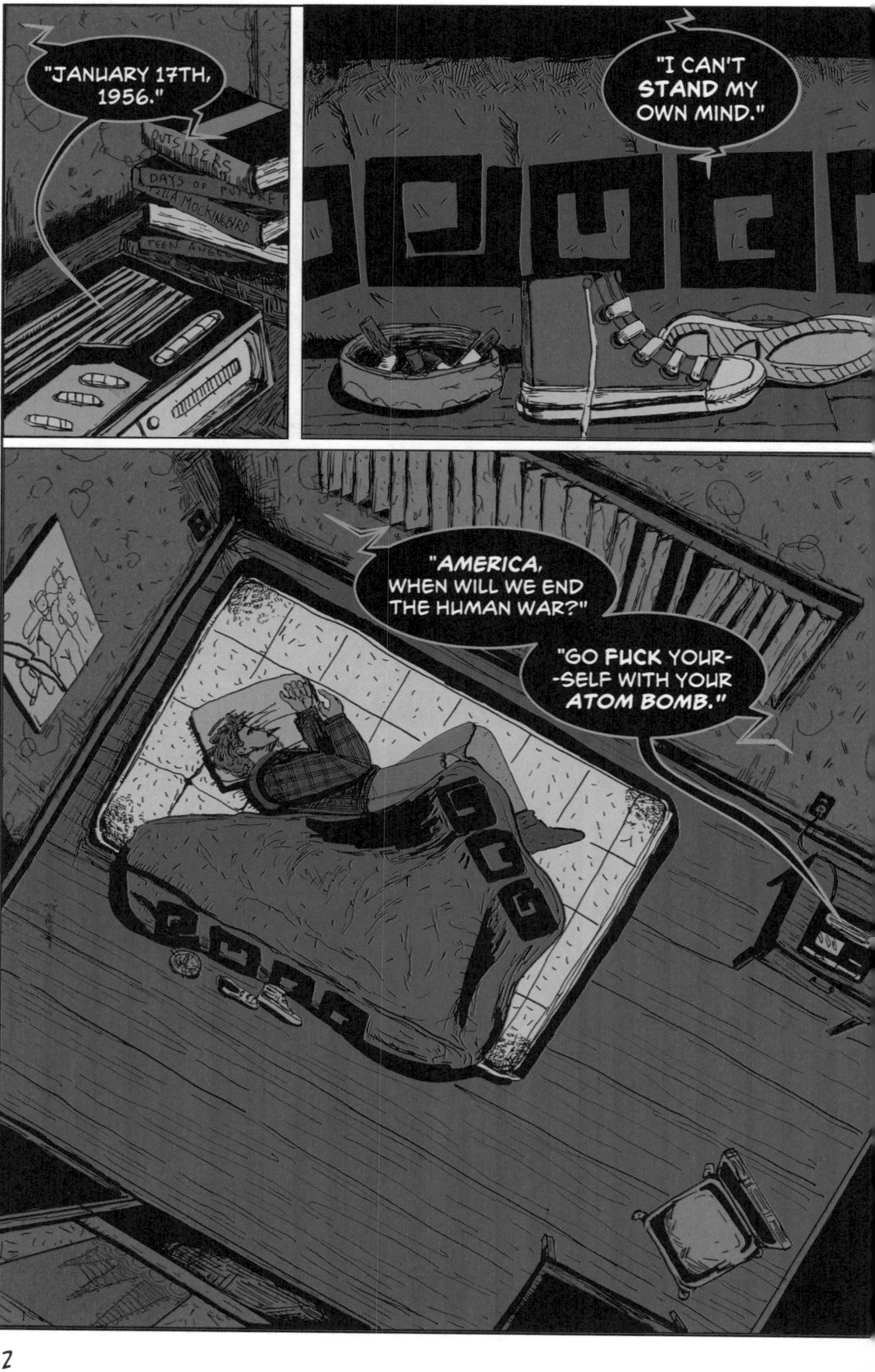
"JANUARY 17TH, 1956."
OUTSIDERS
DAYS OF FUTURE P
TO KILL A MOCKINGBIRD
TEEN ANGEL
"I CAN'T STAND MY OWN MIND."
"AMERICA, WHEN WILL WE END THE HUMAN WAR?"
"GO FUCK YOUR-
-SELF WITH YOUR ATOM BOMB."

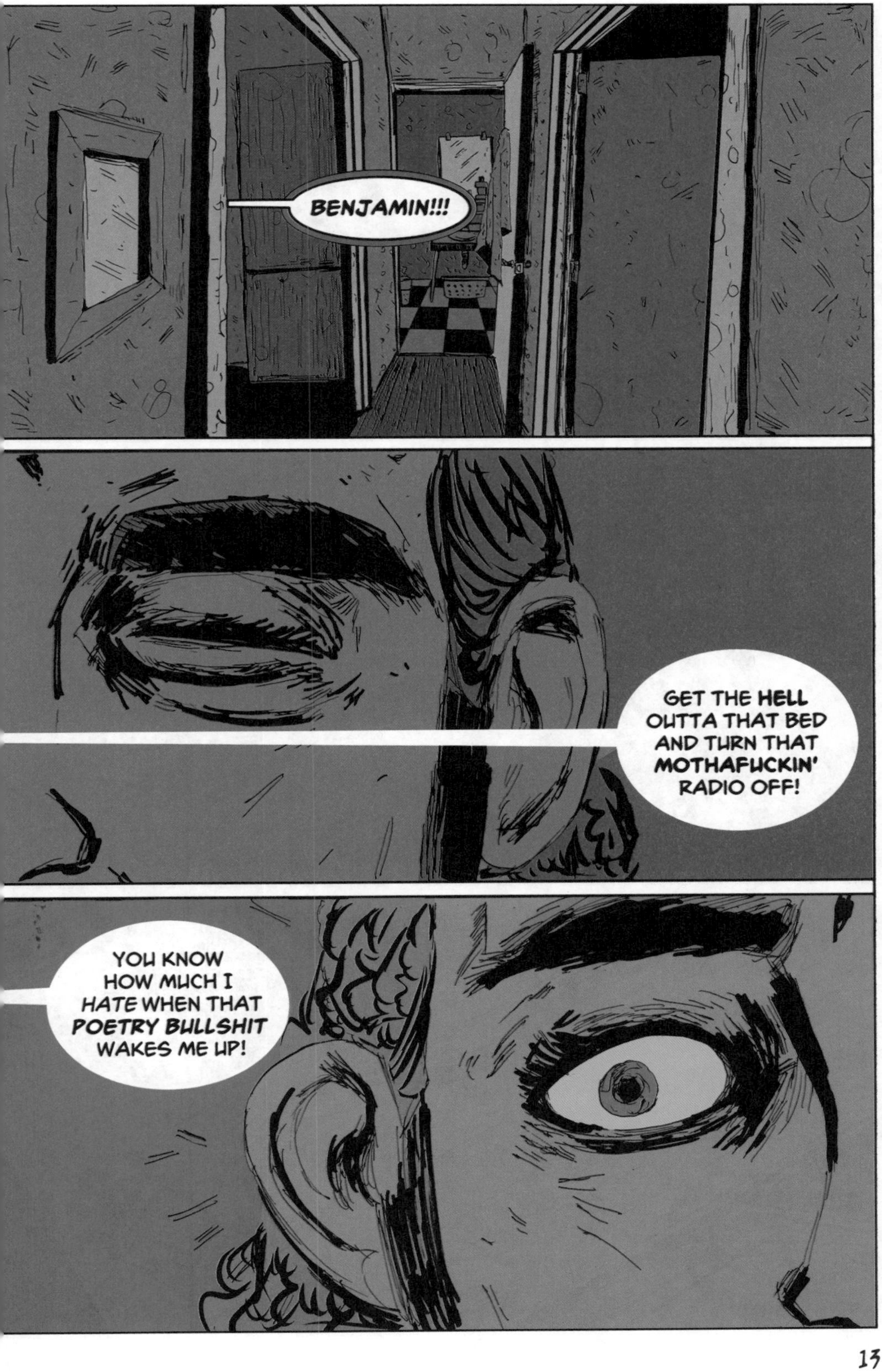
BENJAMIN!!!
GET THE HELL OUTTA THAT BED AND TURN THAT MOTHAFUCKIN' RADIO OFF!
YOU KNOW HOW MUCH I HATE WHEN THAT POETRY BULLSHIT WAKES ME UP!

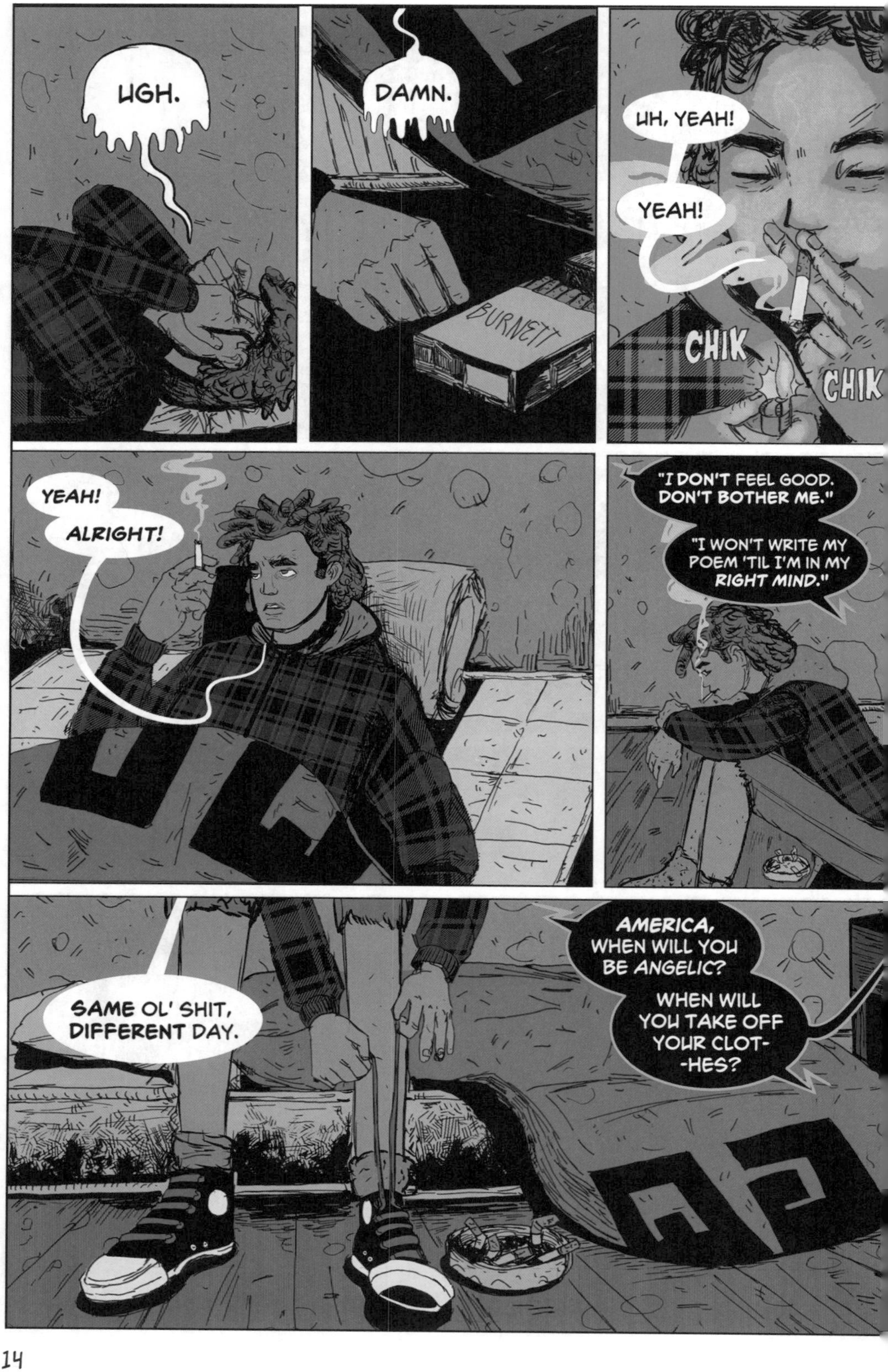
UGH.
DAMN.
BURNETT
UH, YEAH!
YEAH!
CHIK
CHIK
YEAH!
ALRIGHT!
"I DON'T FEEL GOOD. DON'T BOTHER ME."
"I WON'T WRITE MY POEM 'TIL I'M IN MY RIGHT MIND."
SAME OL' SHIT, DIFFERENT DAY.
AMERICA, WHEN WILL YOU BE ANGELIC?
WHEN WILL YOU TAKE OFF YOUR CLOT- -HES?

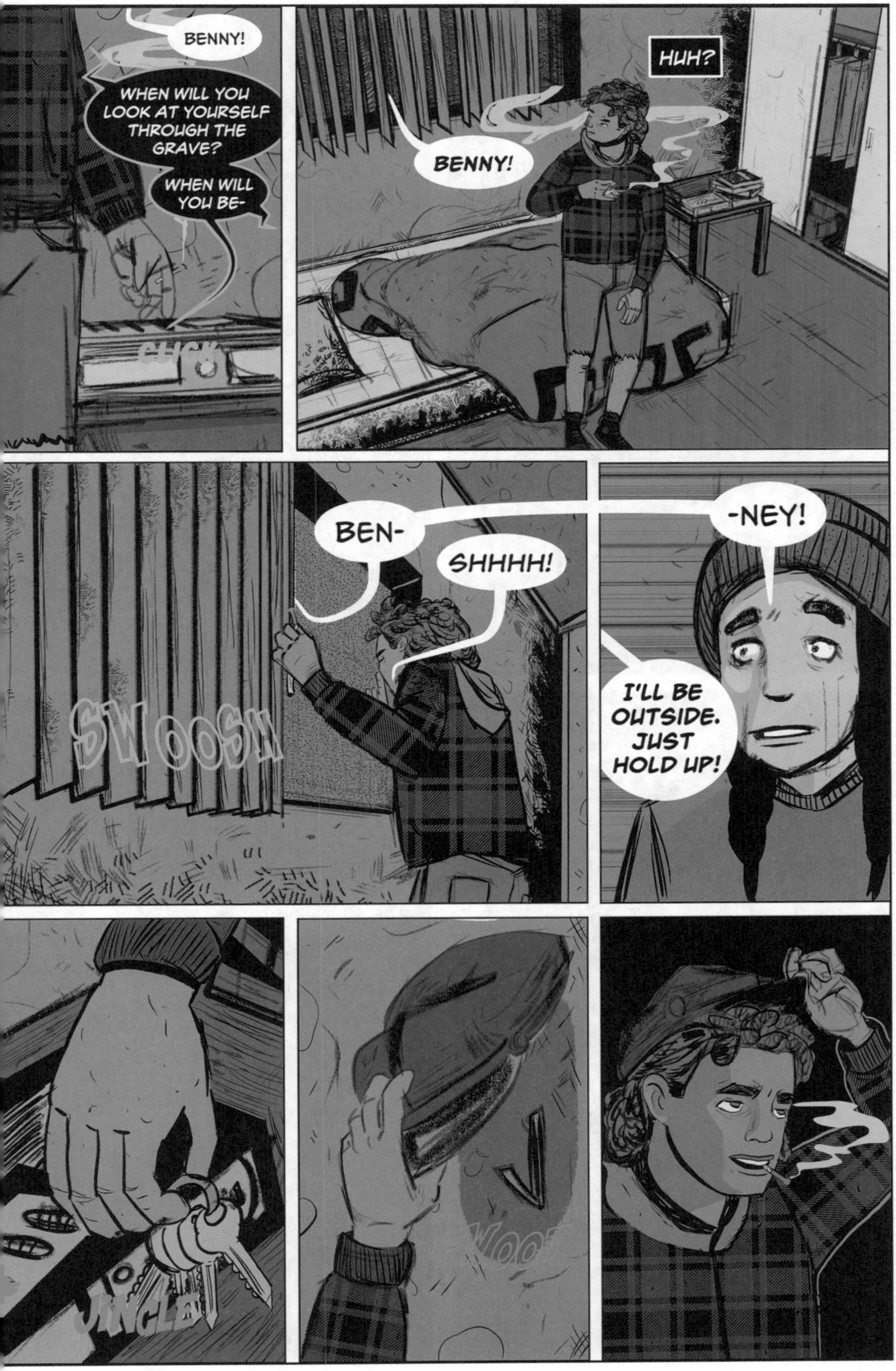
BENNY!
WHEN WILL YOU LOOK AT YOURSELF THROUGH THE GRAVE?
WHEN WILL YOU BE-
HUH?
BENNY!
BEN-
-NEY!
SHHHH!
SWOOSH
I'LL BE OUTSIDE. JUST HOLD UP!
JINGLE

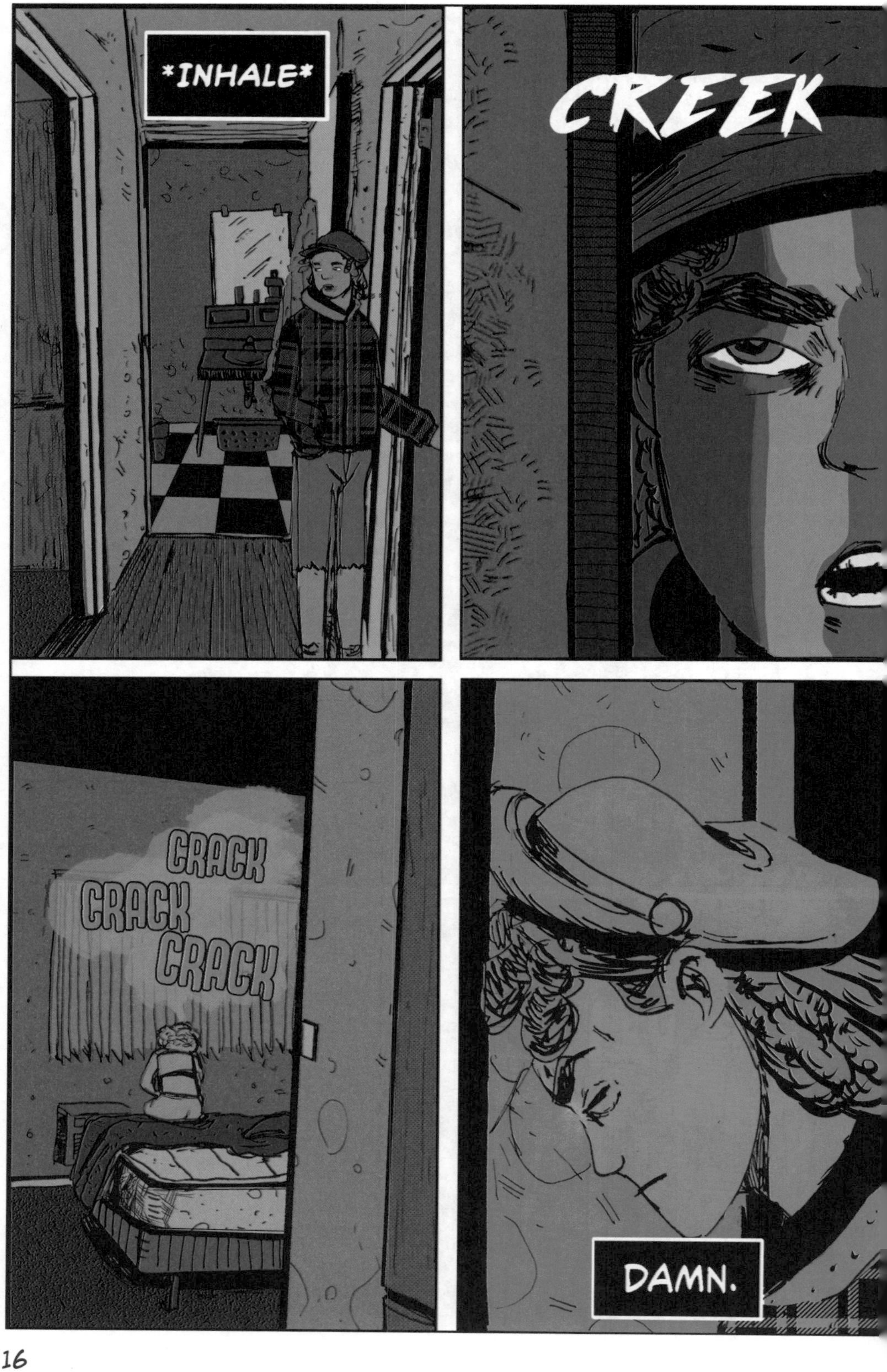
INHALE
CREEK
CRACK
CRACK
CRACK
DAMN.

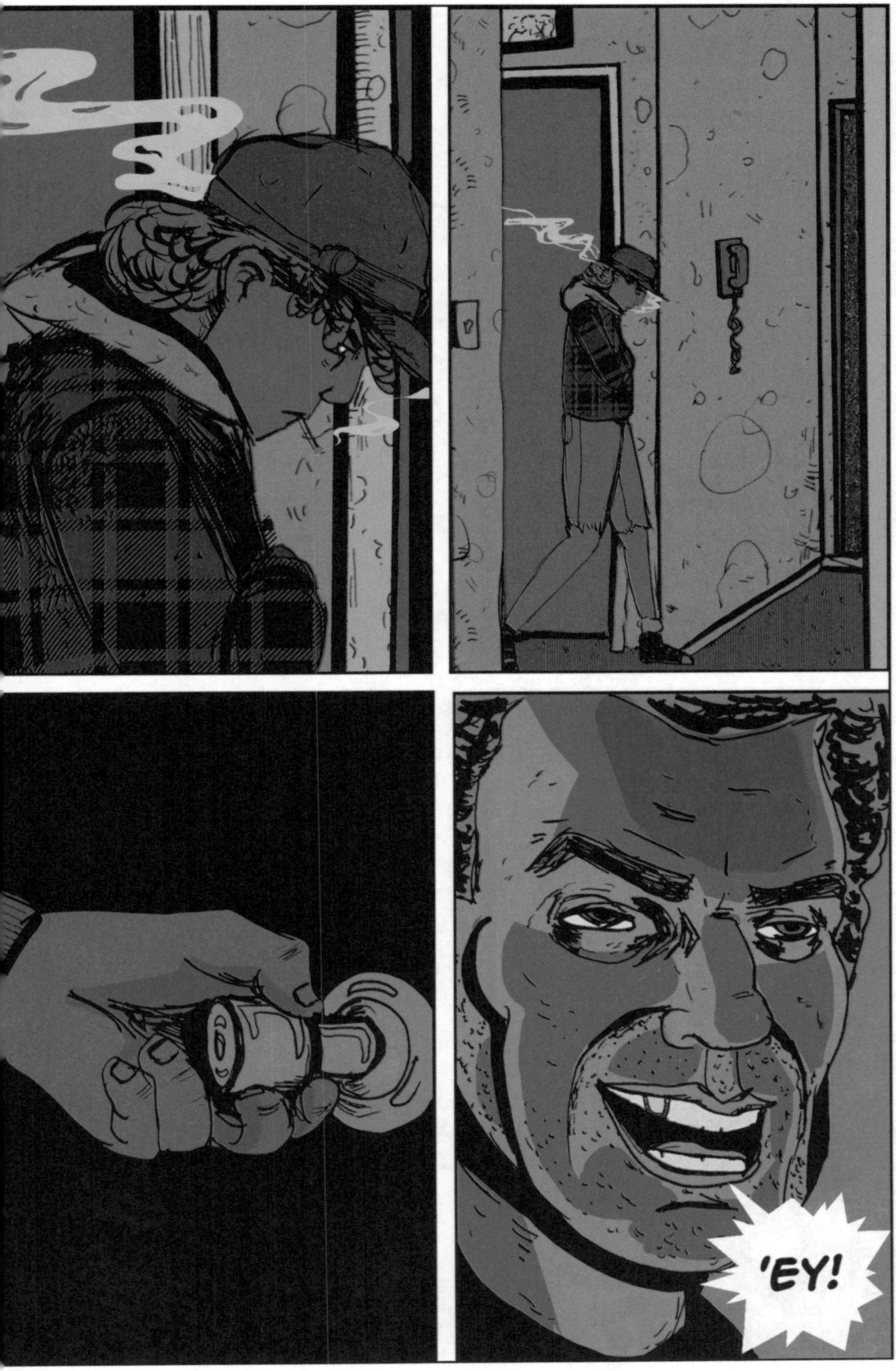
'EY!

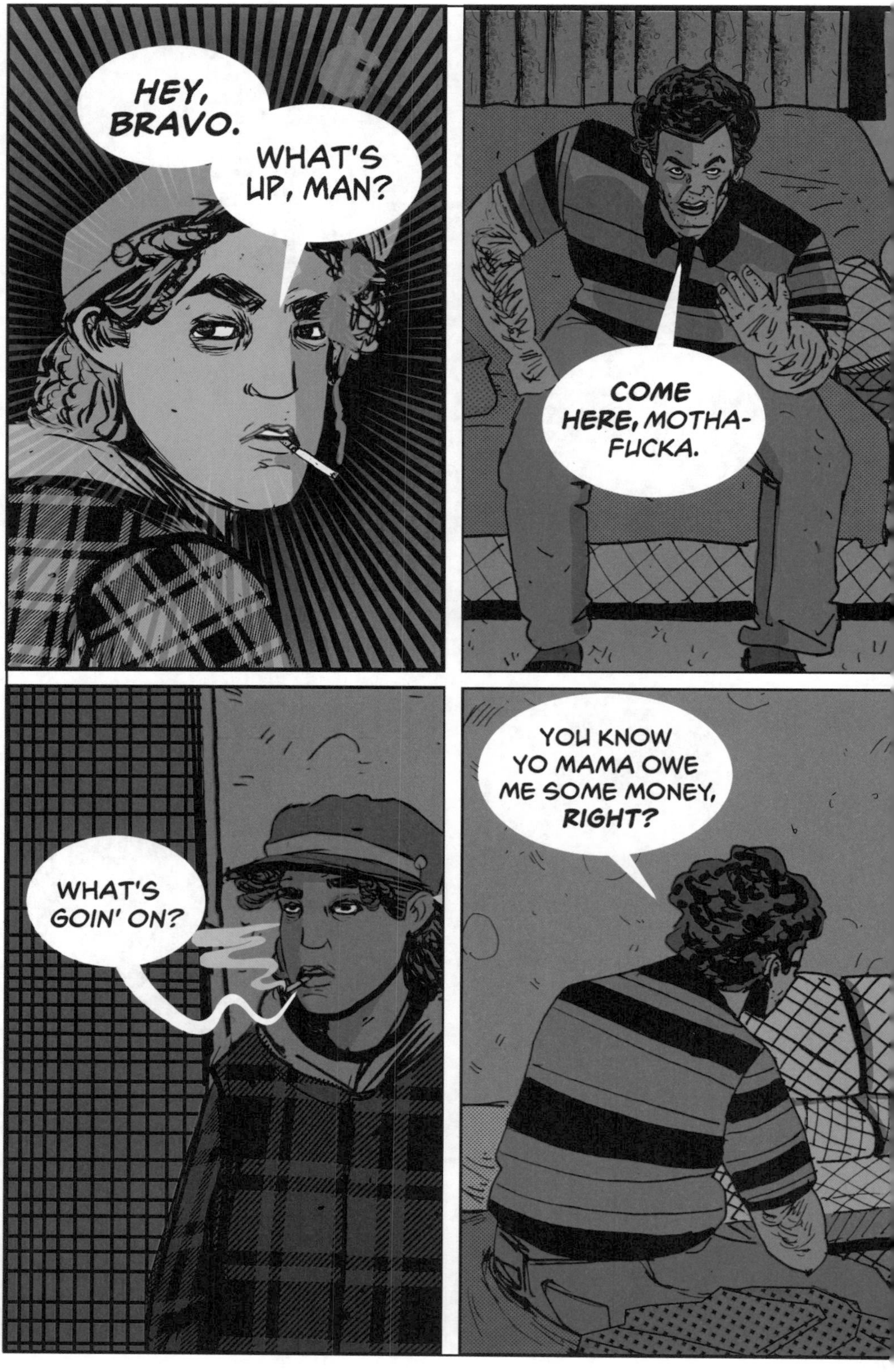
HEY, BRAVO.
WHAT'S UP, MAN?
COME HERE, MOTHA-FUCKA.
WHAT'S GOIN' ON?
YOU KNOW YO MAMA OWE ME SOME MONEY, RIGHT?

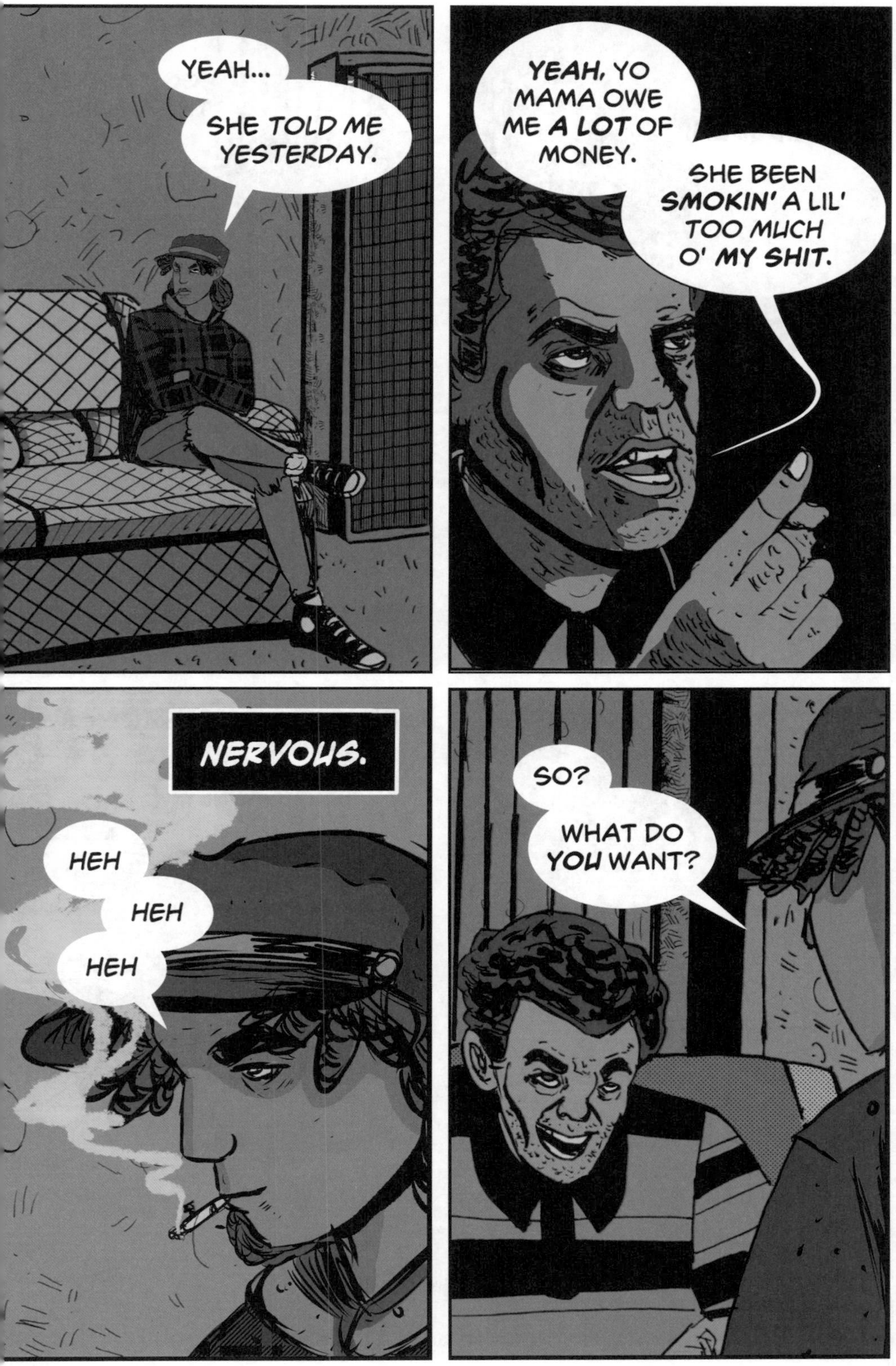
YEAH...
SHE TOLD ME YESTERDAY.
YEAH, YO MAMA OWE ME A LOT OF MONEY.
SHE BEEN SMOKIN' A LIL' TOO MUCH O' MY SHIT.
NERVOUS.
HEH
HEH
HEH
SO?
WHAT DO YOU WANT?

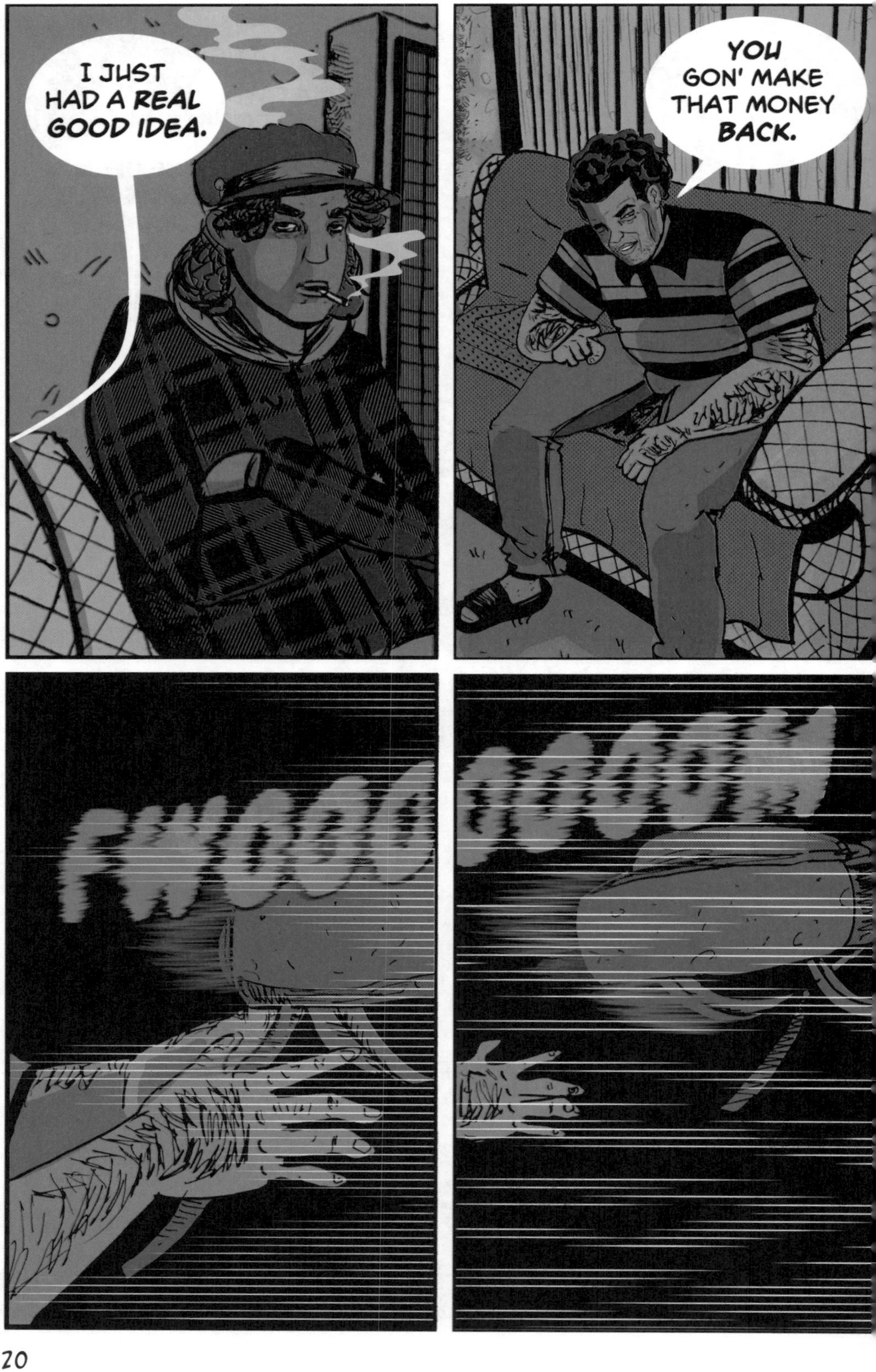
I JUST HAD A REAL GOOD IDEA.
YOU GON' MAKE THAT MONEY BACK.
FWOOOOOOOOM

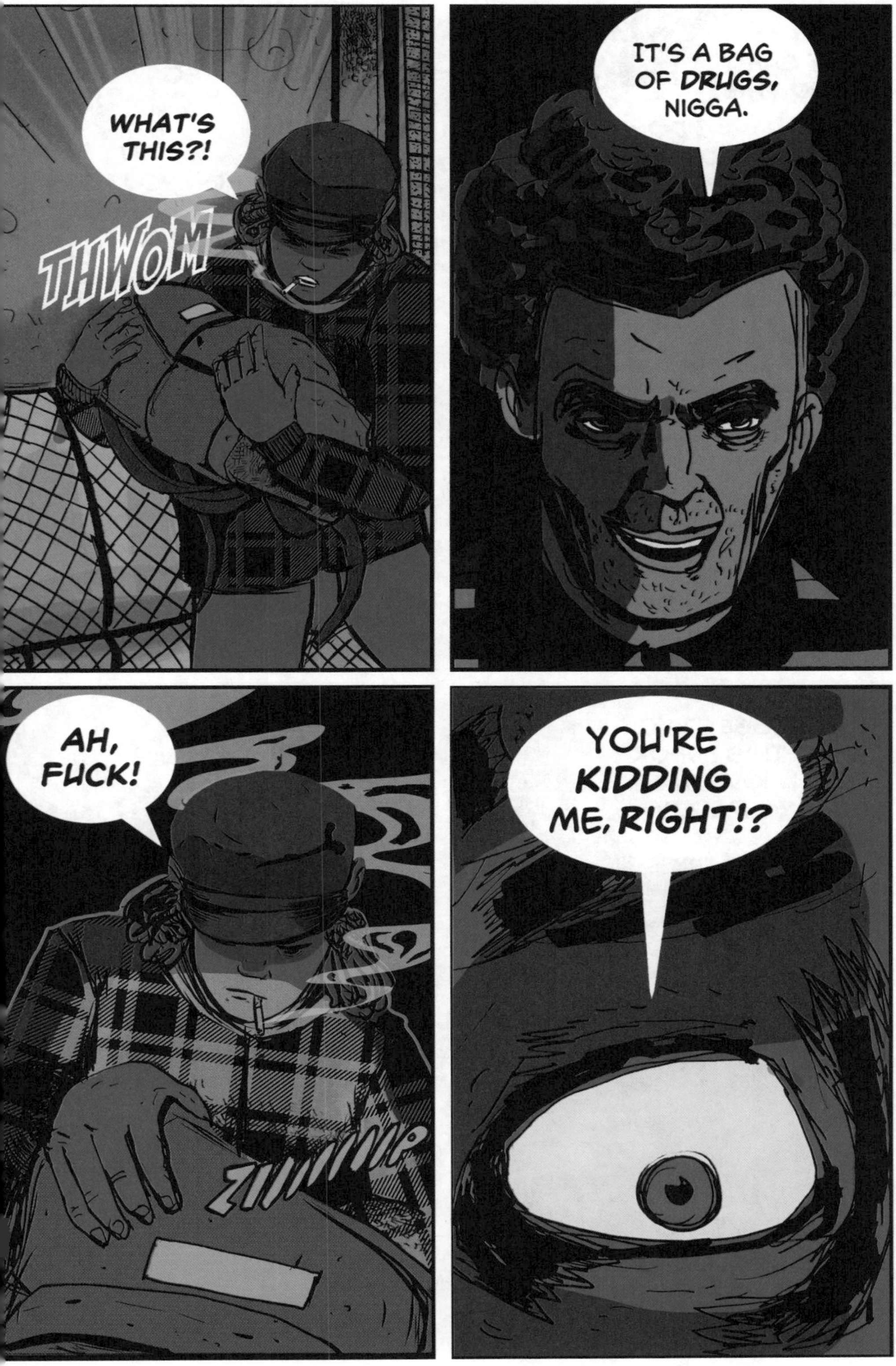
WHAT'S THIS?!
THWOM
IT'S A BAG OF DRUGS, NIGGA.
AH, FUCK!
YOU'RE KIDDING ME, RIGHT!?

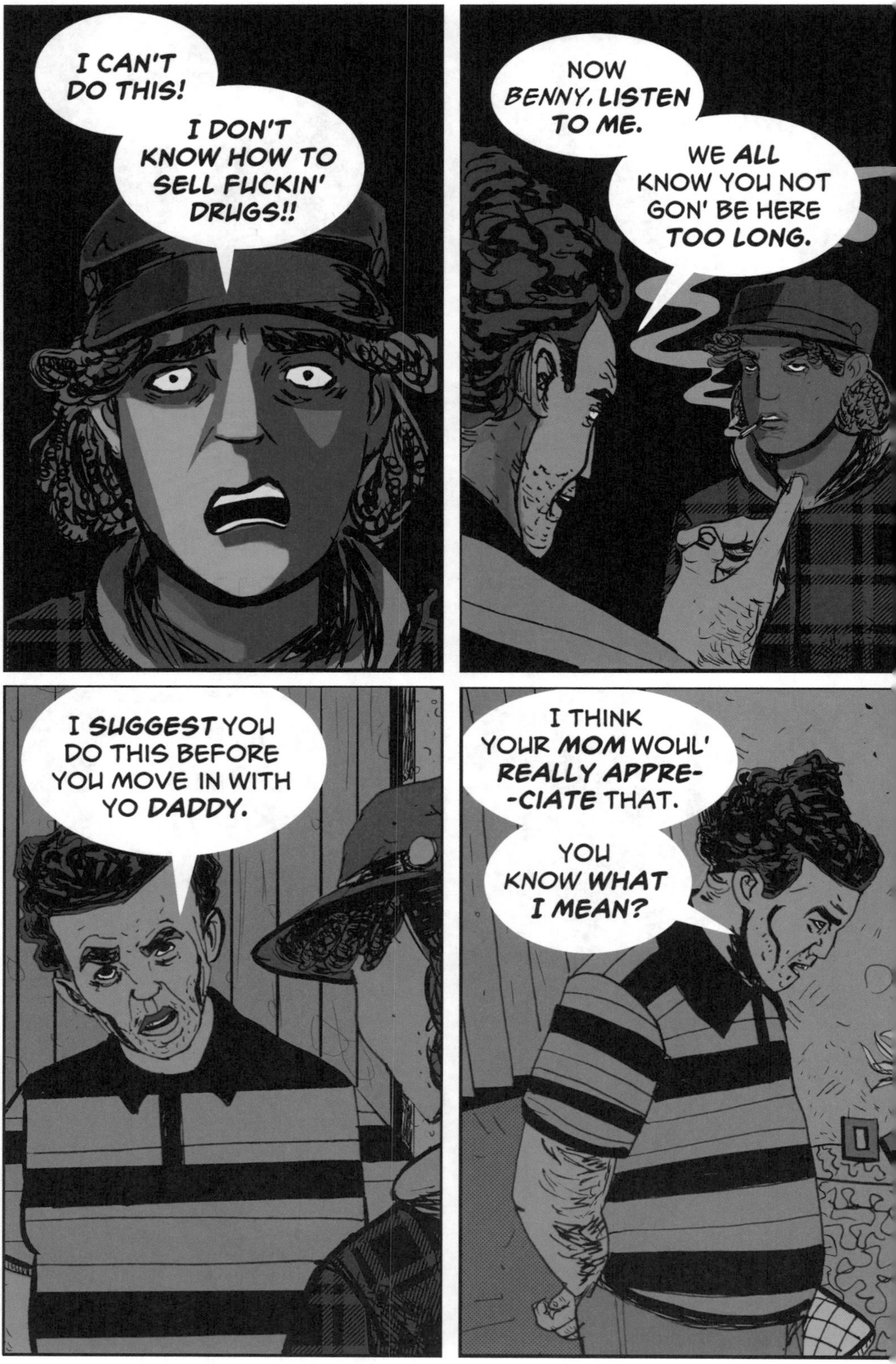
I CAN'T DO THIS!
I DON'T KNOW HOW TO SELL FUCKIN' DRUGS!!
NOW BENNY, LISTEN TO ME.
WE ALL KNOW YOU NOT GON' BE HERE TOO LONG.
I SUGGEST YOU DO THIS BEFORE YOU MOVE IN WITH YO DADDY.
I THINK YOUR MOM WOUL' REALLY APPRE- -CIATE THAT.
YOU KNOW WHAT I MEAN?

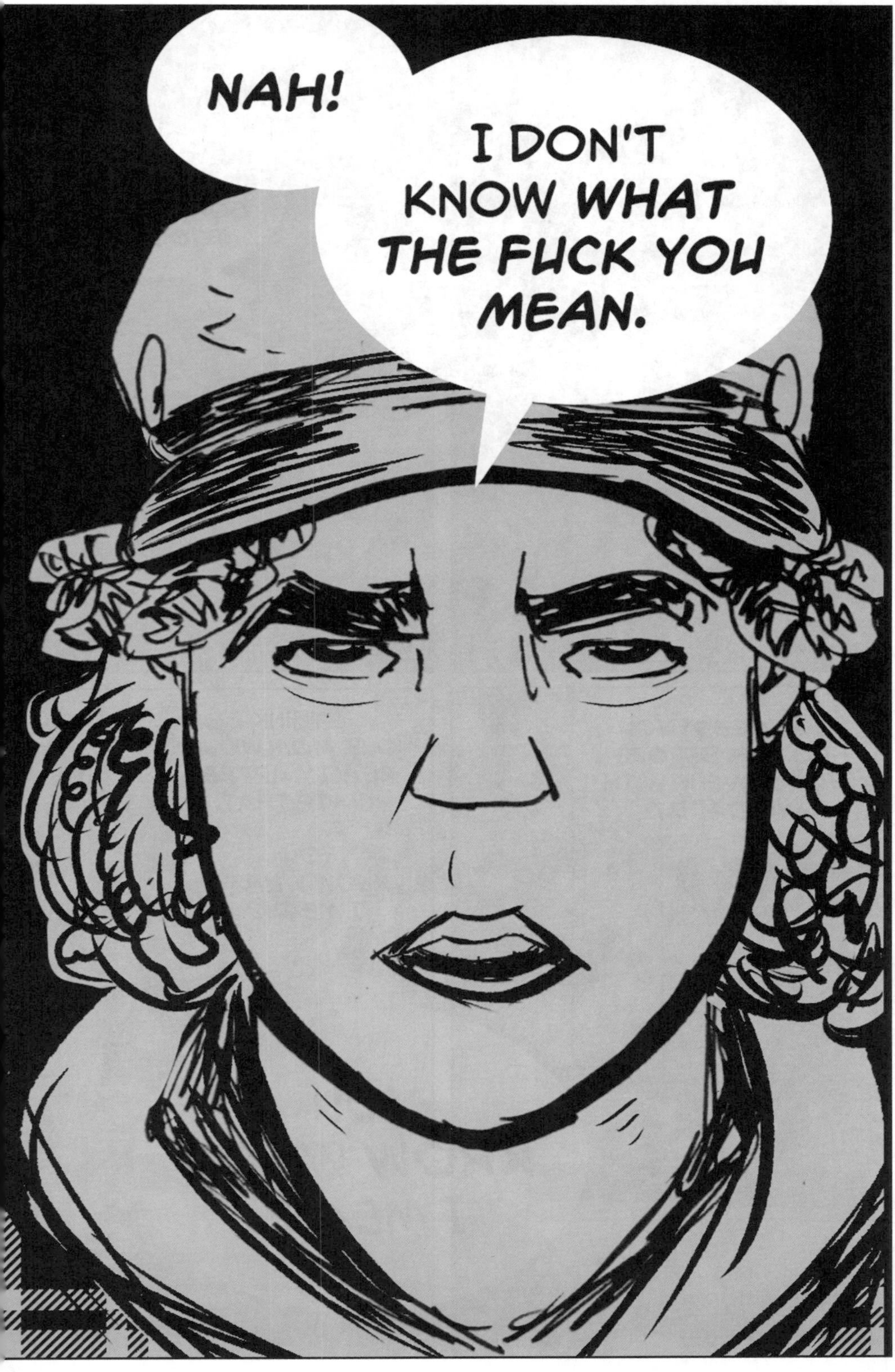
NAH!
I DON'T KNOW WHAT THE FUCK YOU MEAN.

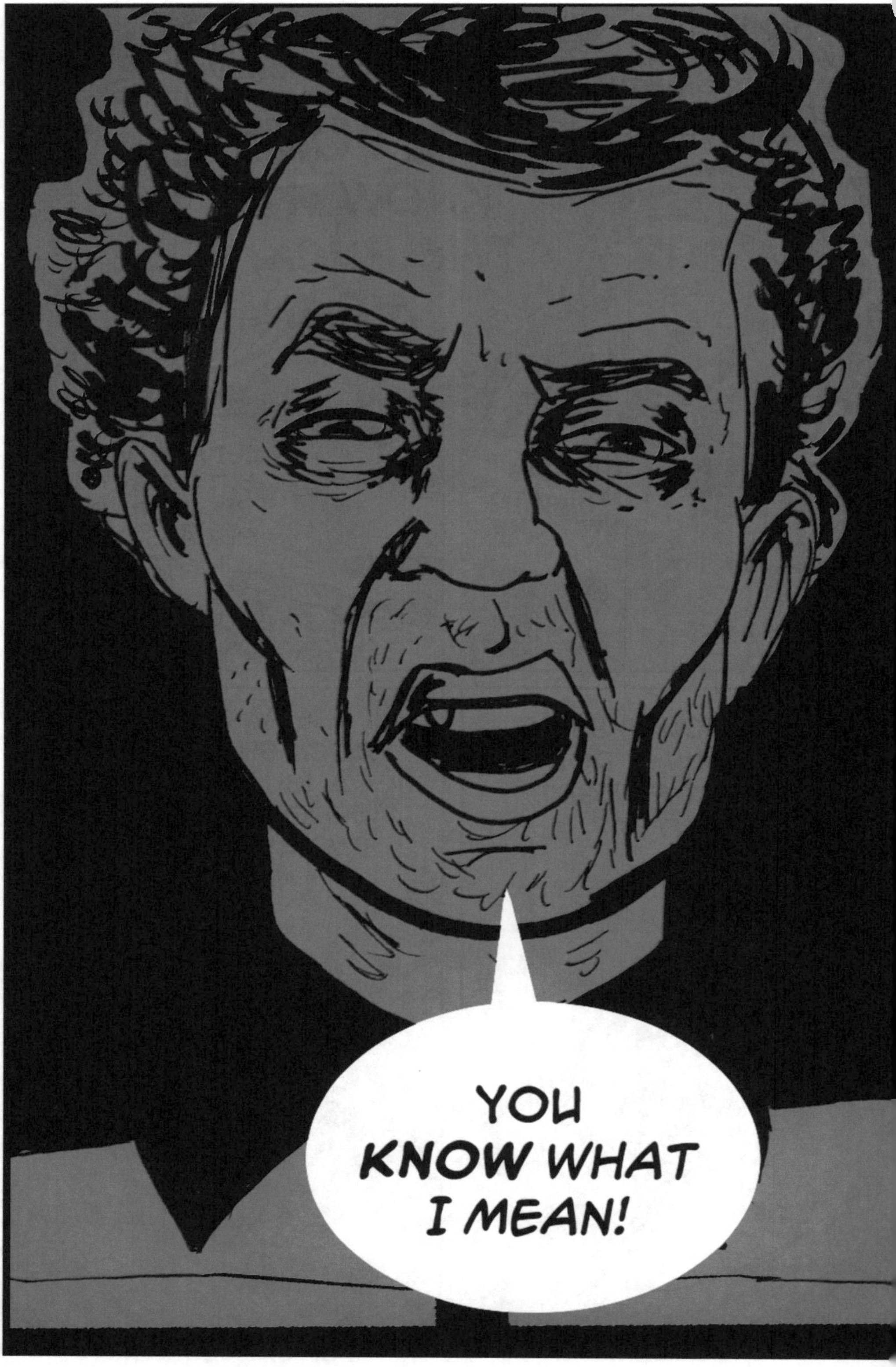
YOU KNOW WHAT I MEAN!

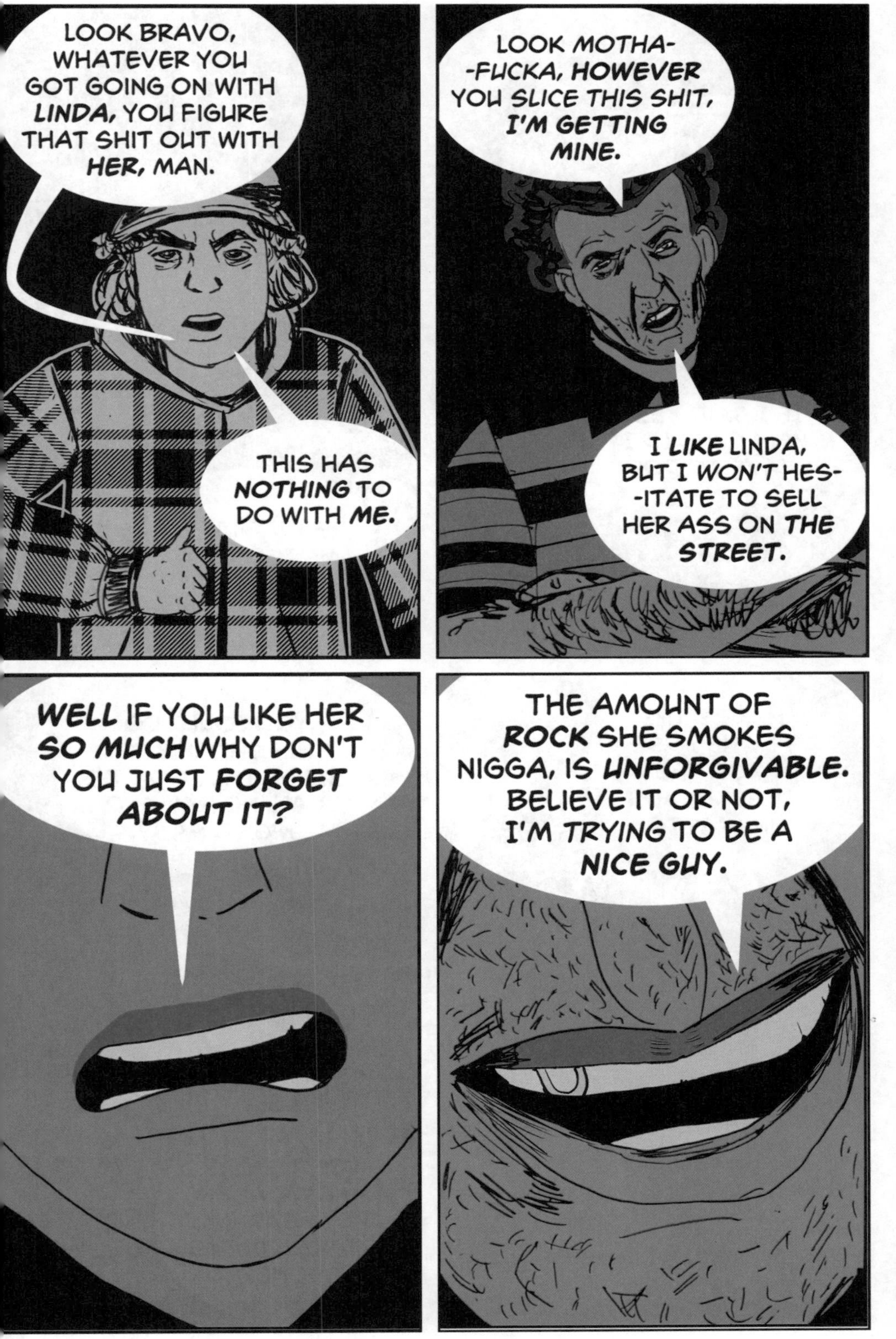
LOOK BRAVO, WHATEVER YOU GOT GOING ON WITH LINDA, YOU FIGURE THAT SHIT OUT WITH HER, MAN.
THIS HAS NOTHING TO DO WITH ME.
LOOK MOTHA--FUCKA, HOWEVER YOU SLICE THIS SHIT, I'M GETTING MINE.
I LIKE LINDA, BUT I WON'T HES--ITATE TO SELL HER ASS ON THE STREET.
WELL IF YOU LIKE HER SO MUCH WHY DON'T YOU JUST FORGET ABOUT IT?
THE AMOUNT OF ROCK SHE SMOKES NIGGA, IS UNFORGIVABLE. BELIEVE IT OR NOT, I'M TRYING TO BE A NICE GUY.

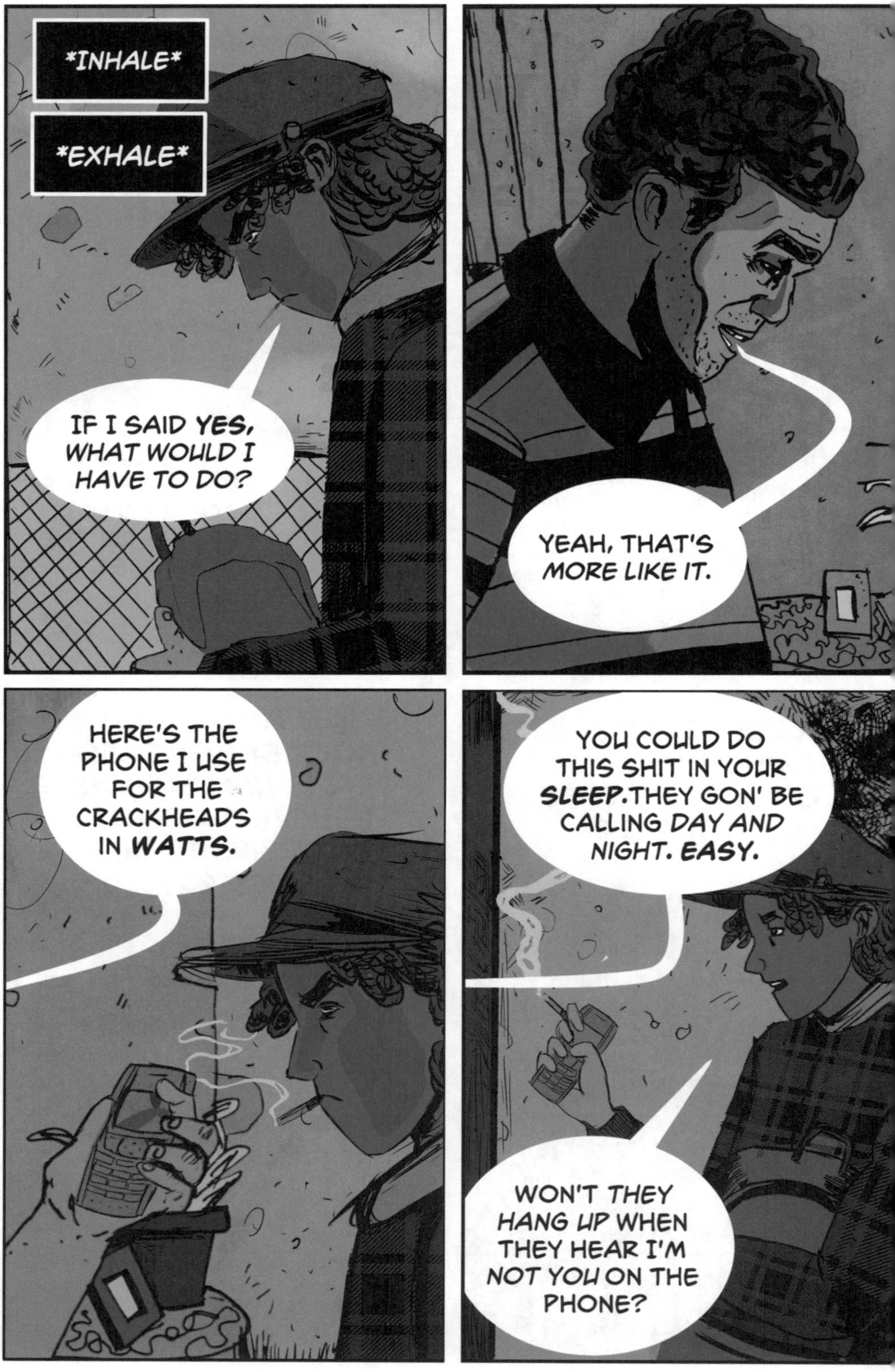
INHALE
EXHALE
IF I SAID YES, WHAT WOULD I HAVE TO DO?
YEAH, THAT'S MORE LIKE IT.
HERE'S THE PHONE I USE FOR THE CRACKHEADS IN WATTS.
YOU COULD DO THIS SHIT IN YOUR SLEEP. THEY GON' BE CALLING DAY AND NIGHT. EASY.
WON'T THEY HANG UP WHEN THEY HEAR I'M NOT YOU ON THE PHONE?

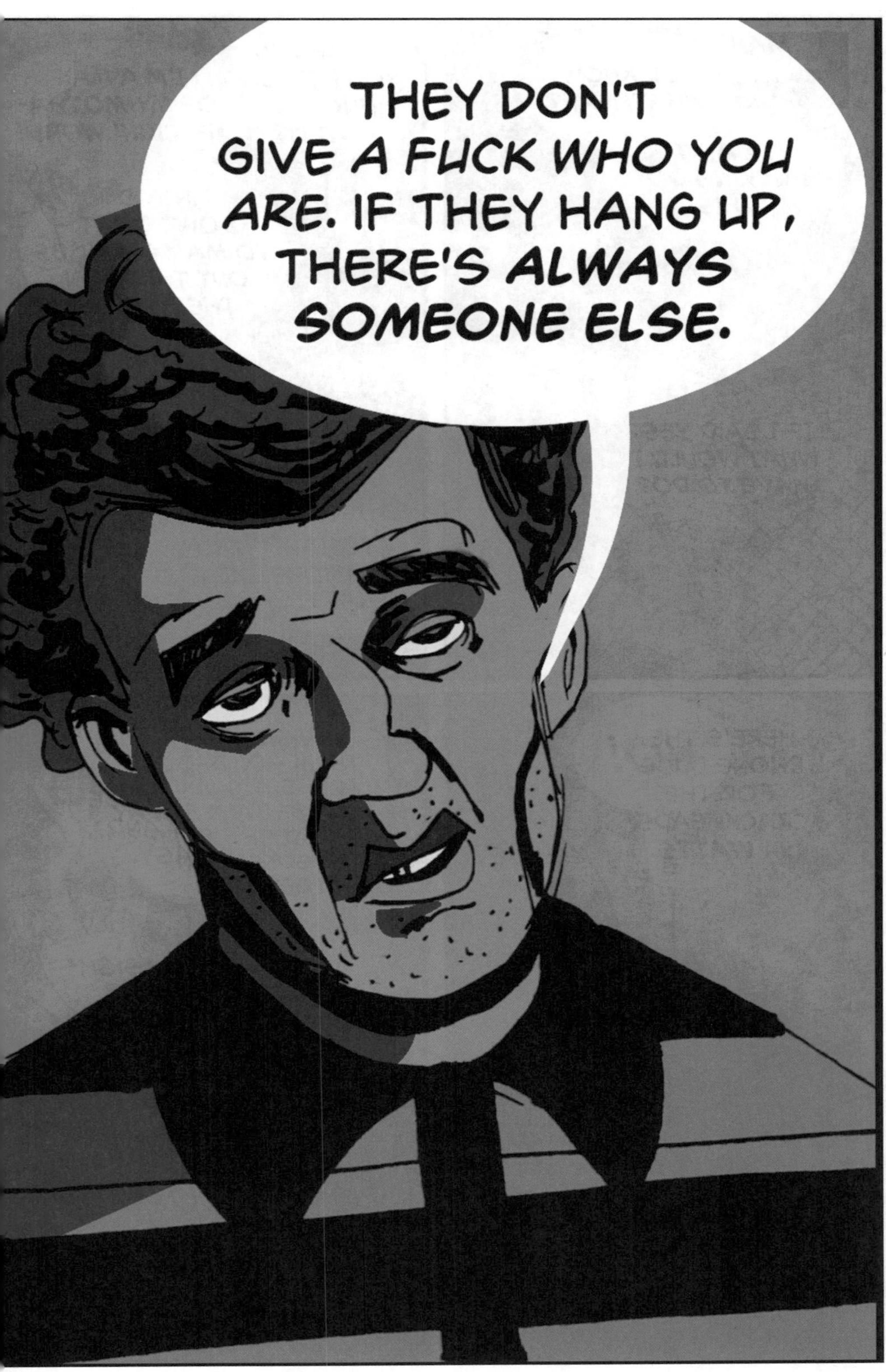
THEY DON'T GIVE A FUCK WHO YOU ARE. IF THEY HANG UP, THERE'S ALWAYS SOMEONE ELSE.

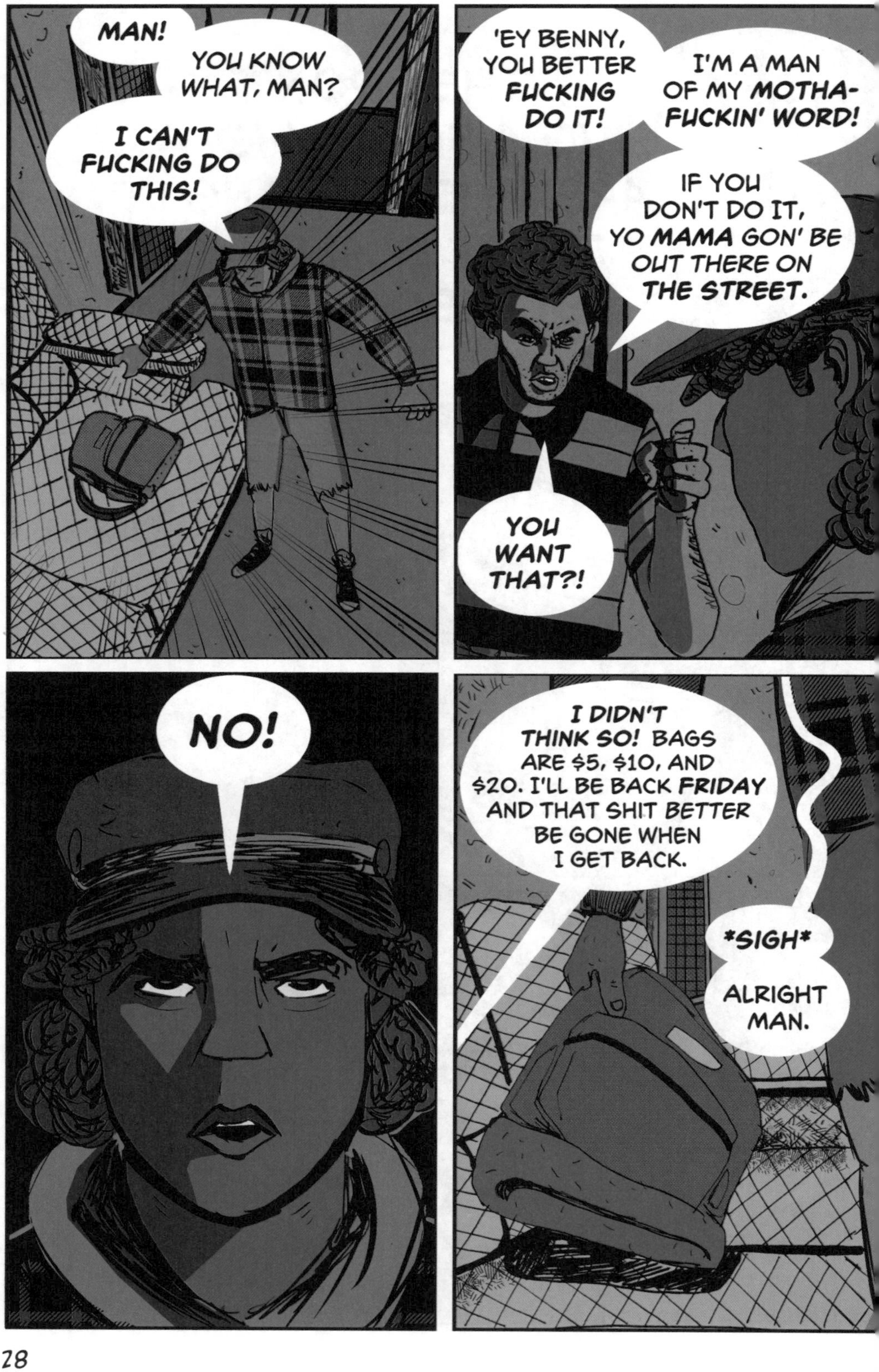
MAN!
YOU KNOW WHAT, MAN?
I CAN'T FUCKING DO THIS!
'EY BENNY, YOU BETTER FUCKING DO IT!
I'M A MAN OF MY MOTHA-FUCKIN' WORD!
IF YOU DON'T DO IT, YO MAMA GON' BE OUT THERE ON THE STREET.
YOU WANT THAT?!
NO!
I DIDN'T THINK SO! BAGS ARE $5, $10, AND $20. I'LL BE BACK FRIDAY AND THAT SHIT BETTER BE GONE WHEN I GET BACK.
SIGH
ALRIGHT MAN.

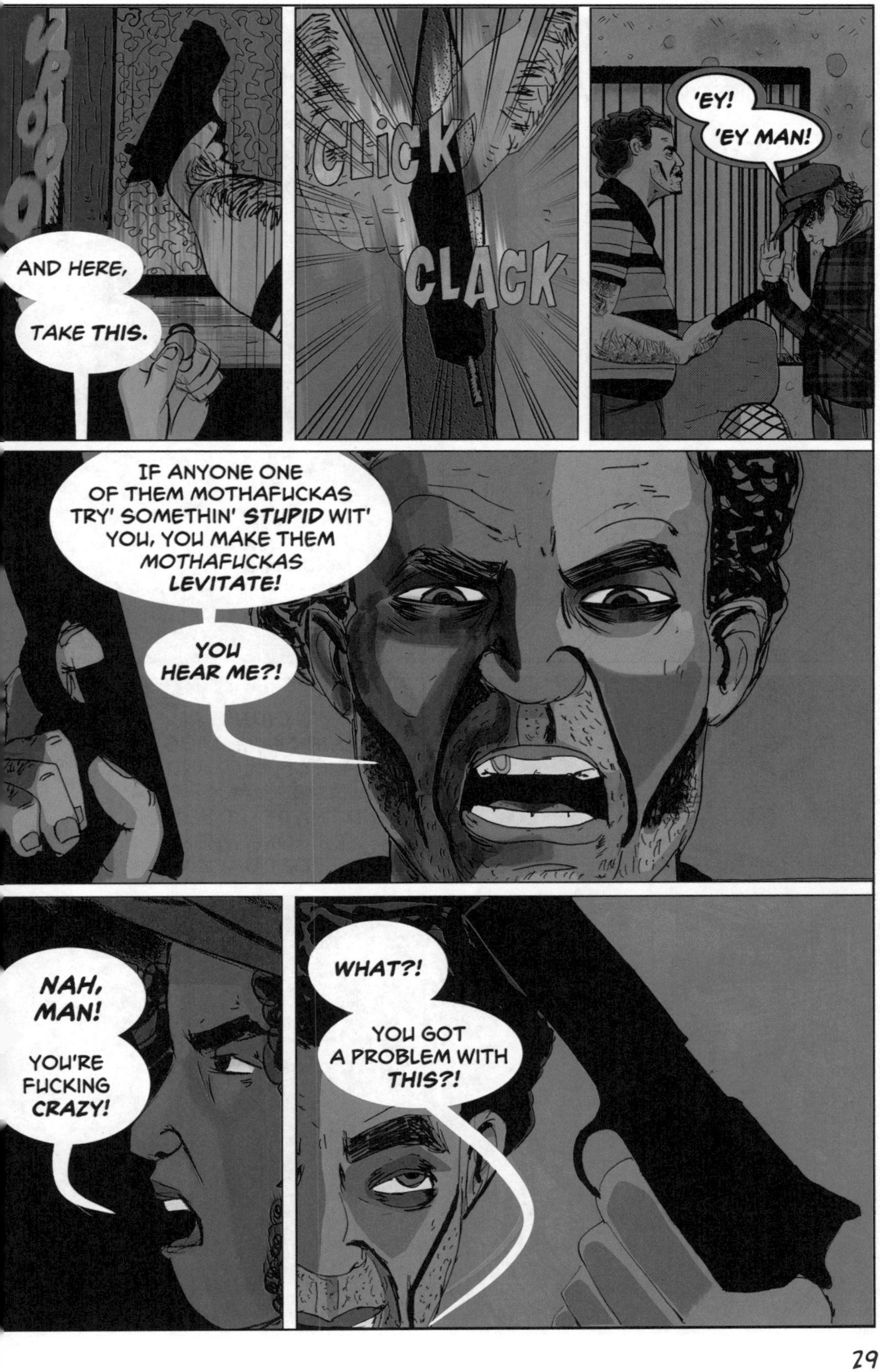
VROOOOM
AND HERE,
TAKE THIS.
CLICK
CLACK
'EY!
'EY MAN!
IF ANYONE ONE OF THEM MOTHAFUCKAS TRY' SOMETHIN' STUPID WIT' YOU, YOU MAKE THEM MOTHAFUCKAS LEVITATE!
YOU HEAR ME?!
NAH, MAN!
YOU'RE FUCKING CRAZY!
WHAT?!
YOU GOT A PROBLEM WITH THIS?!

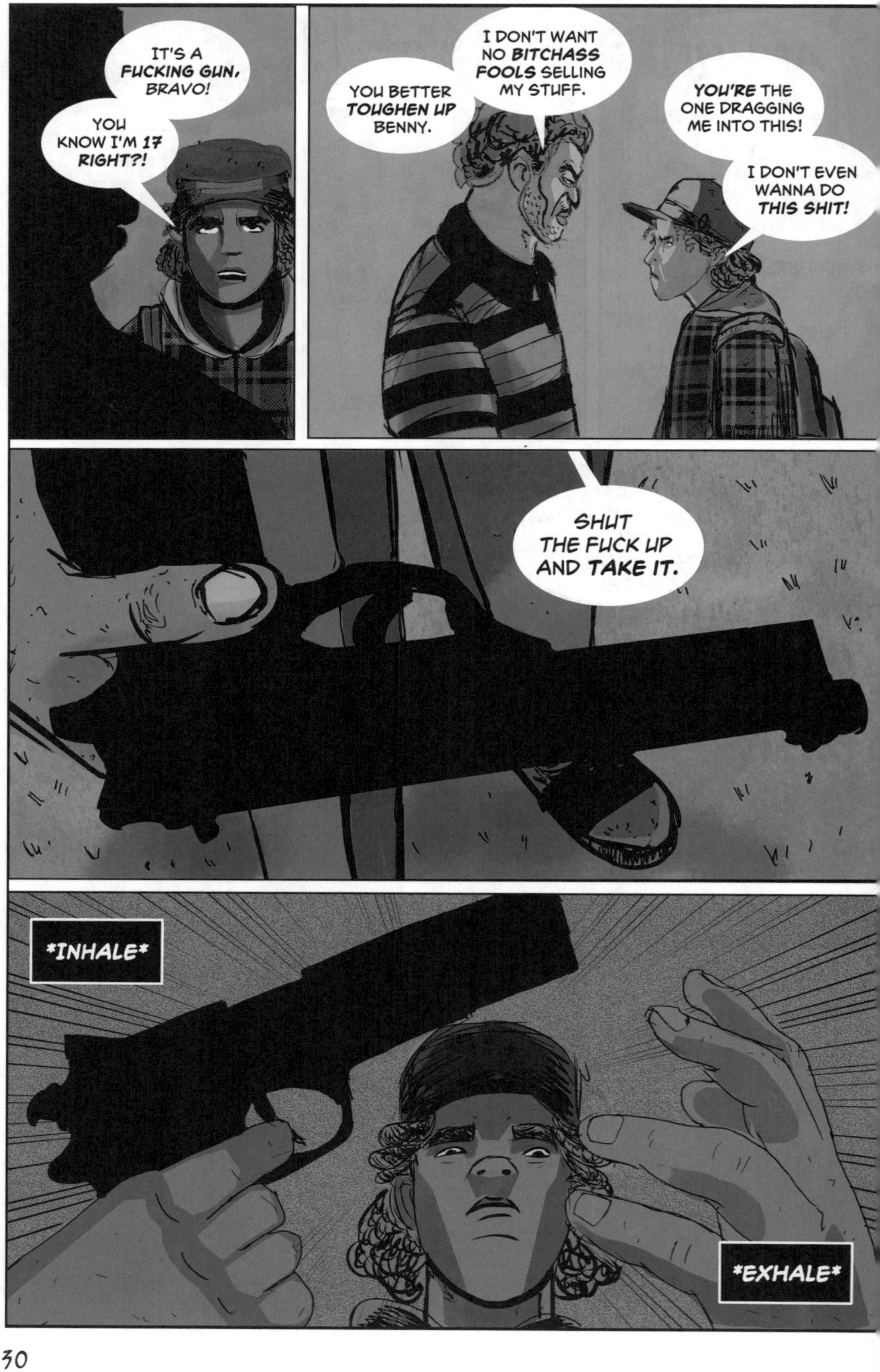
IT'S A FUCKING GUN, BRAVO!
YOU KNOW I'M 17 RIGHT?!
YOU BETTER TOUGHEN UP BENNY.
I DON'T WANT NO BITCHASS FOOLS SELLING MY STUFF.
YOU'RE THE ONE DRAGGING ME INTO THIS!
I DON'T EVEN WANNA DO THIS SHIT!
SHUT THE FUCK UP AND TAKE IT.
INHALE
EXHALE

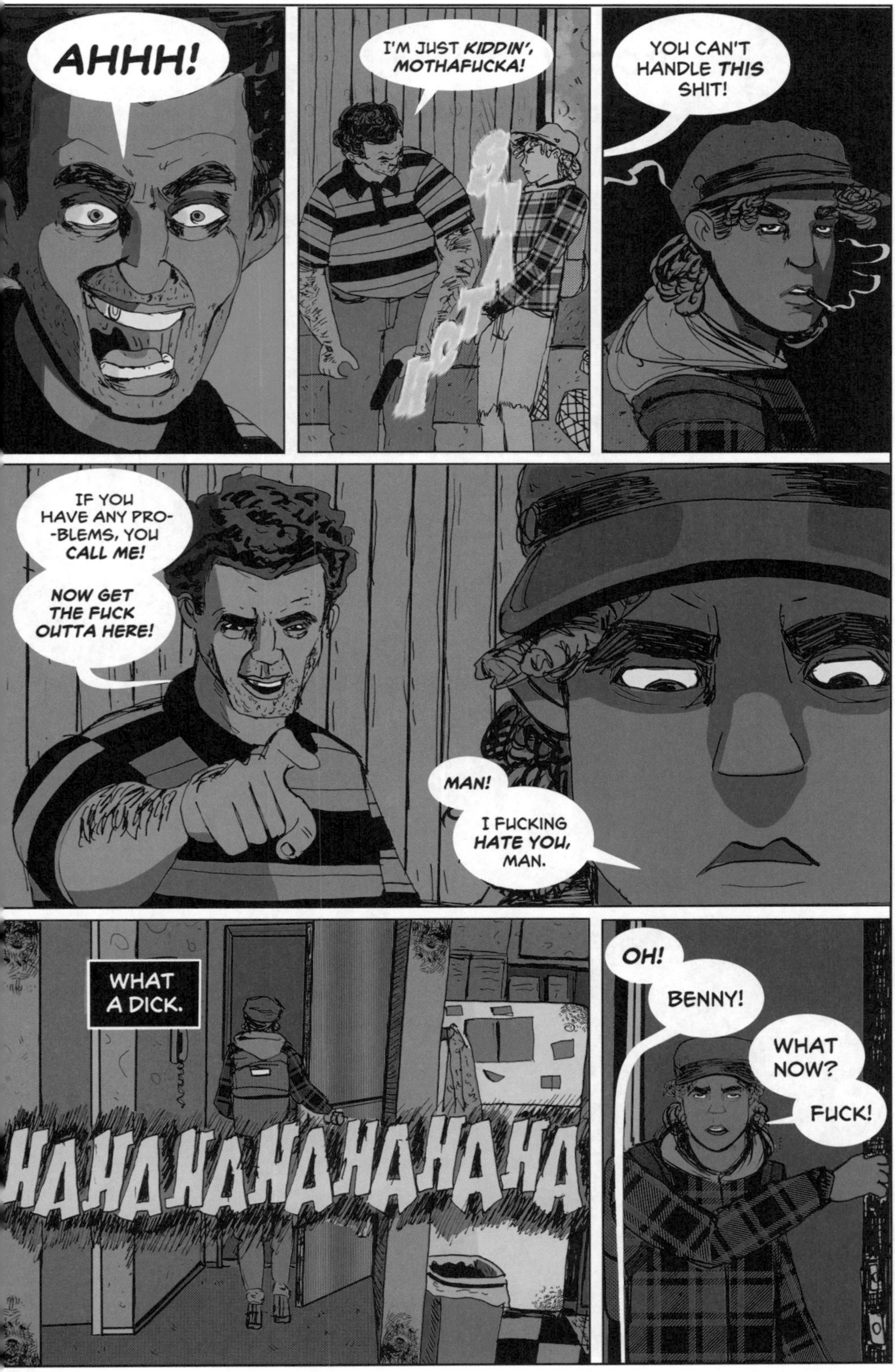
AHHH!
I'M JUST KIDDIN', MOTHAFUCKA!
SNATCH
YOU CAN'T HANDLE THIS SHIT!
IF YOU HAVE ANY PRO- -BLEMS, YOU CALL ME!
NOW GET THE FUCK OUTTA HERE!
MAN!
I FUCKING HATE YOU, MAN.
WHAT A DICK.
HAHAHAHAHAHAHAHAHA
OH!
BENNY!
WHAT NOW?
FUCK!

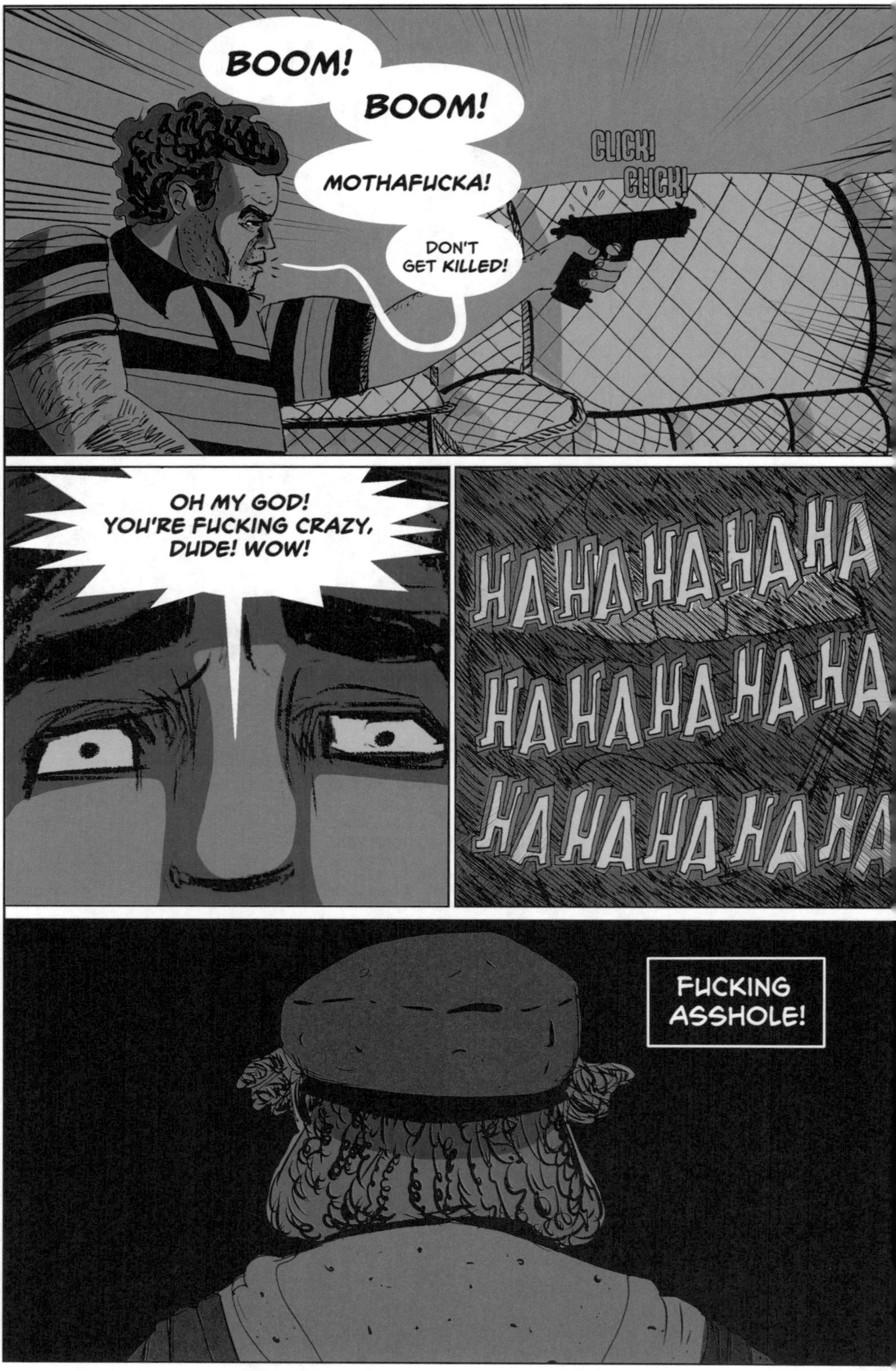
BOOM!
BOOM!
MOTHAFUCKA!
DON'T GET KILLED!
CLICK!
CLICK!
OH MY GOD! YOU'RE FUCKING CRAZY, DUDE! WOW!
HAHAHAHAHAHA
HAHAHAHAHAHA
HAHAHAHAHAHA
FUCKING ASSHOLE!

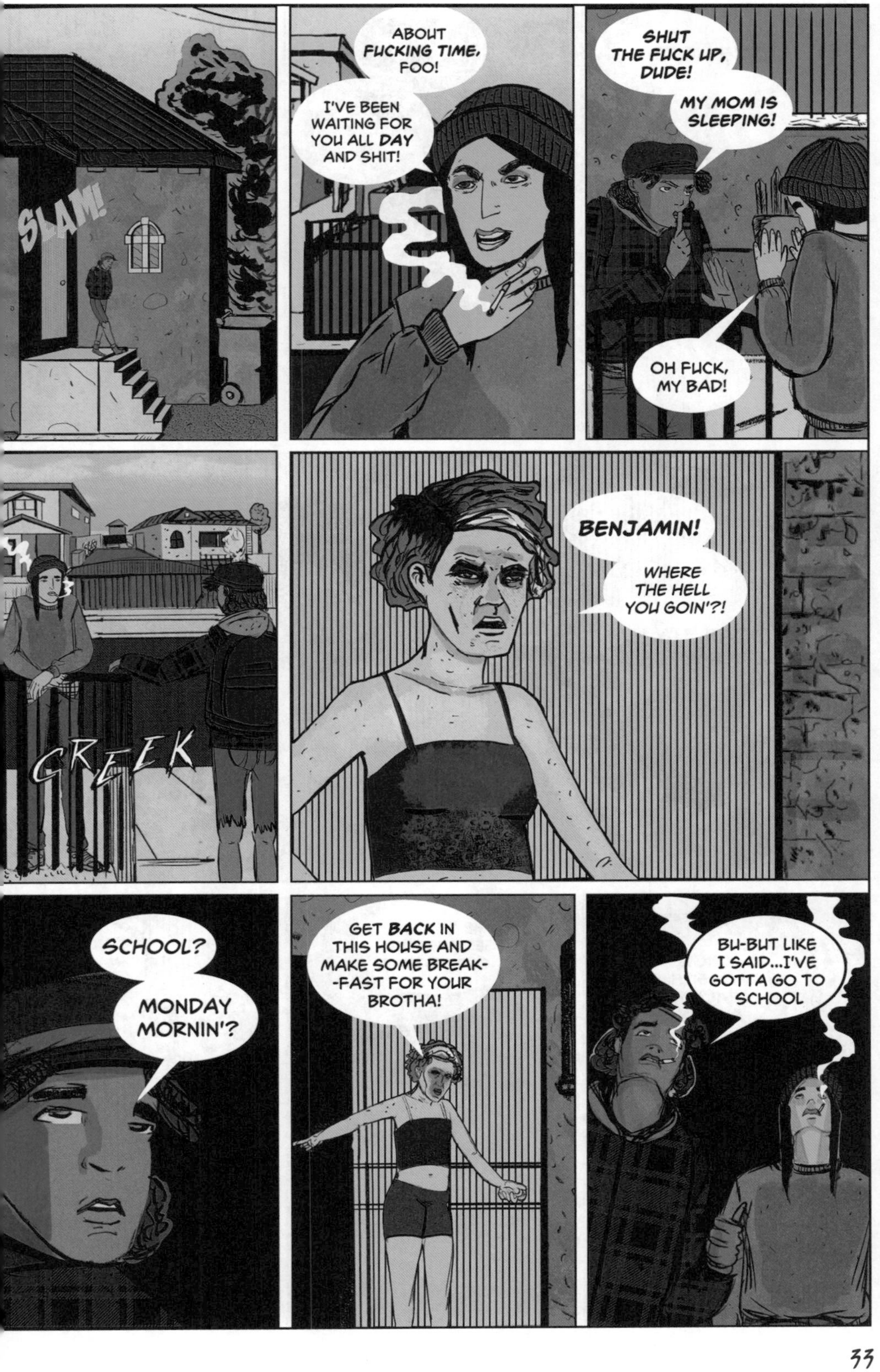
SLAM!
ABOUT FUCKING TIME, FOO!
I'VE BEEN WAITING FOR YOU ALL DAY AND SHIT!
SHUT THE FUCK UP, DUDE!
MY MOM IS SLEEPING!
OH FUCK, MY BAD!
CREEK
BENJAMIN!
WHERE THE HELL YOU GOIN'?!
SCHOOL?
MONDAY MORNIN'?
GET BACK IN THIS HOUSE AND MAKE SOME BREAK-
-FAST FOR YOUR BROTHA!
BU-BUT LIKE I SAID...I'VE GOTTA GO TO SCHOOL

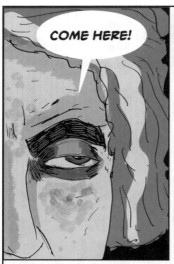

COME HERE!

SIGH

I'M NOT STUPID BOY. I KNOW WHAT'S IN THE BAG.

FORGET WHATEVER THIS MOTHAFUCKA TOLD YOU.

I CAN PAY 'EM BACK MYSELF!

NOW YOU EITHER LEAVE THAT SHIT HERE--

HEY LINDA, SHUT THE FUCK UP AND LET 'EM GO!

HEY BENNY! GET THE FUCK OUTTA HERE!

YOU'RE GON--NA GET 'EM KILLED!

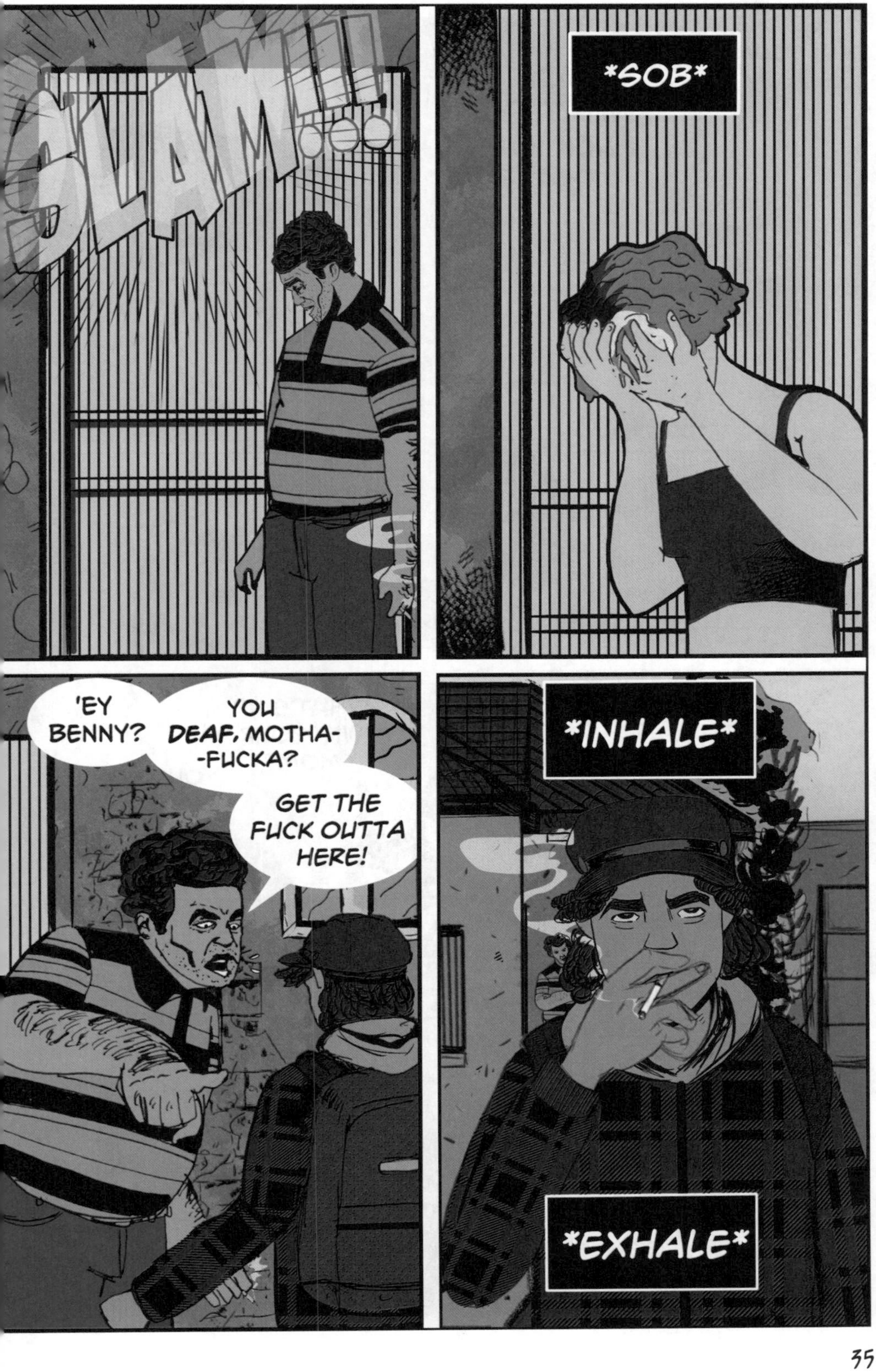
SLAM!!!...
SOB
'EY BENNY?
YOU DEAF, MOTHA- -FUCKA?
GET THE FUCK OUTTA HERE!
INHALE
EXHALE

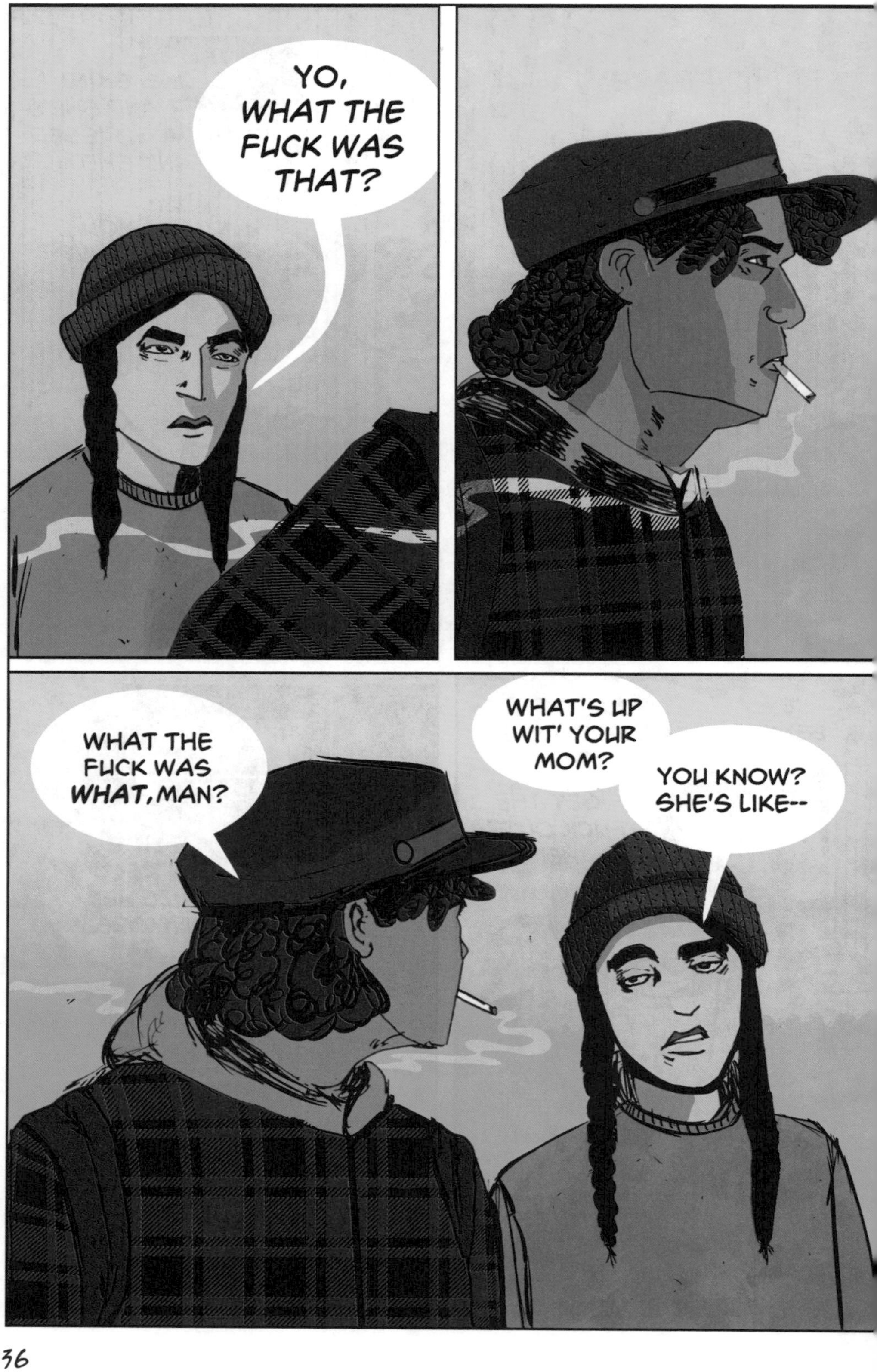
YO, WHAT THE FUCK WAS THAT?
WHAT THE FUCK WAS WHAT, MAN?
WHAT'S UP WIT' YOUR MOM?
YOU KNOW? SHE'S LIKE--

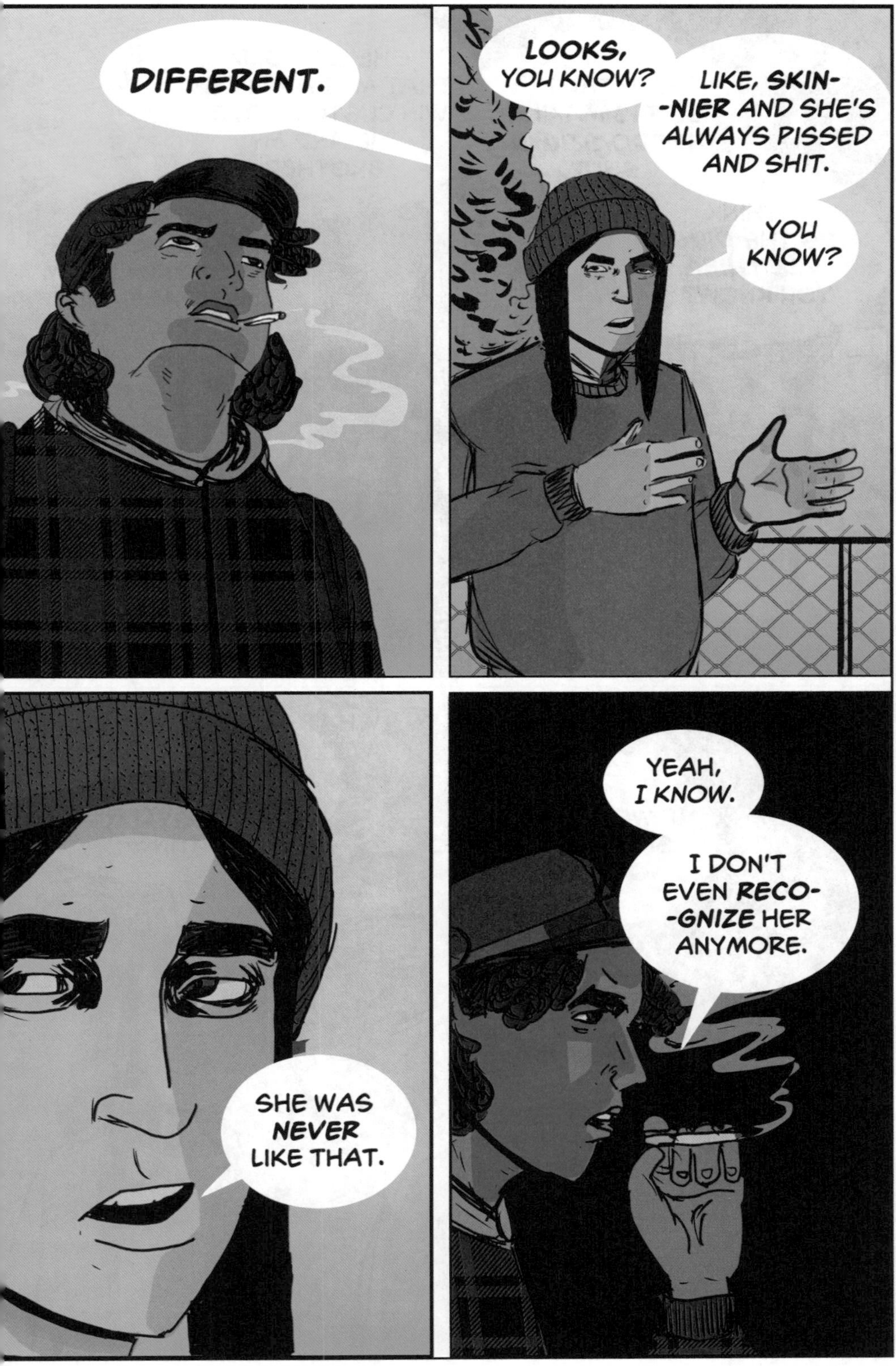
DIFFERENT.
LOOKS, YOU KNOW?
LIKE, SKIN- -NIER AND SHE'S ALWAYS PISSED AND SHIT.
YOU KNOW?
SHE WAS NEVER LIKE THAT.
YEAH, I KNOW.
I DON'T EVEN RECO- -GNIZE HER ANYMORE.

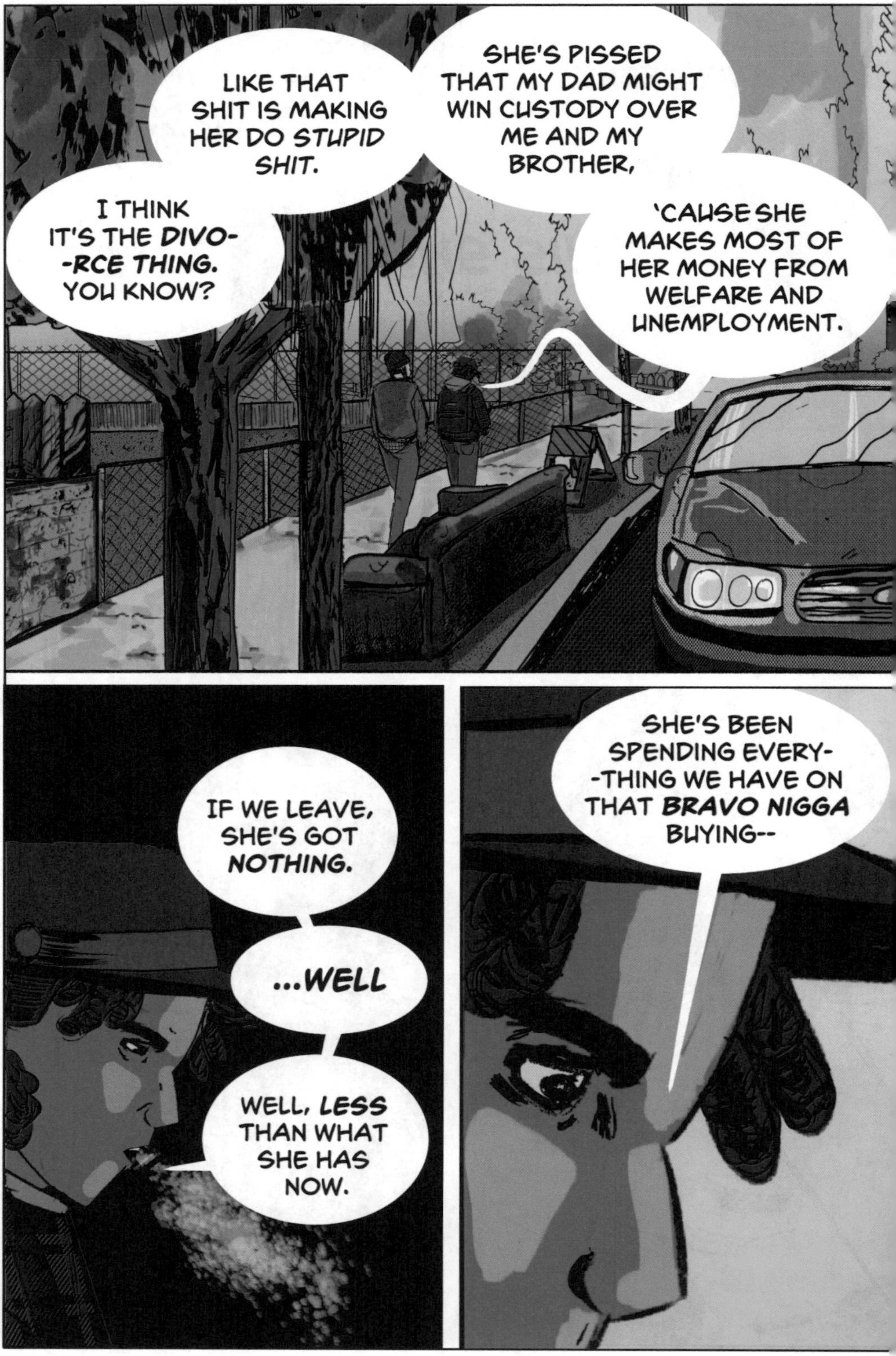
I THINK IT'S THE DIVO-RCE THING. YOU KNOW?
LIKE THAT SHIT IS MAKING HER DO STUPID SHIT.
SHE'S PISSED THAT MY DAD MIGHT WIN CUSTODY OVER ME AND MY BROTHER,
'CAUSE SHE MAKES MOST OF HER MONEY FROM WELFARE AND UNEMPLOYMENT.
IF WE LEAVE, SHE'S GOT NOTHING.
...WELL
WELL, LESS THAN WHAT SHE HAS NOW.
SHE'S BEEN SPENDING EVERY-THING WE HAVE ON THAT BRAVO NIGGA BUYING--

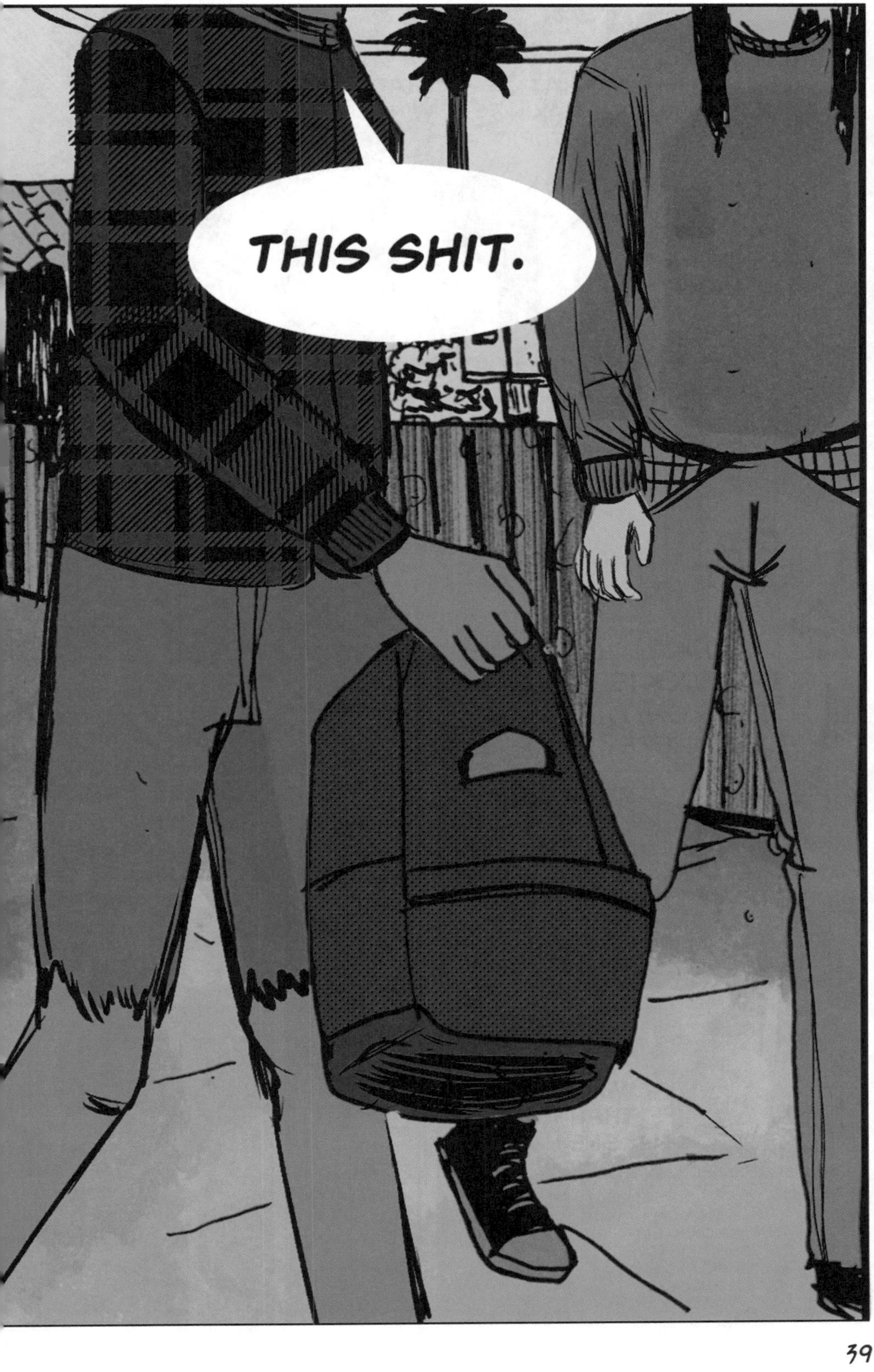
THIS SHIT.

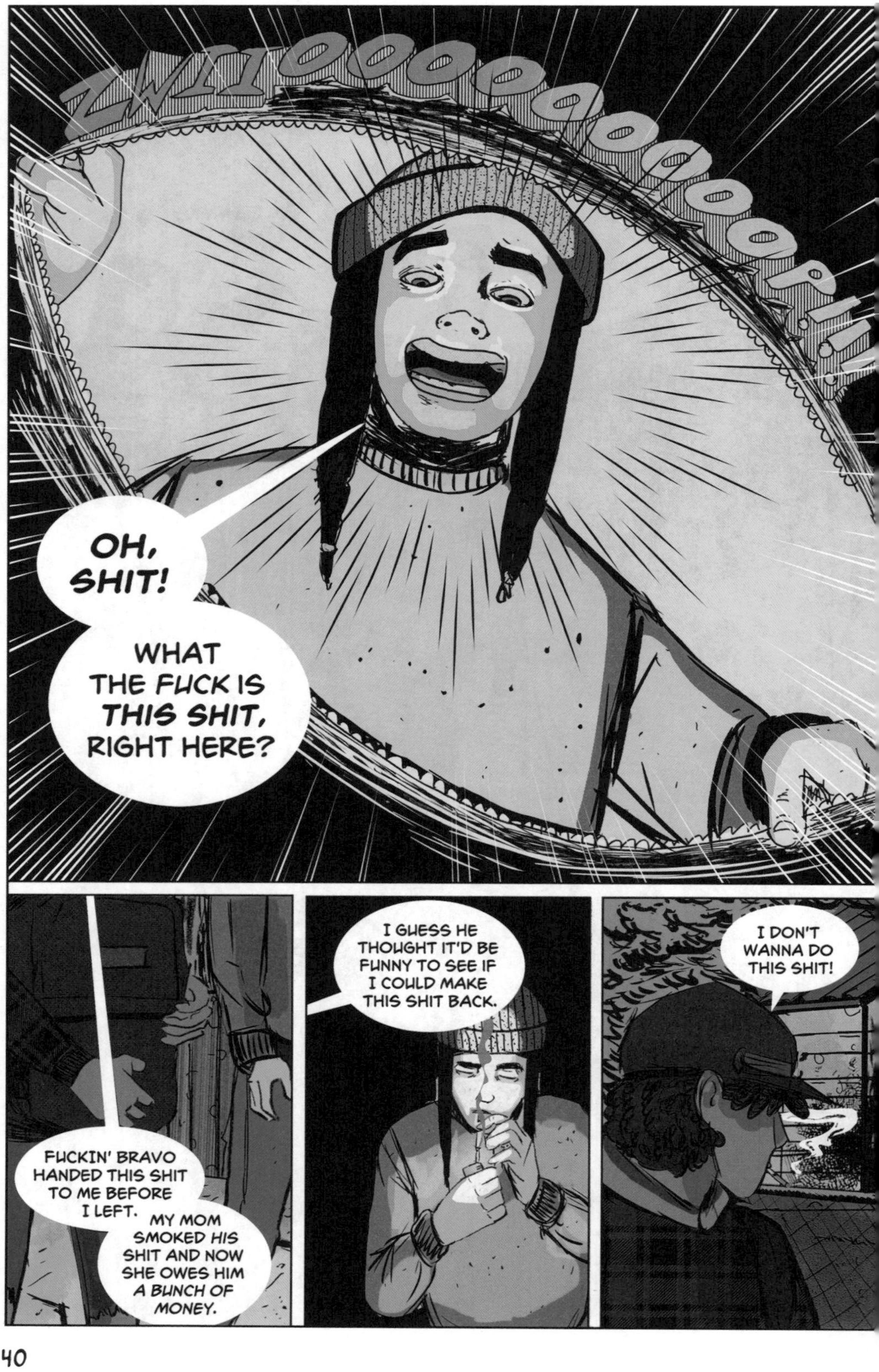
ZWIIOOOOOOOOOOOP!!!
OH, SHIT!
WHAT THE FUCK IS THIS SHIT, RIGHT HERE?
FUCKIN' BRAVO HANDED THIS SHIT TO ME BEFORE I LEFT.
MY MOM SMOKED HIS SHIT AND NOW SHE OWES HIM A BUNCH OF MONEY.
I GUESS HE THOUGHT IT'D BE FUNNY TO SEE IF I COULD MAKE THIS SHIT BACK.
I DON'T WANNA DO THIS SHIT!

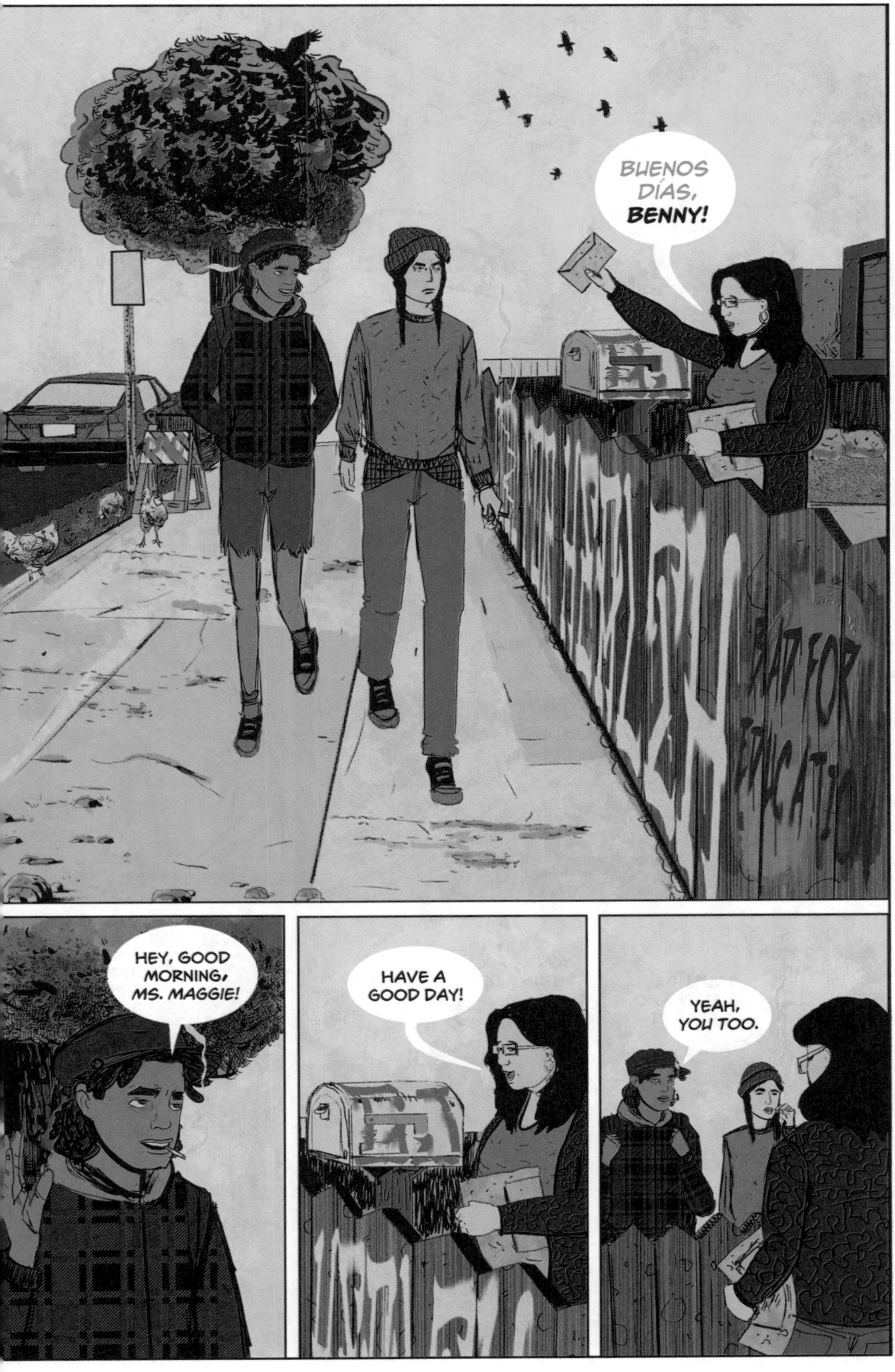
BUENOS DÍAS, BENNY!
HEY, GOOD MORNING, MS. MAGGIE!
HAVE A GOOD DAY!
YEAH, YOU TOO.

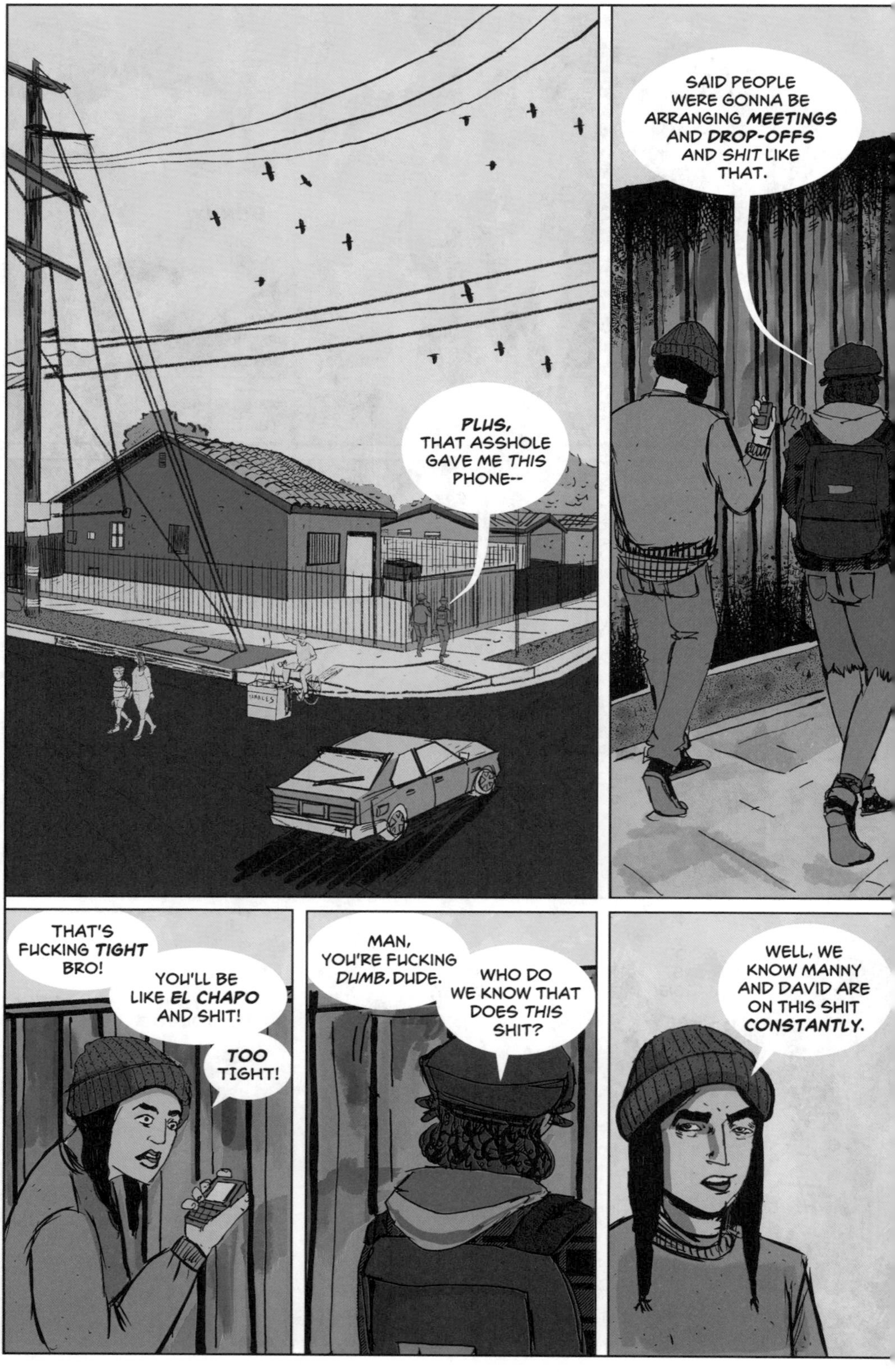
PLUS, THAT ASSHOLE GAVE ME THIS PHONE--
SAID PEOPLE WERE GONNA BE ARRANGING MEETINGS AND DROP-OFFS AND SHIT LIKE THAT.
THAT'S FUCKING TIGHT BRO!
YOU'LL BE LIKE EL CHAPO AND SHIT!
TOO TIGHT!
MAN, YOU'RE FUCKING DUMB, DUDE.
WHO DO WE KNOW THAT DOES THIS SHIT?
WELL, WE KNOW MANNY AND DAVID ARE ON THIS SHIT CONSTANTLY.

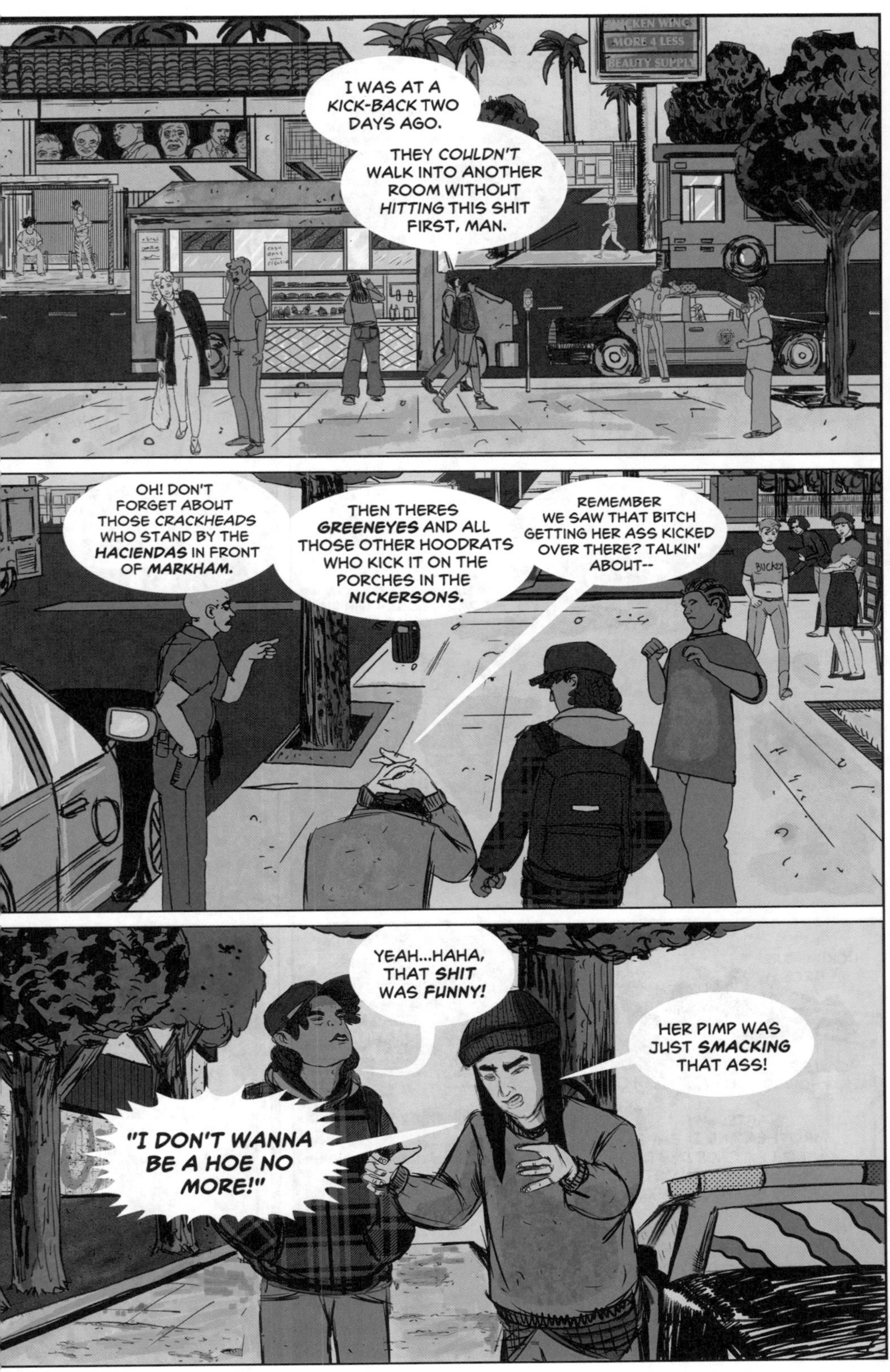

CHICKEN WINGS
MORE 4 LESS
BEAUTY SUPPLY
I WAS AT A KICK-BACK TWO DAYS AGO.
THEY COULDN'T WALK INTO ANOTHER ROOM WITHOUT HITTING THIS SHIT FIRST, MAN.
OH! DON'T FORGET ABOUT THOSE CRACKHEADS WHO STAND BY THE HACIENDAS IN FRONT OF MARKHAM.
THEN THERES GREENEYES AND ALL THOSE OTHER HOODRATS WHO KICK IT ON THE PORCHES IN THE NICKERSONS.
REMEMBER WE SAW THAT BITCH GETTING HER ASS KICKED OVER THERE? TALKIN' ABOUT--
BUCKEY
YEAH...HAHA, THAT SHIT WAS FUNNY!
HER PIMP WAS JUST SMACKING THAT ASS!
"I DON'T WANNA BE A HOE NO MORE!"

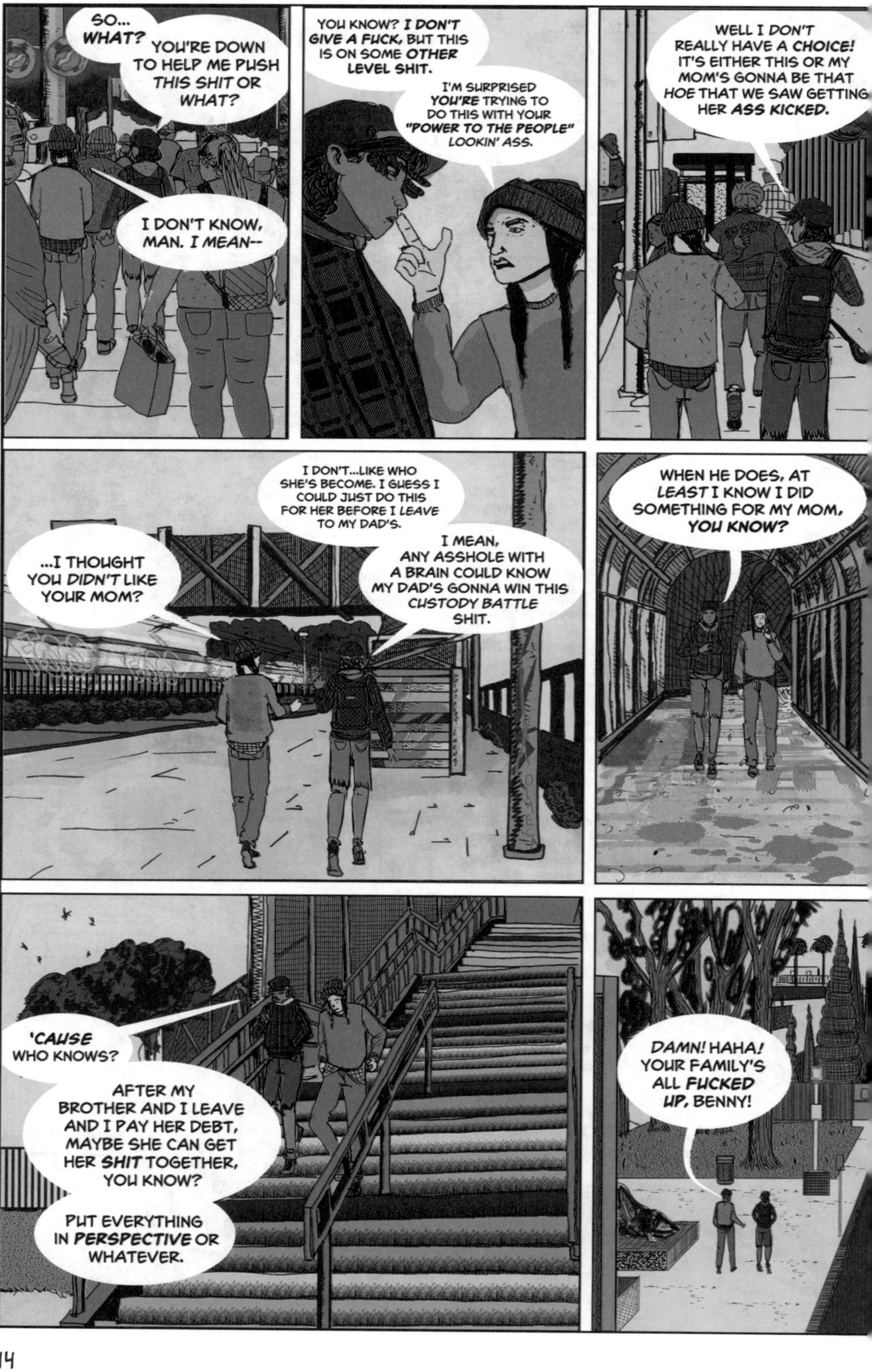

SO... WHAT? YOU'RE DOWN TO HELP ME PUSH THIS SHIT OR WHAT?
I DON'T KNOW, MAN. I MEAN--
YOU KNOW? I DON'T GIVE A FUCK, BUT THIS IS ON SOME OTHER LEVEL SHIT.
I'M SURPRISED YOU'RE TRYING TO DO THIS WITH YOUR "POWER TO THE PEOPLE" LOOKIN' ASS.
WELL I DON'T REALLY HAVE A CHOICE! IT'S EITHER THIS OR MY MOM'S GONNA BE THAT HOE THAT WE SAW GETTING HER ASS KICKED.
...I THOUGHT YOU DIDN'T LIKE YOUR MOM?
I DON'T...LIKE WHO SHE'S BECOME. I GUESS I COULD JUST DO THIS FOR HER BEFORE I LEAVE TO MY DAD'S.
I MEAN, ANY ASSHOLE WITH A BRAIN COULD KNOW MY DAD'S GONNA WIN THIS CUSTODY BATTLE SHIT.
WHEN HE DOES, AT LEAST I KNOW I DID SOMETHING FOR MY MOM, YOU KNOW?
'CAUSE WHO KNOWS?
AFTER MY BROTHER AND I LEAVE AND I PAY HER DEBT, MAYBE SHE CAN GET HER SHIT TOGETHER, YOU KNOW?
PUT EVERYTHING IN PERSPECTIVE OR WHATEVER.
DAMN! HAHA! YOUR FAMILY'S ALL FUCKED UP, BENNY!

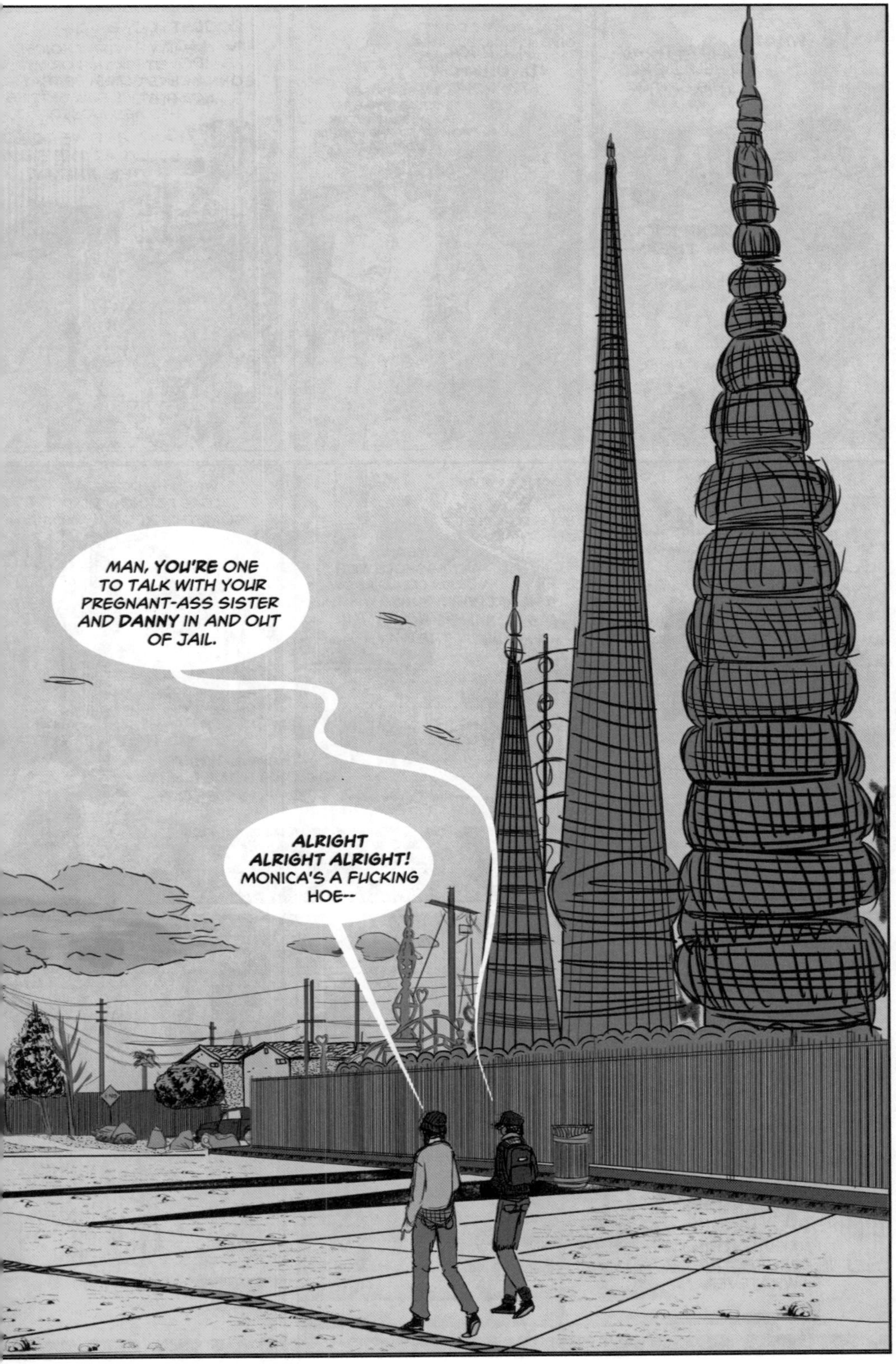
MAN, YOU'RE ONE TO TALK WITH YOUR PREGNANT-ASS SISTER AND DANNY IN AND OUT OF JAIL.
ALRIGHT ALRIGHT ALRIGHT! MONICA'S A FUCKING HOE--

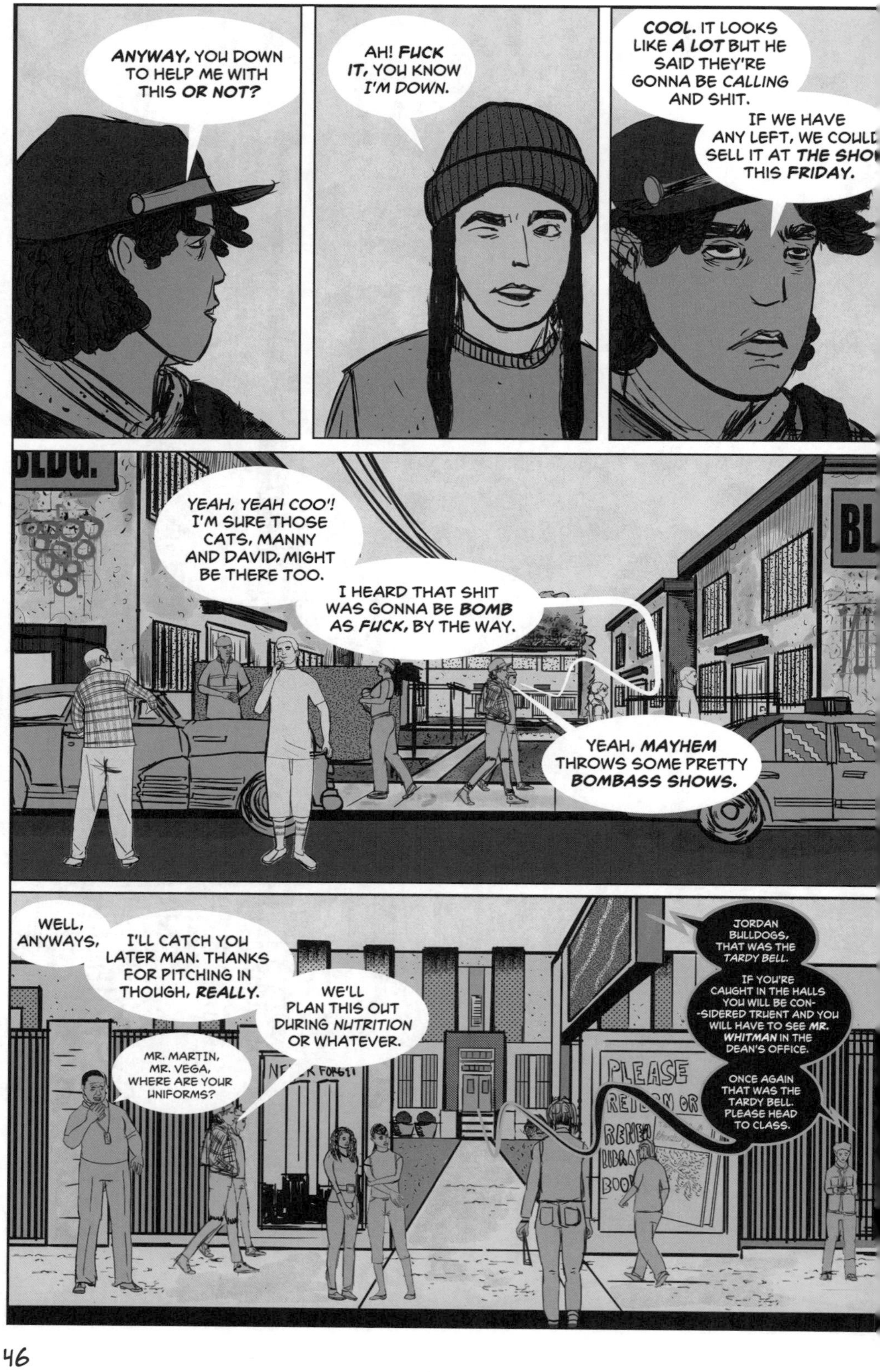
ANYWAY, YOU DOWN TO HELP ME WITH THIS OR NOT?
AH! FUCK IT, YOU KNOW I'M DOWN.
COOL. IT LOOKS LIKE A LOT BUT HE SAID THEY'RE GONNA BE CALLING AND SHIT.
IF WE HAVE ANY LEFT, WE COULD SELL IT AT THE SHOW THIS FRIDAY.
YEAH, YEAH COO'! I'M SURE THOSE CATS, MANNY AND DAVID, MIGHT BE THERE TOO.
I HEARD THAT SHIT WAS GONNA BE BOMB AS FUCK, BY THE WAY.
YEAH, MAYHEM THROWS SOME PRETTY BOMBASS SHOWS.
WELL, ANYWAYS,
I'LL CATCH YOU LATER MAN. THANKS FOR PITCHING IN THOUGH, REALLY.
WE'LL PLAN THIS OUT DURING NUTRITION OR WHATEVER.
MR. MARTIN, MR. VEGA, WHERE ARE YOUR UNIFORMS?
JORDAN BULLDOGS, THAT WAS THE TARDY BELL.
IF YOU'RE CAUGHT IN THE HALLS YOU WILL BE CON-SIDERED TRUENT AND YOU WILL HAVE TO SEE MR. WHITMAN IN THE DEAN'S OFFICE.
ONCE AGAIN THAT WAS THE TARDY BELL. PLEASE HEAD TO CLASS.
PLEASE

MONDAY
NIGHT

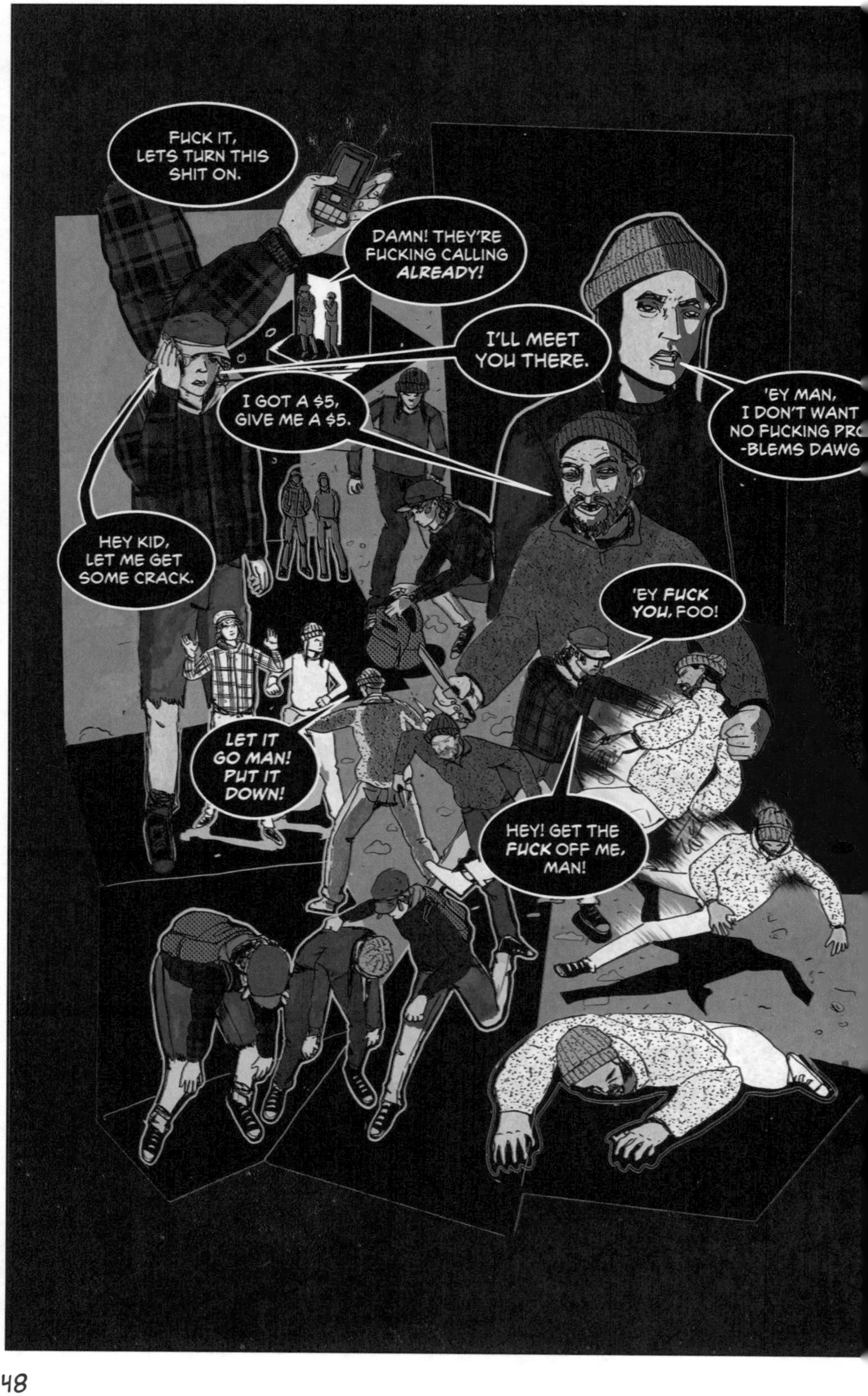
FUCK IT, LETS TURN THIS SHIT ON.
DAMN! THEY'RE FUCKING CALLING ALREADY!
I'LL MEET YOU THERE.
'EY MAN, I DON'T WANT NO FUCKING PRO -BLEMS DAWG
I GOT A $5, GIVE ME A $5.
HEY KID, LET ME GET SOME CRACK.
'EY FUCK YOU, FOO!
LET IT GO MAN! PUT IT DOWN!
HEY! GET THE FUCK OFF ME, MAN!

TUESDAY
COMPTON AVE. & 111th ST.

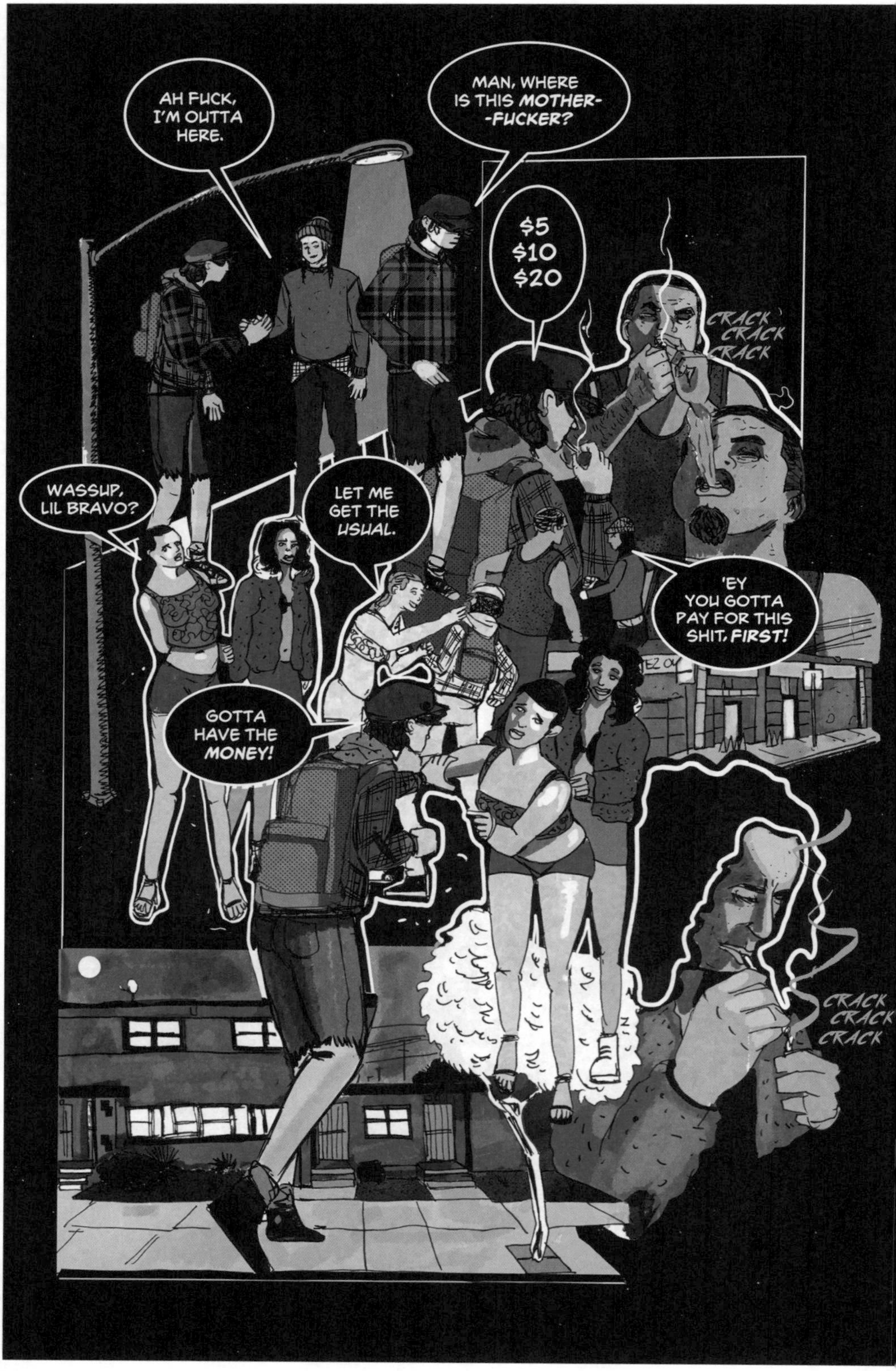
AH FUCK, I'M OUTTA HERE.
MAN, WHERE IS THIS MOTHER- -FUCKER?
$5 $10 $20
CRACK CRACK CRACK
WASSUP, LIL BRAVO?
LET ME GET THE USUAL.
'EY YOU GOTTA PAY FOR THIS SHIT, FIRST!
GOTTA HAVE THE MONEY!
CRACK CRACK CRACK

WEDNESDAY
JORDAN DOWNS HOUSING PROJECTS
101st ST. & GRAPE ST.

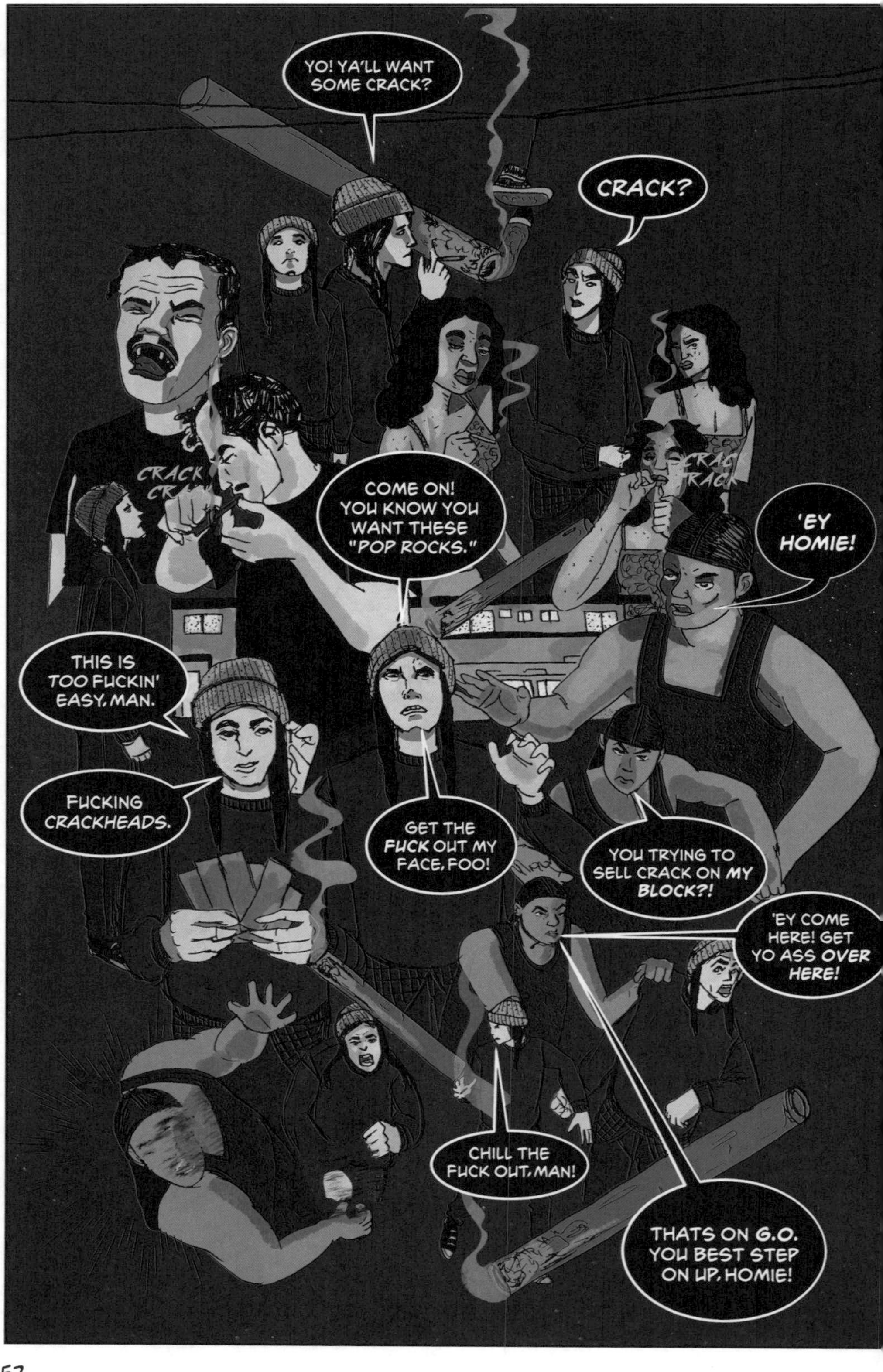

YO! YA'LL WANT SOME CRACK?
CRACK?
CRACK CRACK
CRAC RACK
COME ON! YOU KNOW YOU WANT THESE "POP ROCKS."
'EY HOMIE!
THIS IS TOO FUCKIN' EASY, MAN.
FUCKING CRACKHEADS.
GET THE FUCK OUT MY FACE, FOO!
YOU TRYING TO SELL CRACK ON MY BLOCK?!
'EY COME HERE! GET YO ASS OVER HERE!
CHILL THE FUCK OUT, MAN!
THATS ON G.O. YOU BEST STEP ON UP, HOMIE!

THURSDAY
RAINBOW BRIDGE
SANTA ANA BLVD. & GRAHAM AVE.

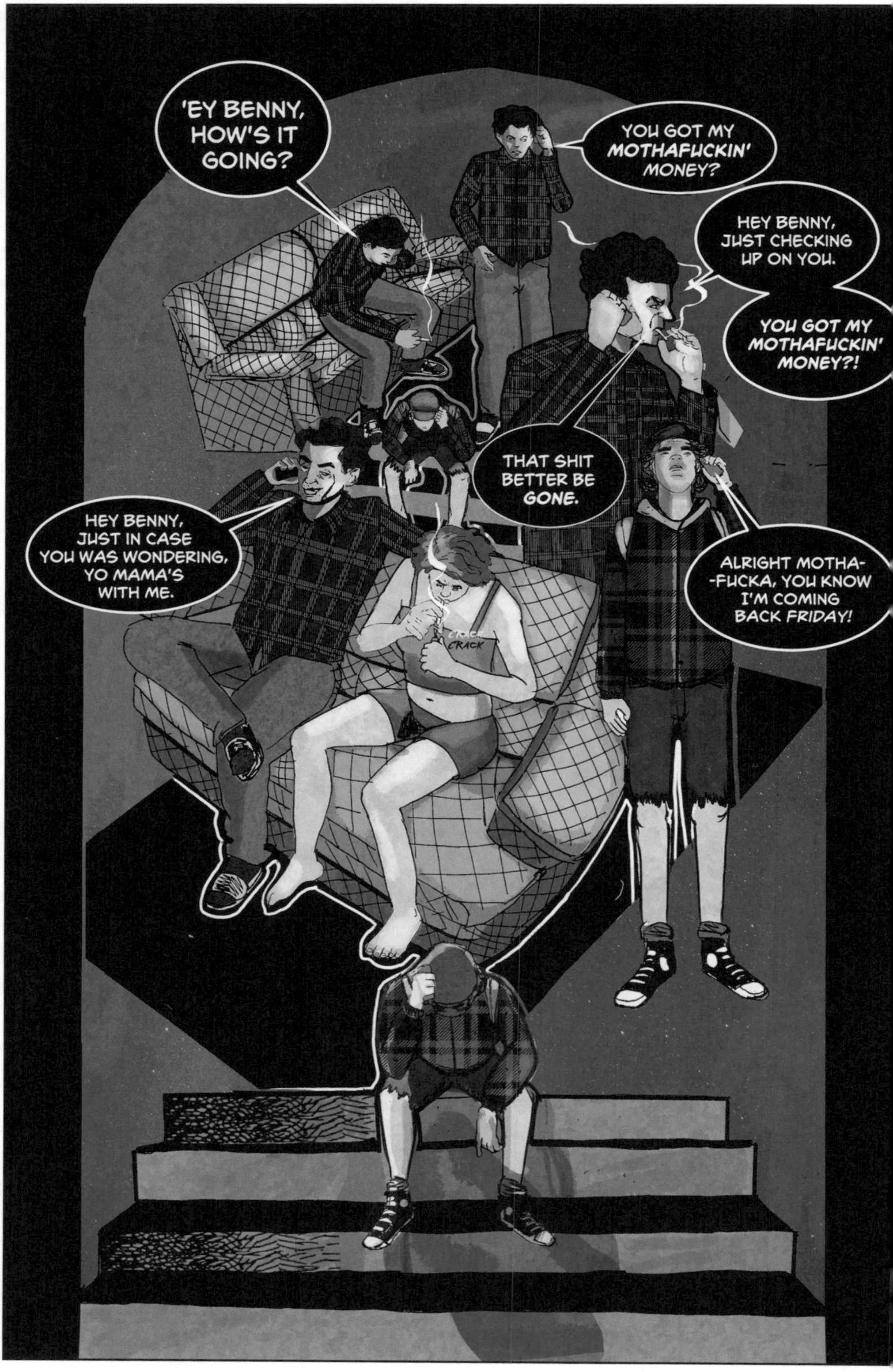
'EY BENNY, HOW'S IT GOING?
YOU GOT MY *MOTHAFUCKIN'* MONEY?
HEY BENNY, JUST CHECKING UP ON YOU.
YOU GOT MY MOTHAFUCKIN' MONEY?!
THAT SHIT BETTER BE **GONE.**
HEY BENNY, JUST IN CASE YOU WAS WONDERING, YO MAMA'S WITH ME.
ALRIGHT MOTHA--FUCKA, YOU KNOW I'M COMING BACK FRIDAY!
CRACK CRACK

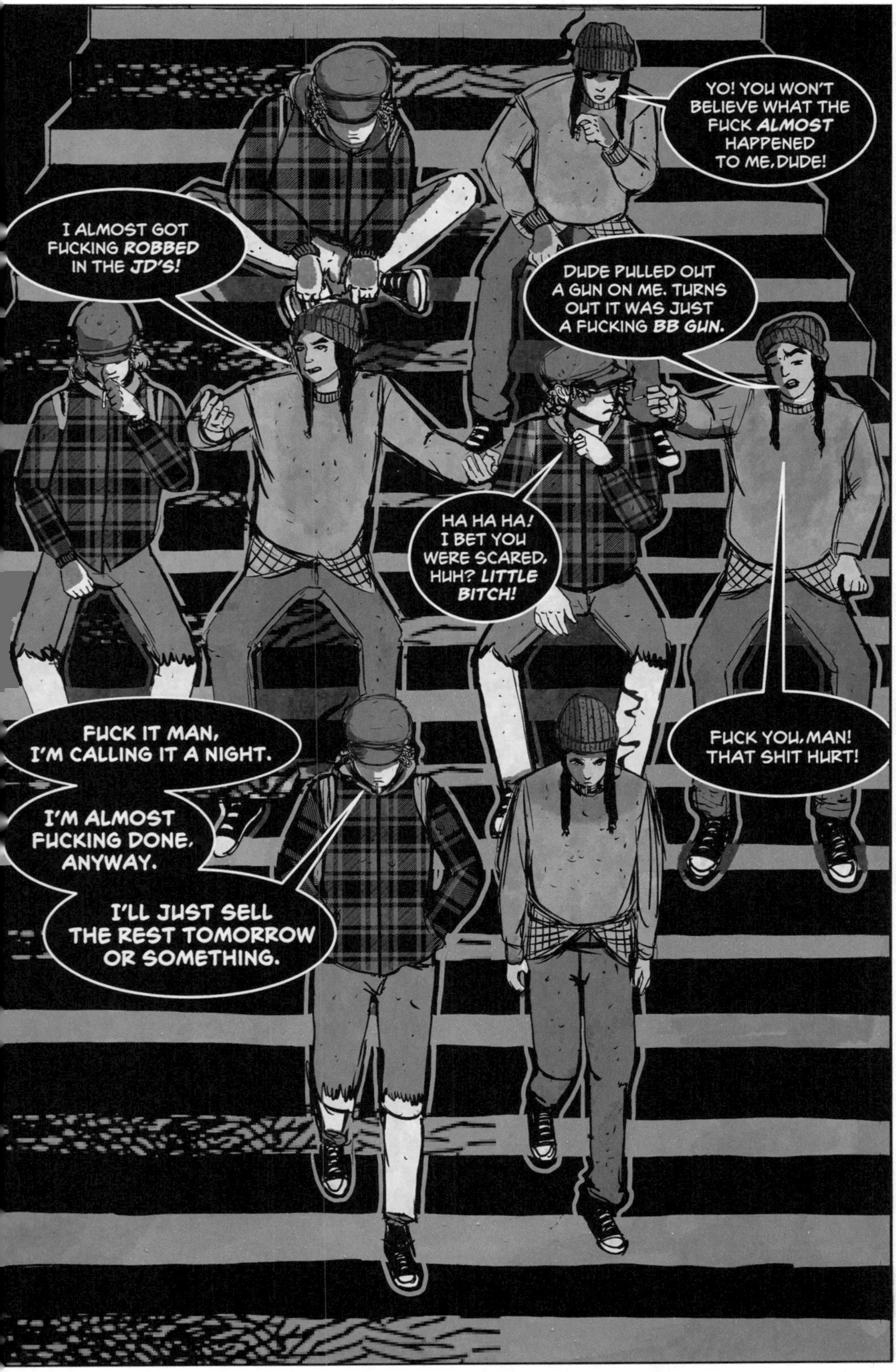
YO! YOU WON'T BELIEVE WHAT THE FUCK ALMOST HAPPENED TO ME, DUDE!
I ALMOST GOT FUCKING ROBBED IN THE JD'S!
DUDE PULLED OUT A GUN ON ME. TURNS OUT IT WAS JUST A FUCKING BB GUN.
HA HA HA! I BET YOU WERE SCARED, HUH? LITTLE BITCH!
FUCK YOU, MAN! THAT SHIT HURT!
FUCK IT MAN, I'M CALLING IT A NIGHT.
I'M ALMOST FUCKING DONE, ANYWAY.
I'LL JUST SELL THE REST TOMORROW OR SOMETHING.

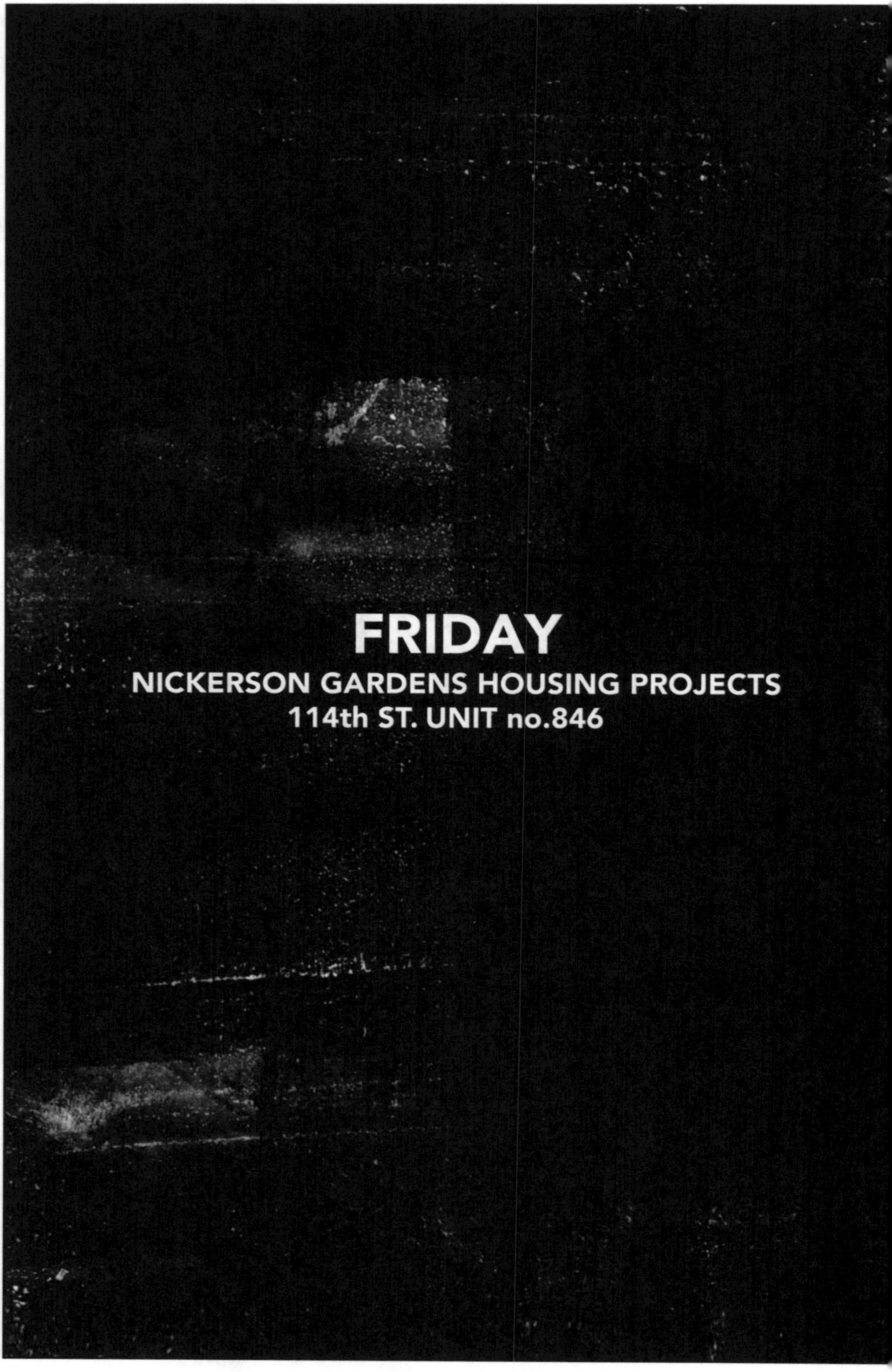

FRIDAY

NICKERSON GARDENS HOUSING PROJECTS
114th ST. UNIT no.846

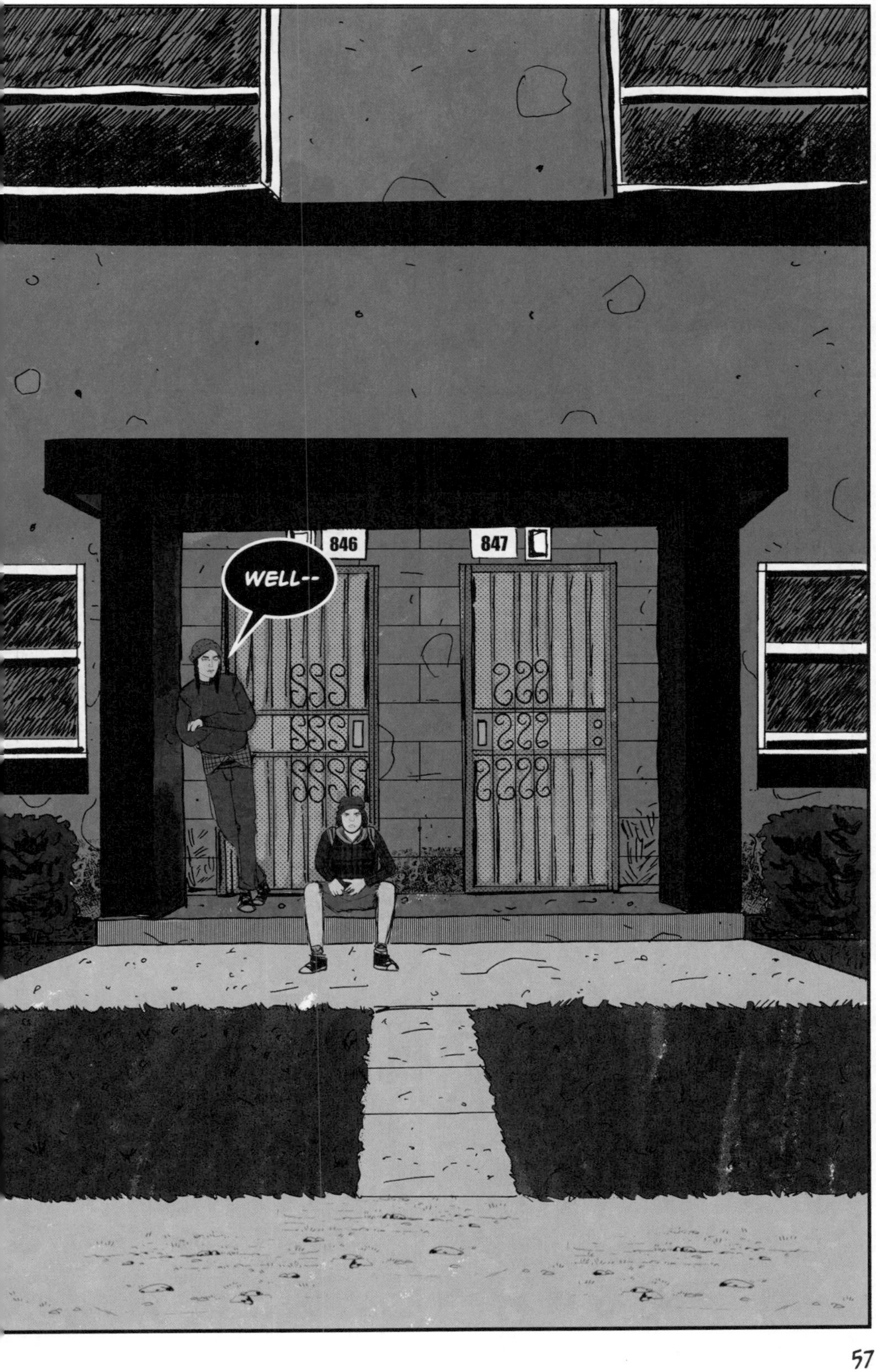
846
847
WELL--

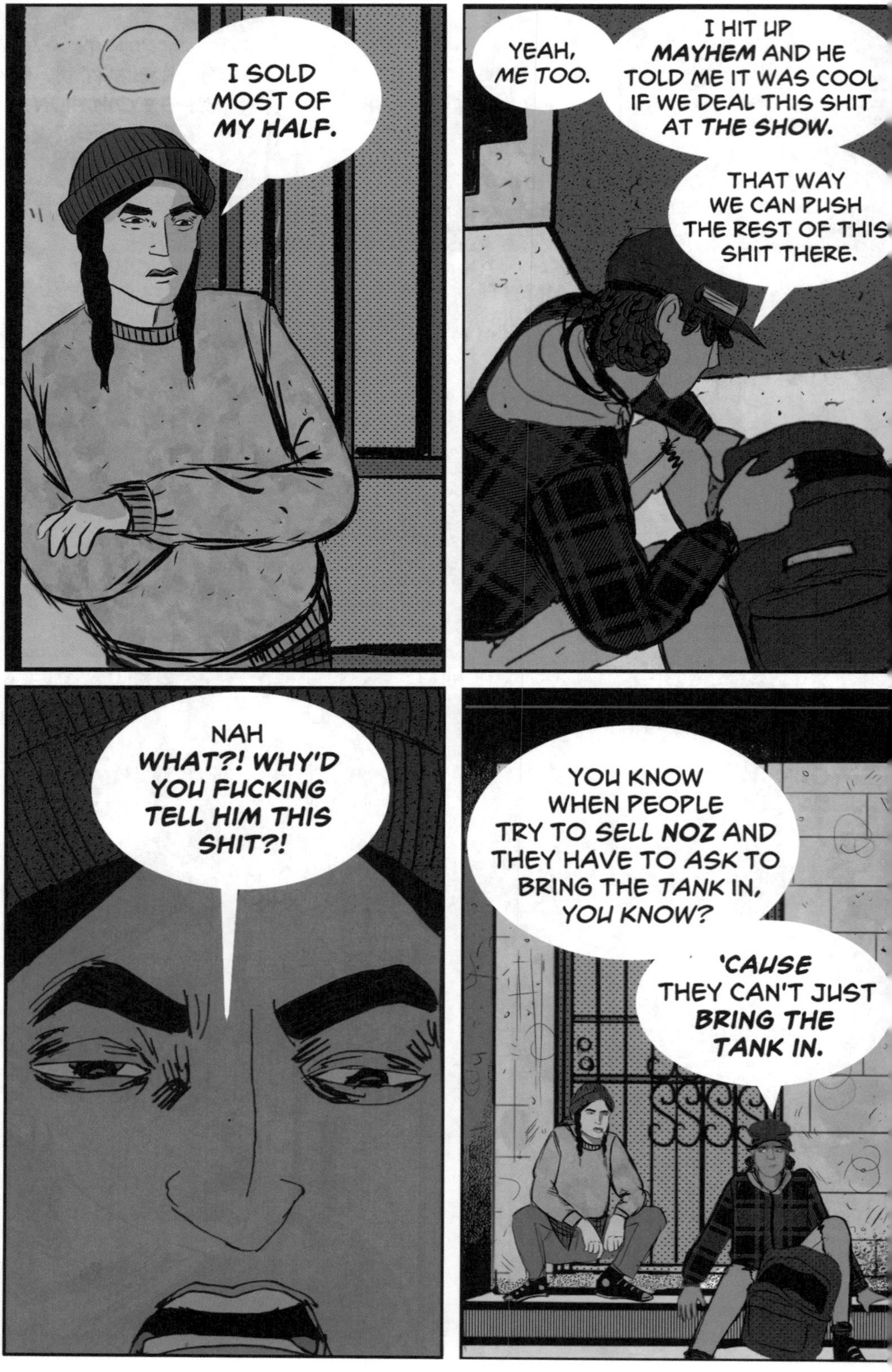
I SOLD MOST OF MY HALF.
YEAH, ME TOO.
I HIT UP MAYHEM AND HE TOLD ME IT WAS COOL IF WE DEAL THIS SHIT AT THE SHOW.
THAT WAY WE CAN PUSH THE REST OF THIS SHIT THERE.
NAH WHAT?! WHY'D YOU FUCKING TELL HIM THIS SHIT?!
YOU KNOW WHEN PEOPLE TRY TO SELL NOZ AND THEY HAVE TO ASK TO BRING THE TANK IN, YOU KNOW?
'CAUSE THEY CAN'T JUST BRING THE TANK IN.

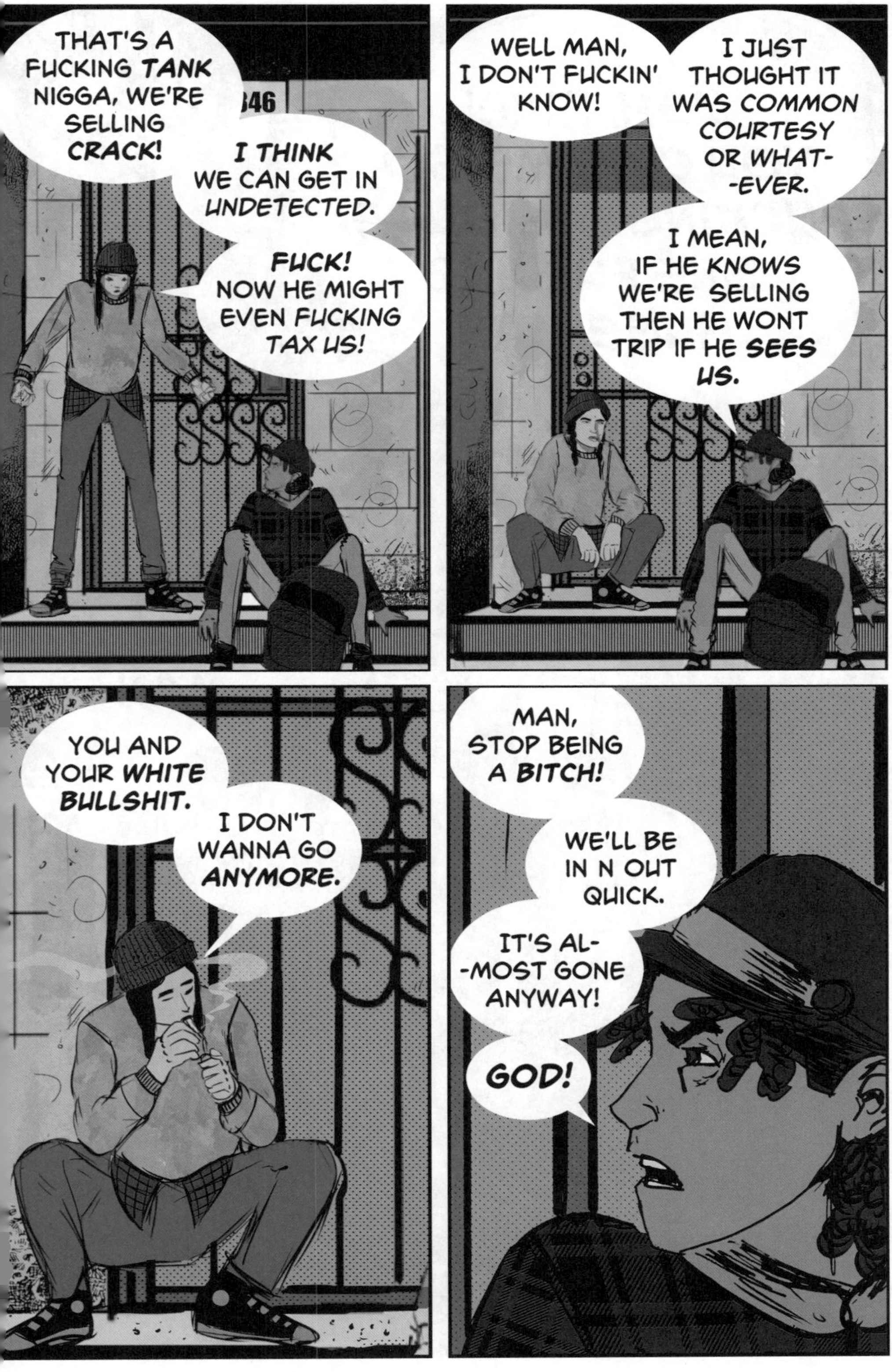
THAT'S A FUCKING **TANK** NIGGA, WE'RE SELLING **CRACK!**
I THINK WE CAN GET IN UNDETECTED.
FUCK! NOW HE MIGHT EVEN *FUCKING* *TAX US!*
WELL MAN, I DON'T FUCKIN' KNOW!
I JUST THOUGHT IT WAS COMMON COURTESY OR WHAT- -EVER.
I MEAN, IF HE KNOWS WE'RE SELLING THEN HE WONT TRIP IF HE **SEES US.**
YOU AND YOUR **WHITE BULLSHIT.**
I DON'T WANNA GO **ANYMORE.**
MAN, STOP BEING A **BITCH!**
WE'LL BE IN N OUT QUICK.
IT'S AL- -MOST GONE ANYWAY!
GOD!

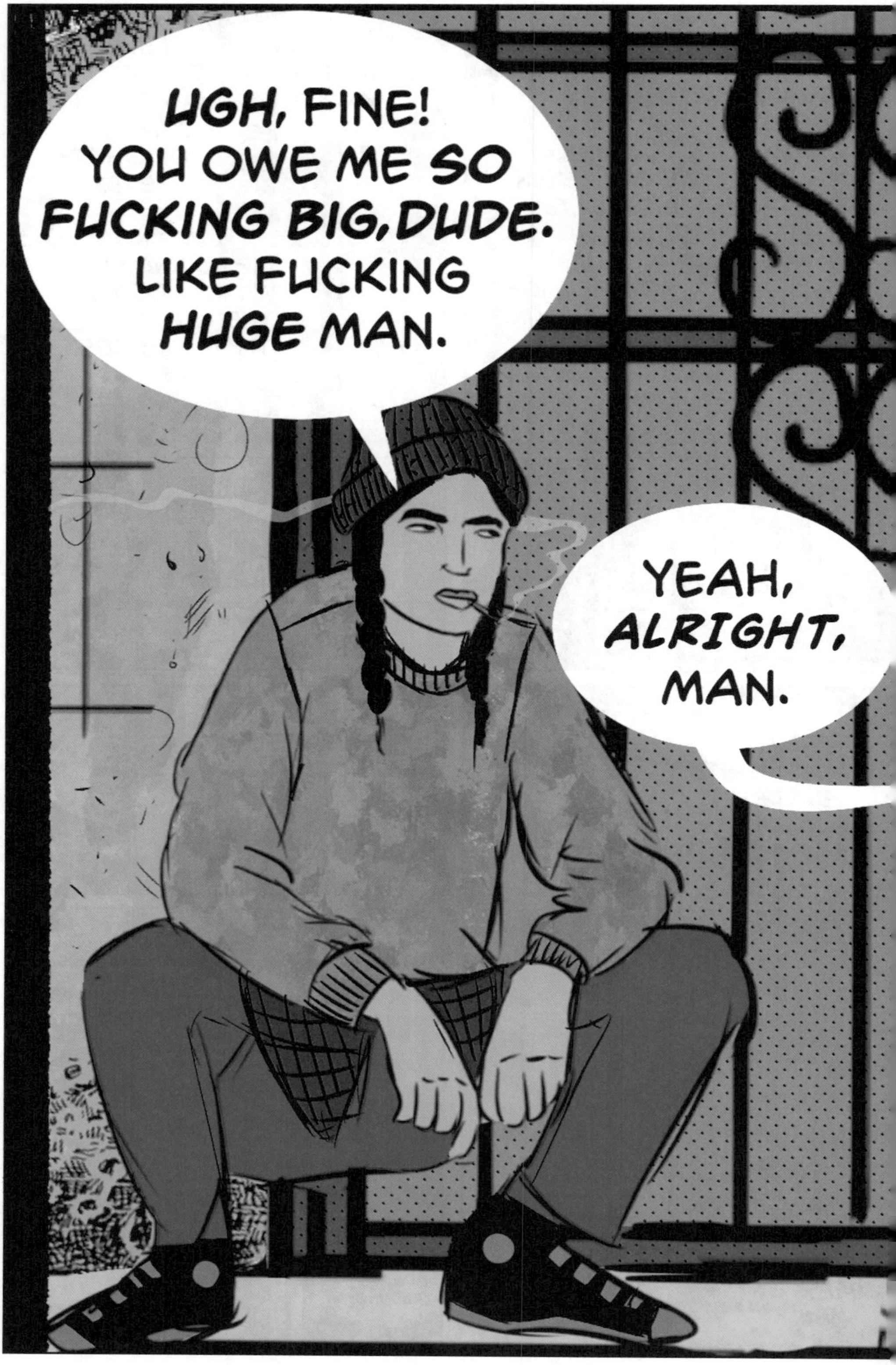
UGH, FINE! YOU OWE ME SO FUCKING BIG, DUDE. LIKE FUCKING HUGE MAN.
YEAH, ALRIGHT, MAN.

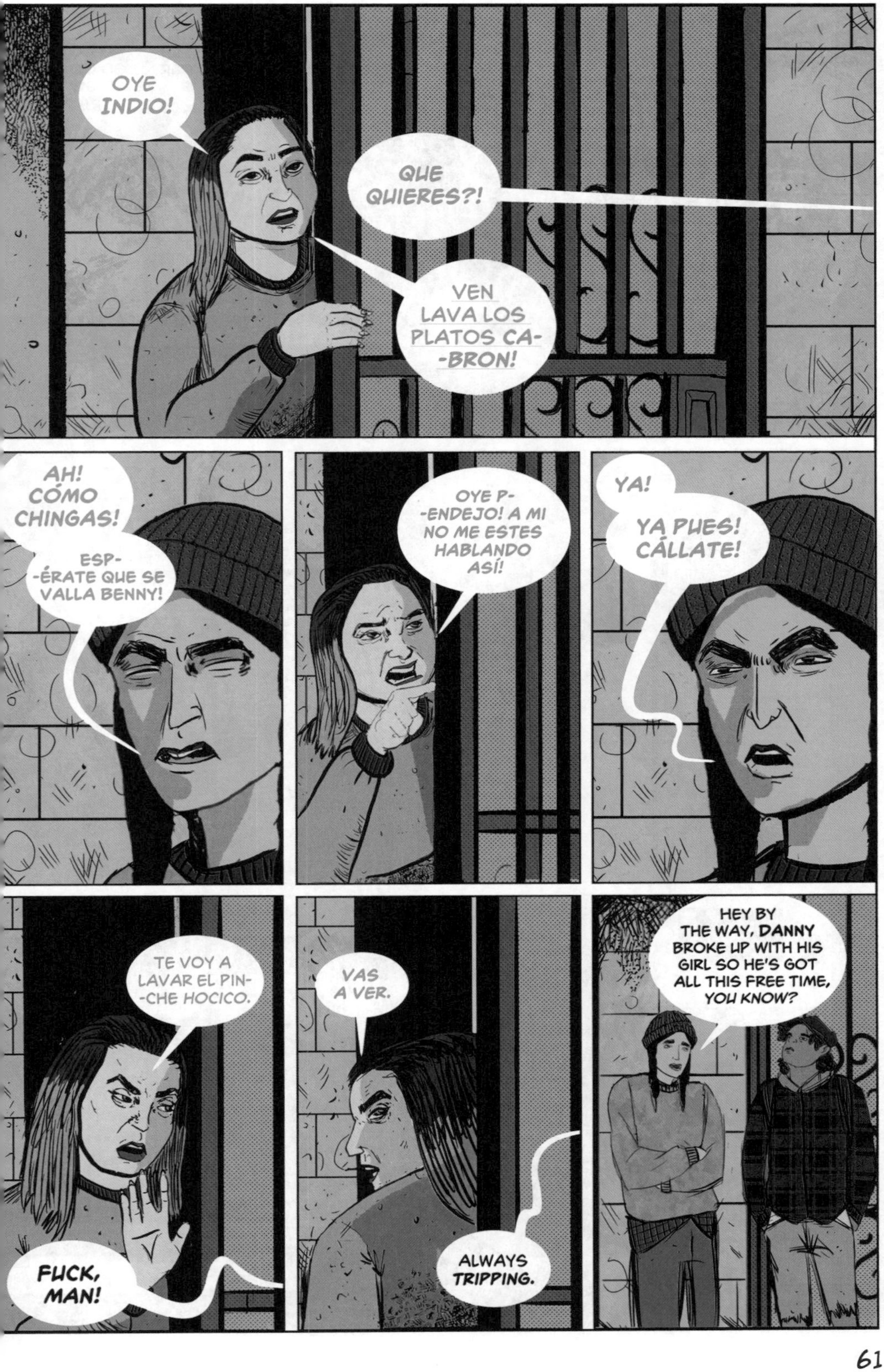
OYE INDIO!
QUE QUIERES?!
VEN LAVA LOS PLATOS CA- -BRON!
AH! CÓMO CHINGAS!
ESP- -ÉRATE QUE SE VALLA BENNY!
OYE P- -ENDEJO! A MI NO ME ESTES HABLANDO ASÍ!
YA!
YA PUES! CÁLLATE!
TE VOY A LAVAR EL PIN- -CHE HOCICO.
VAS A VER.
FUCK, MAN!
ALWAYS TRIPPING.
HEY BY THE WAY, DANNY BROKE UP WITH HIS GIRL SO HE'S GOT ALL THIS FREE TIME, YOU KNOW?

HE SAID HE'LL GIVE US A RIDE TO THAT SHOW AND SHIT.

WE CAN PICK YOU UP LATER, BUT *BE READY NIGGA, YOU ALWAYS TAKE FOREVER! I'M SERIOUS.*

MAN, SHUT THE FUCK UP, MAN. I'LL BE QUICK.

ALRIGHT, I'LL CATCH YOU LATER DAWG.

I GOTTA GO DO SOME SHIT, *MY MOM'S TRIPPING.*

PEACE.

CLAP

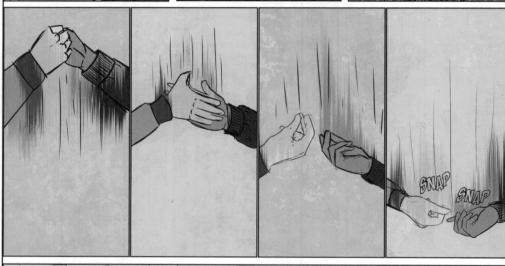

SNAP

SNAP

SIGH

SLAM!!

847

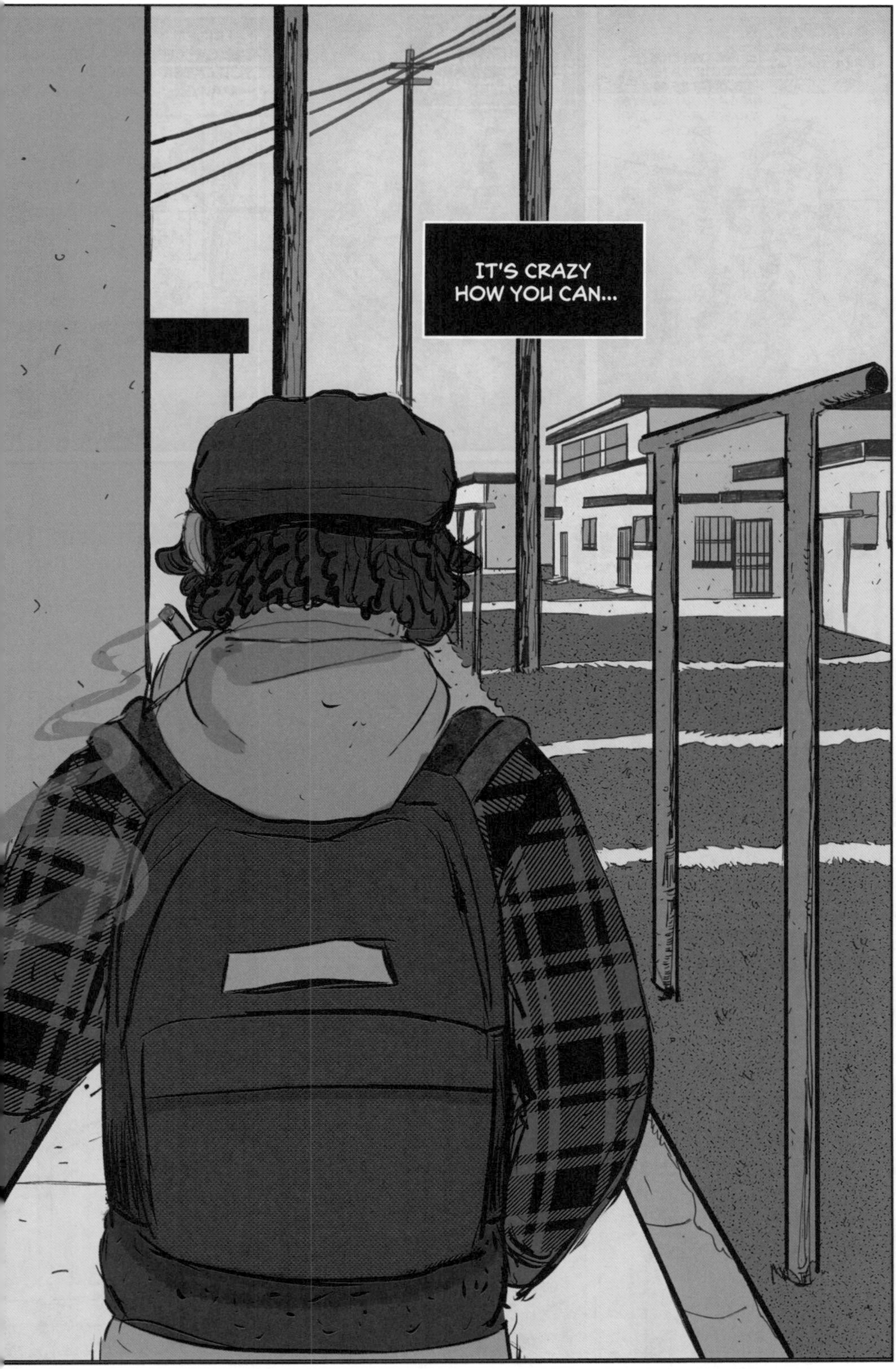
IT'S CRAZY HOW YOU CAN...

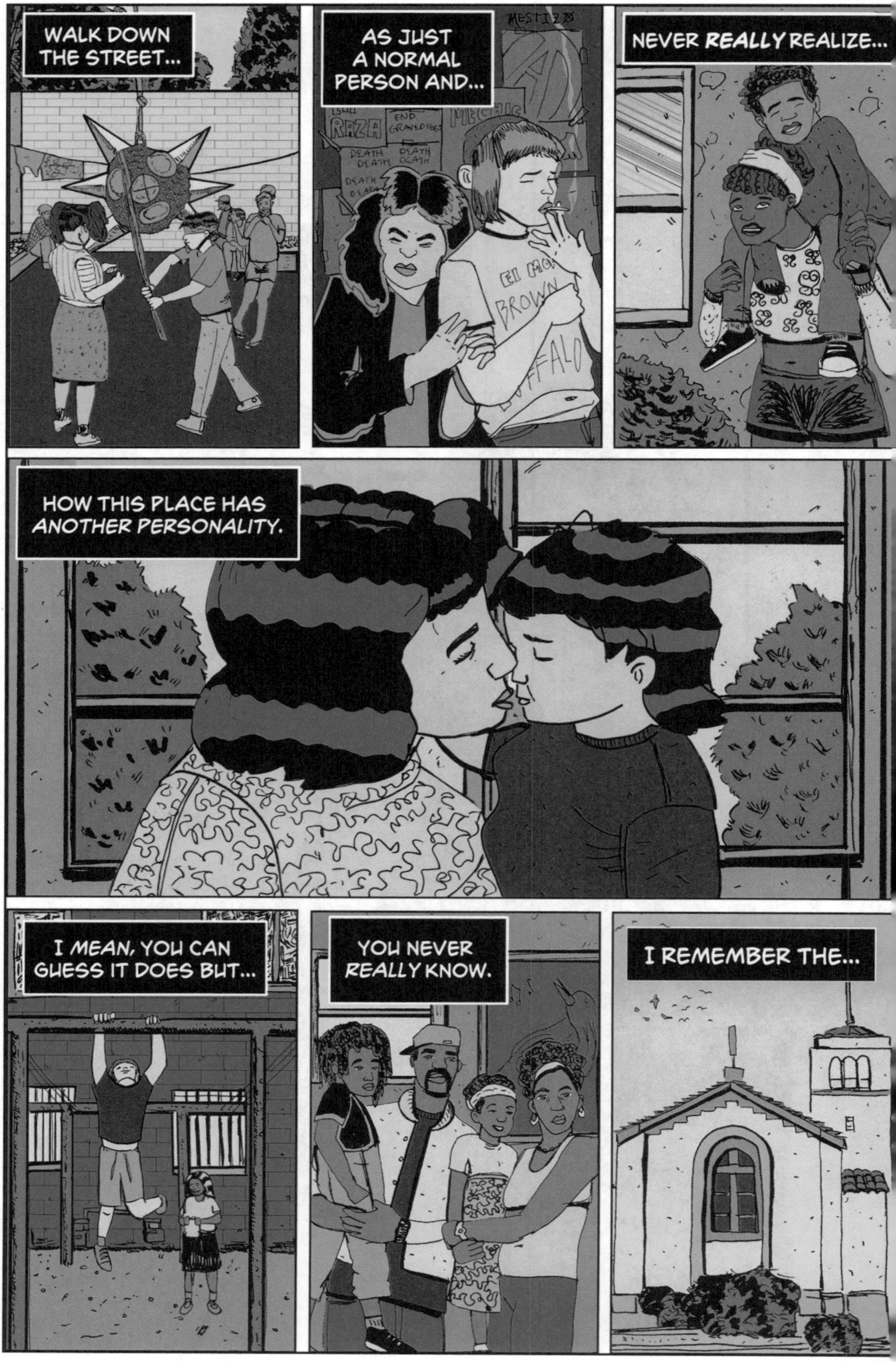
WALK DOWN THE STREET...
AS JUST A NORMAL PERSON AND...
NEVER *REALLY* REALIZE...
HOW THIS PLACE HAS *ANOTHER PERSONALITY.*
I *MEAN,* YOU CAN GUESS IT DOES BUT...
YOU NEVER *REALLY* KNOW.
I REMEMBER THE...

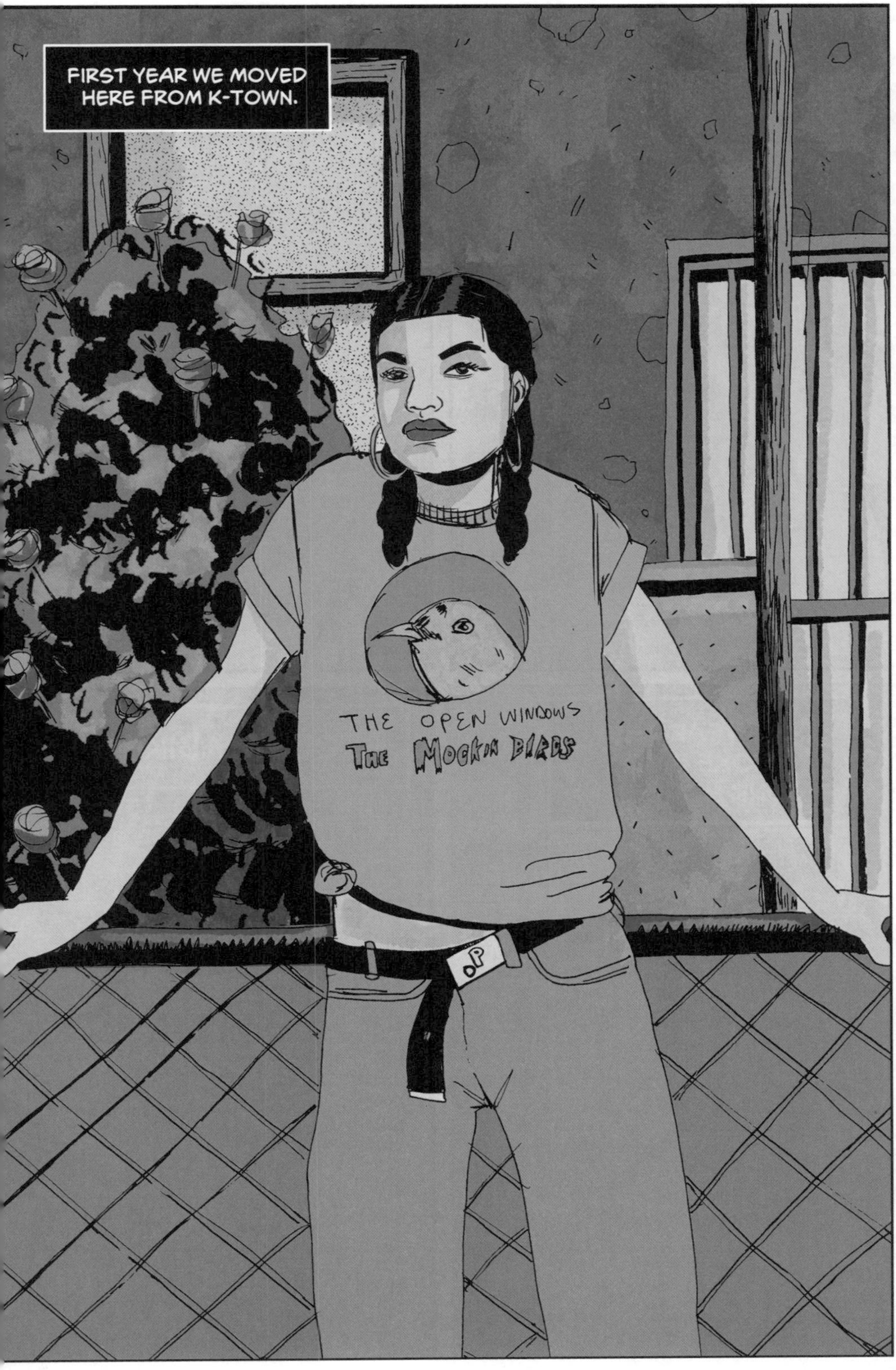
FIRST YEAR WE MOVED HERE FROM K-TOWN.
THE OPEN WINDOWS
THE MOCKIN BIRDS

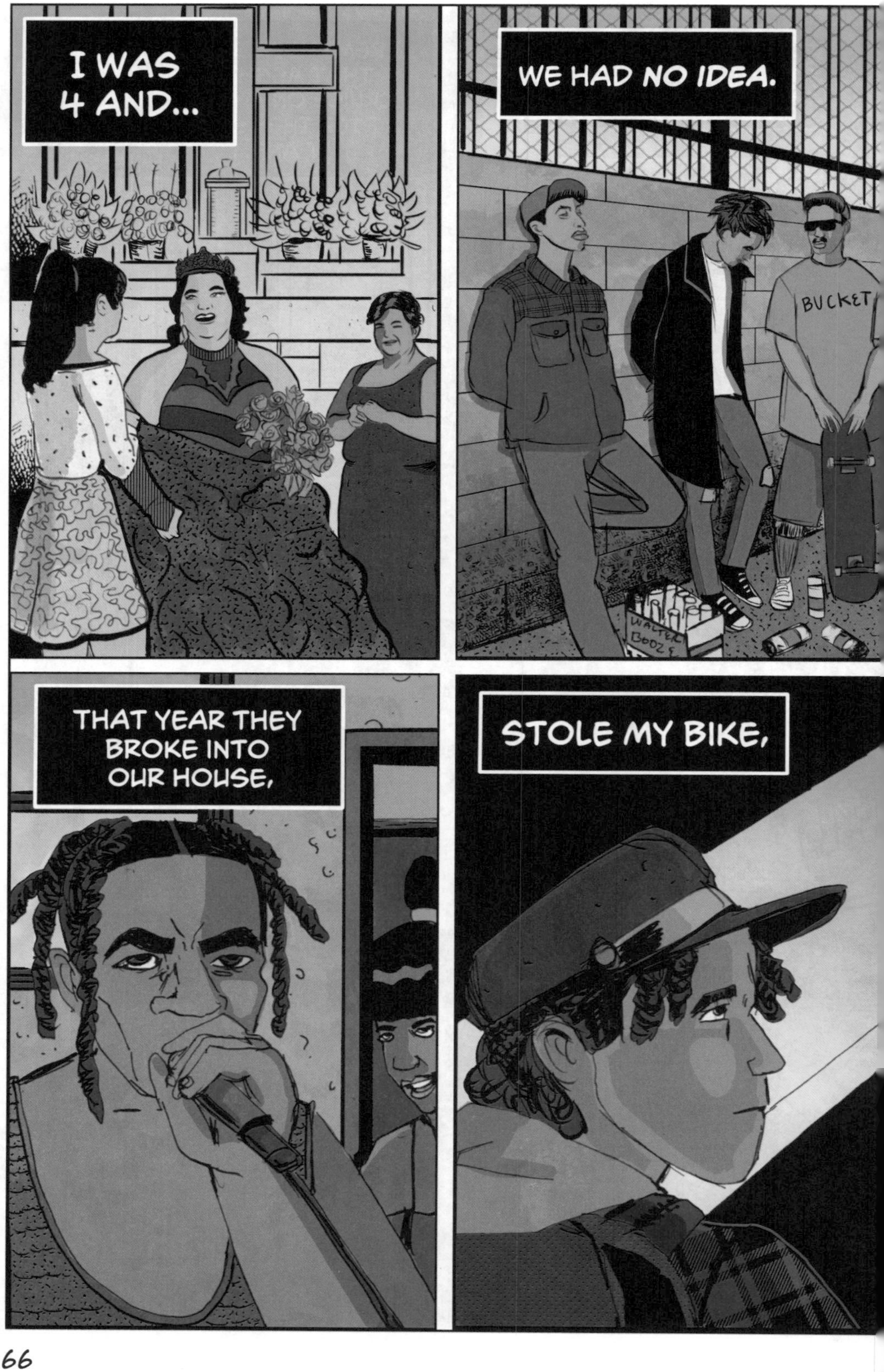
I WAS 4 AND...
WE HAD NO IDEA.
BUCKET
WALTER BOOZE
THAT YEAR THEY BROKE INTO OUR HOUSE,
STOLE MY BIKE,

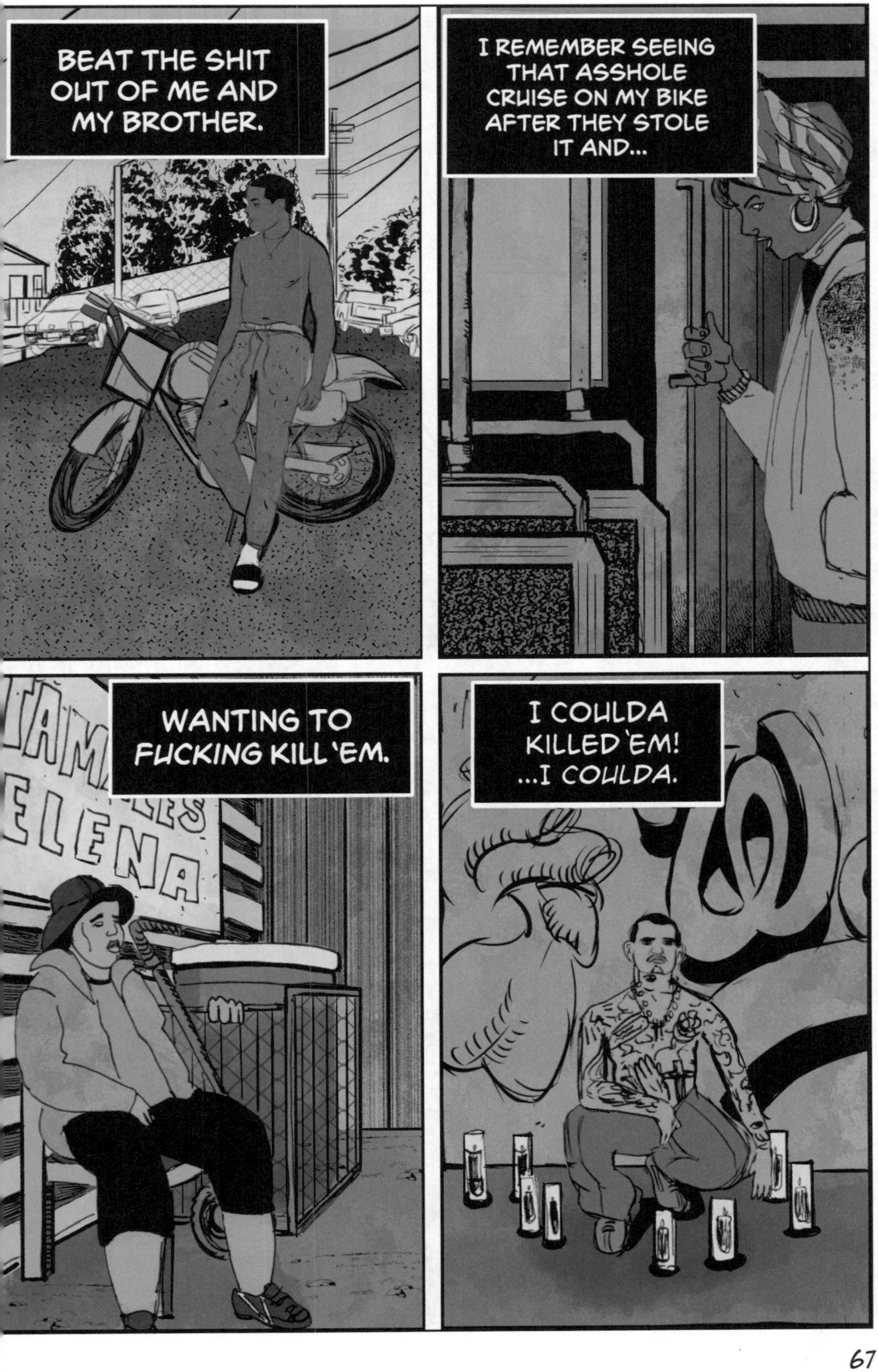
BEAT THE SHIT OUT OF ME AND MY BROTHER.
I REMEMBER SEEING THAT ASSHOLE CRUISE ON MY BIKE AFTER THEY STOLE IT AND...
WANTING TO FUCKING KILL 'EM.
ELENA
I COULDA KILLED 'EM! ...I COULDA.

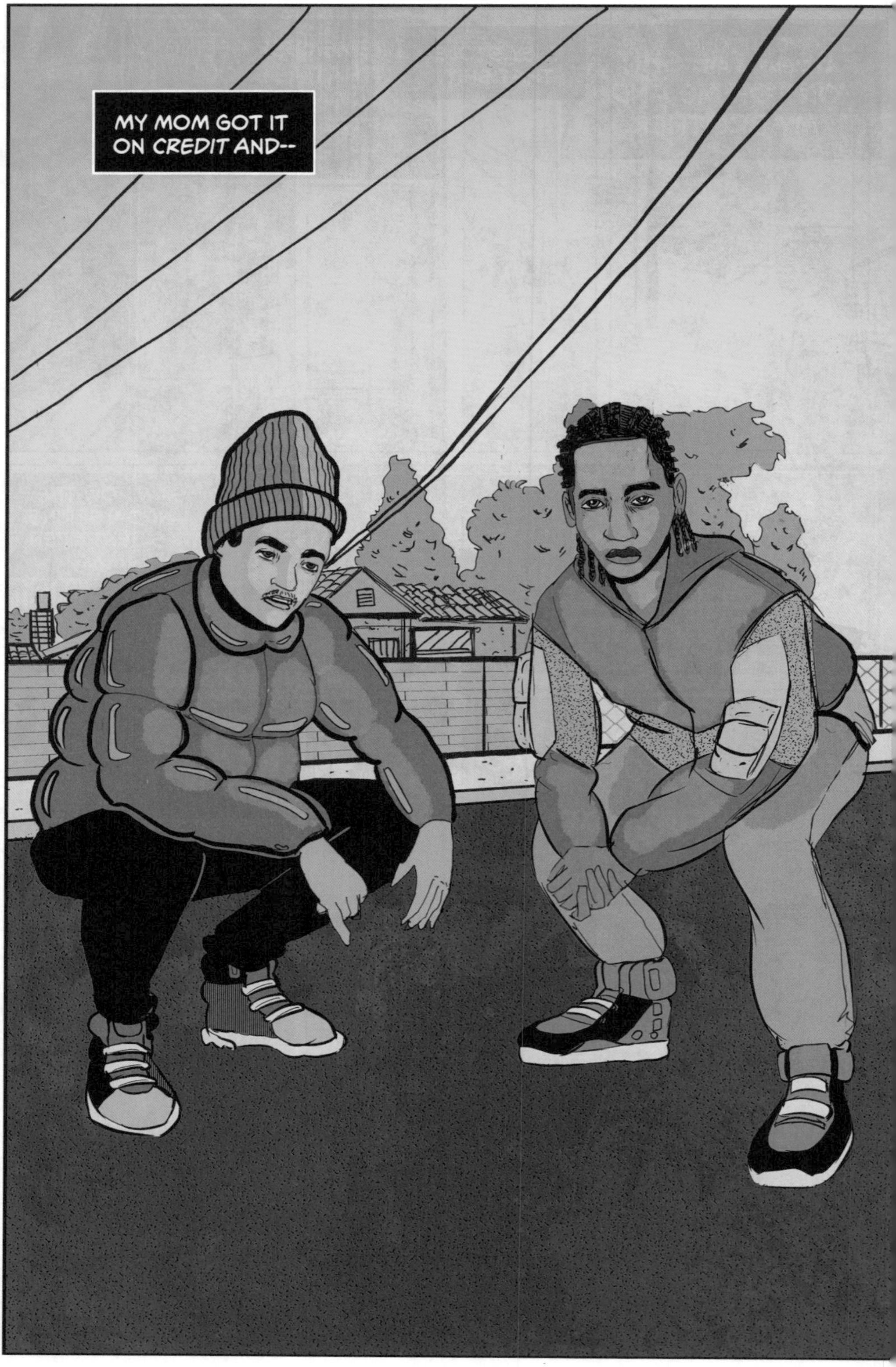
MY MOM GOT IT ON CREDIT AND--

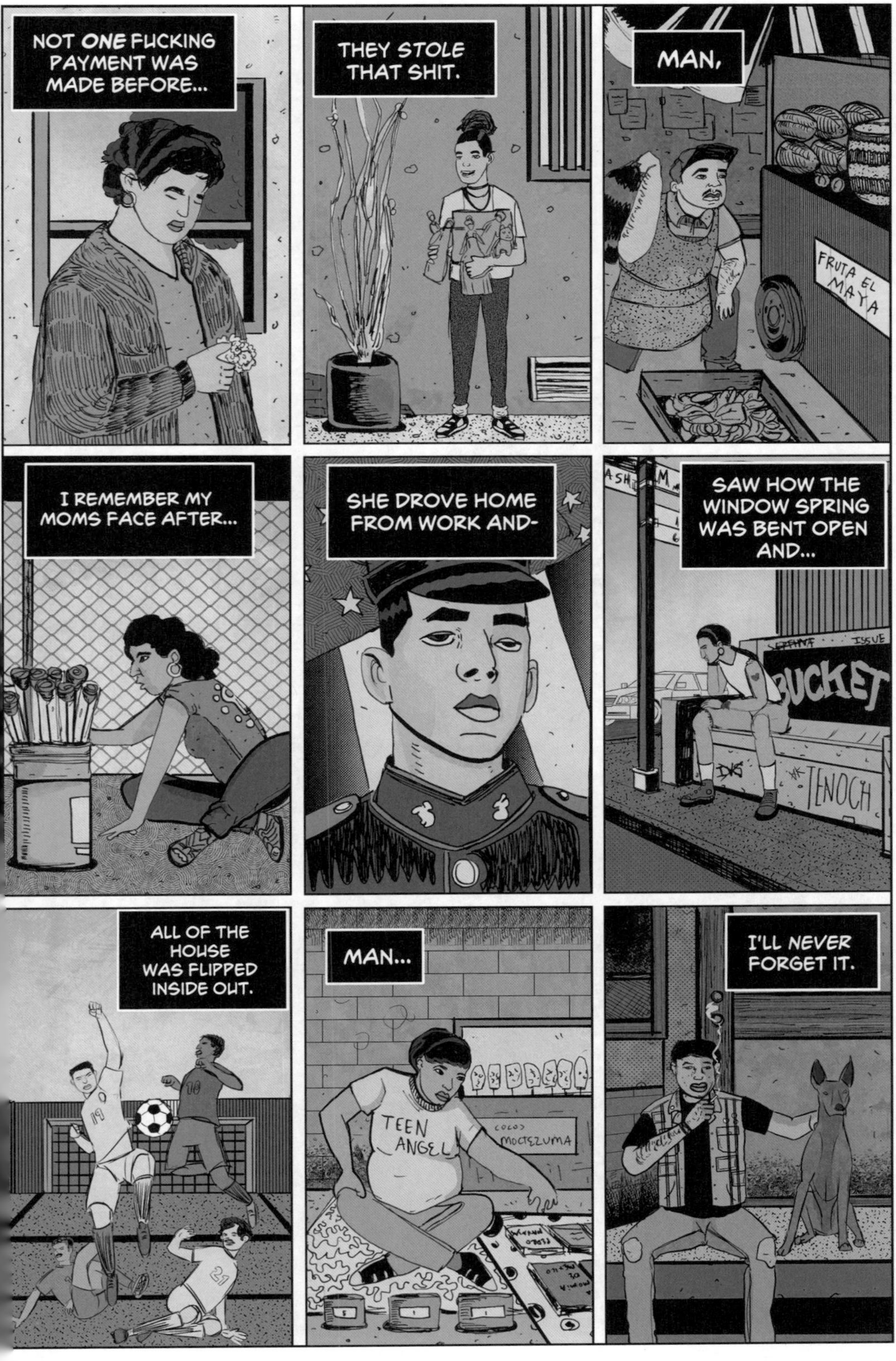
NOT ONE FUCKING PAYMENT WAS MADE BEFORE...
THEY STOLE THAT SHIT.
MAN,
FRUTA EL MAYA
I REMEMBER MY MOMS FACE AFTER...
SHE DROVE HOME FROM WORK AND-
SAW HOW THE WINDOW SPRING WAS BENT OPEN AND...
ISSUE
BUCKET
TENOCH
ALL OF THE HOUSE WAS FLIPPED INSIDE OUT.
MAN...
TEEN ANGEL
MOCTEZUMA
I'LL NEVER FORGET IT.

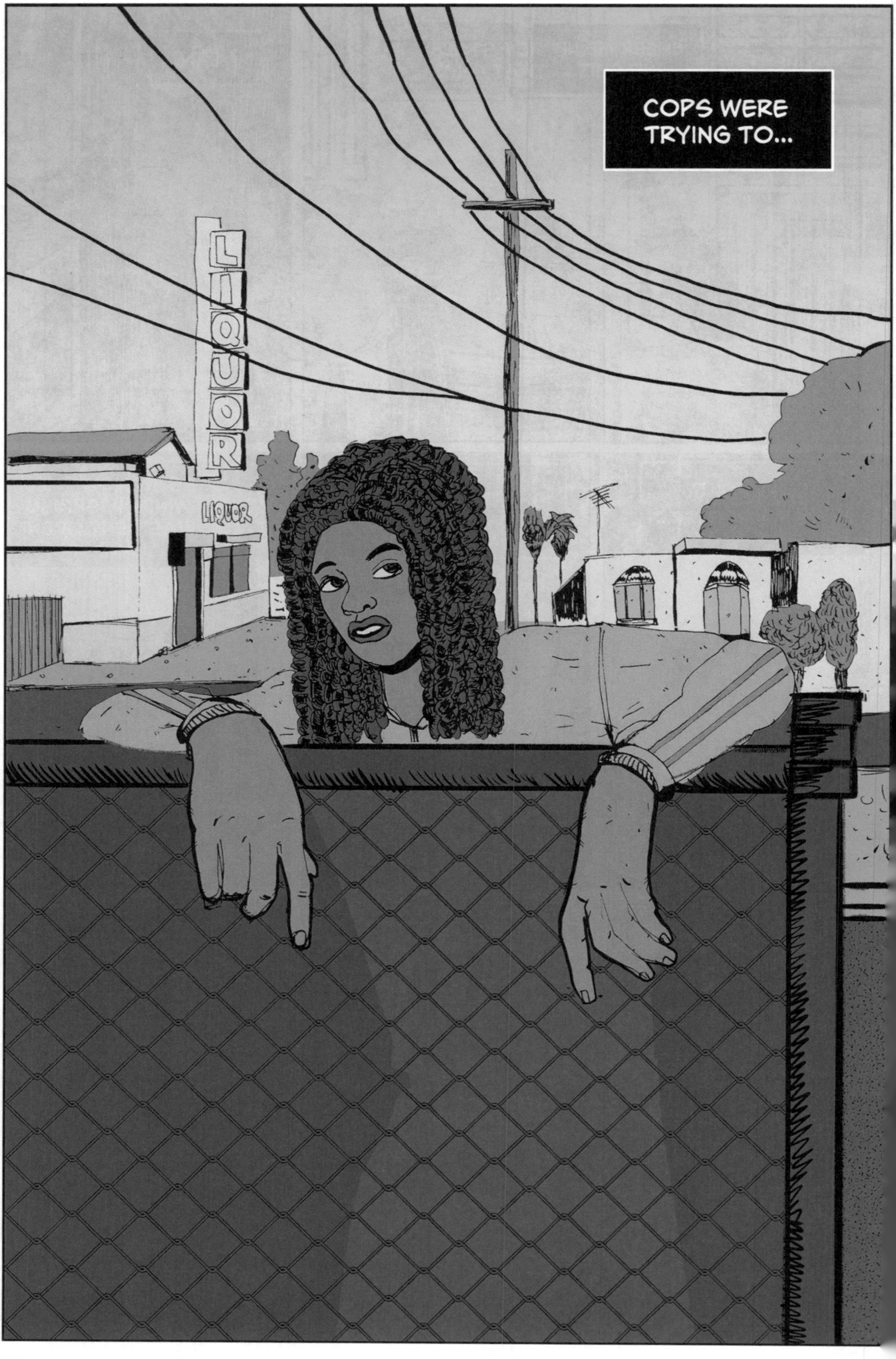
COPS WERE TRYING TO...
LIQUOR
LIQUOR

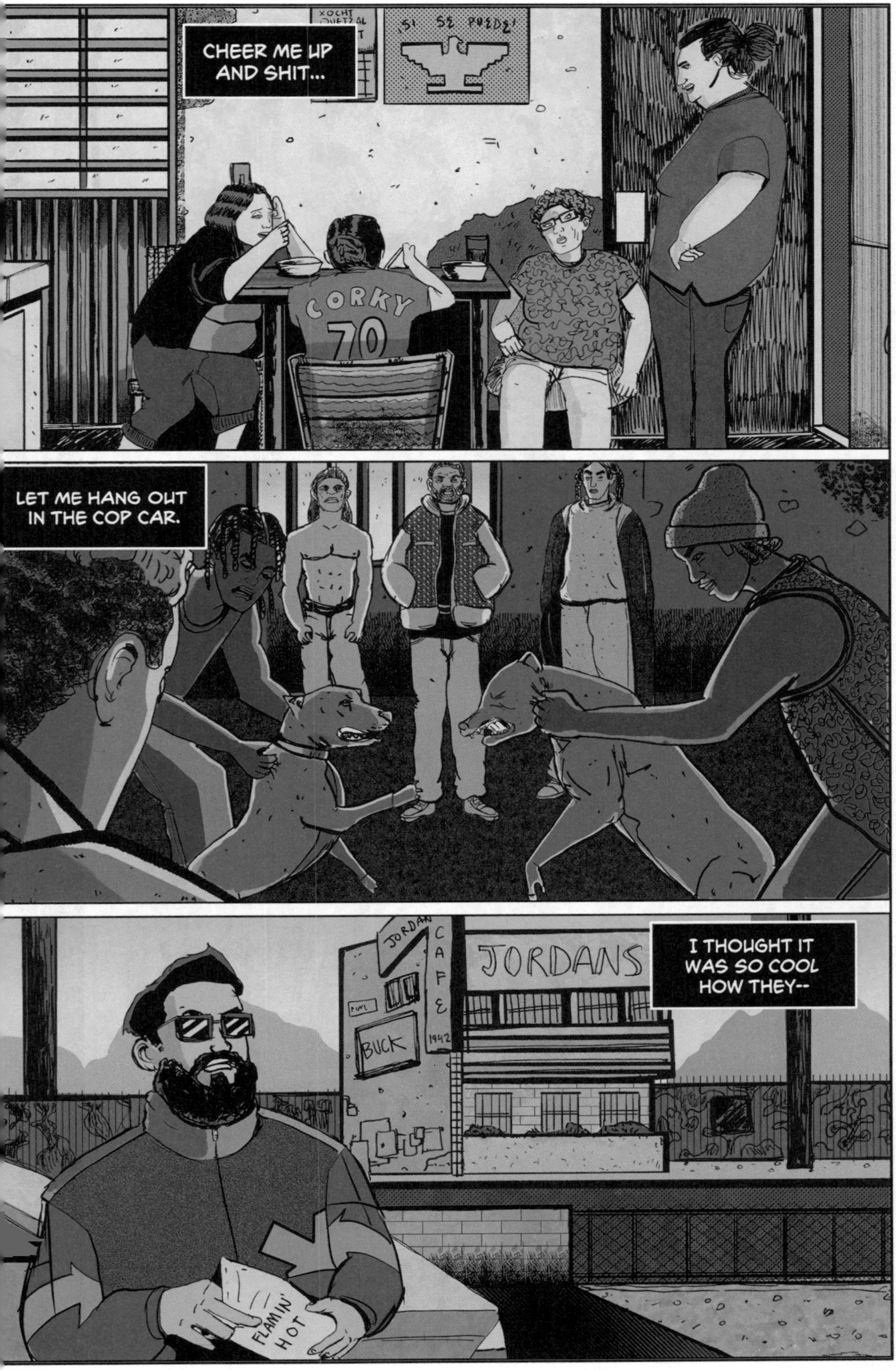
CHEER ME UP AND SHIT...
CORKY 70
LET ME HANG OUT IN THE COP CAR.
JORDAN
CAFE
JORDANS
BUCK
1942
I THOUGHT IT WAS SO COOL HOW THEY--
FLAMIN' HOT

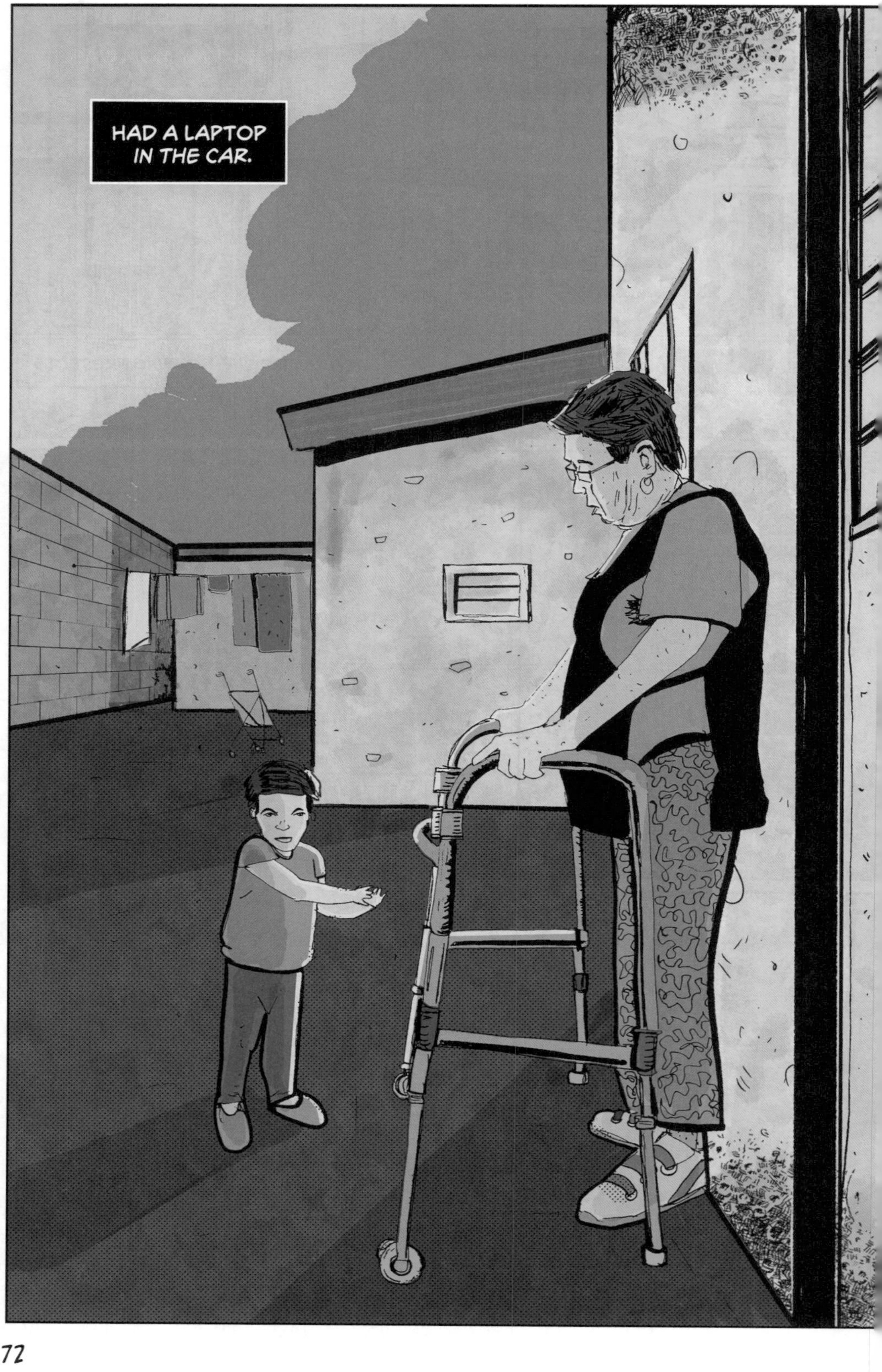
HAD A LAPTOP IN THE CAR.

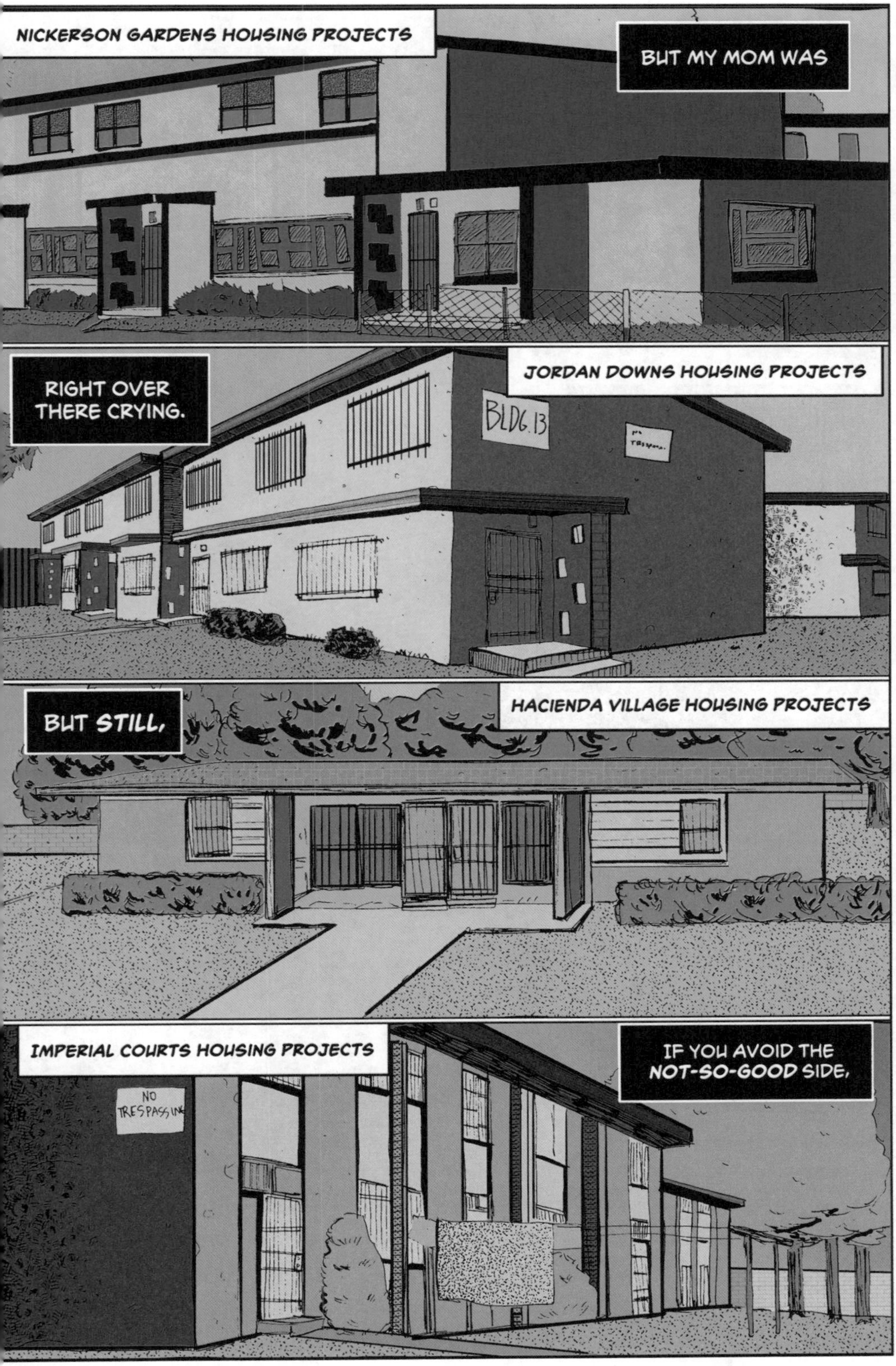
NICKERSON GARDENS HOUSING PROJECTS
BUT MY MOM WAS
RIGHT OVER THERE CRYING.
JORDAN DOWNS HOUSING PROJECTS
BLDG. 13
BUT STILL,
HACIENDA VILLAGE HOUSING PROJECTS
IMPERIAL COURTS HOUSING PROJECTS
IF YOU AVOID THE NOT-SO-GOOD SIDE,
NO TRESPASSIN

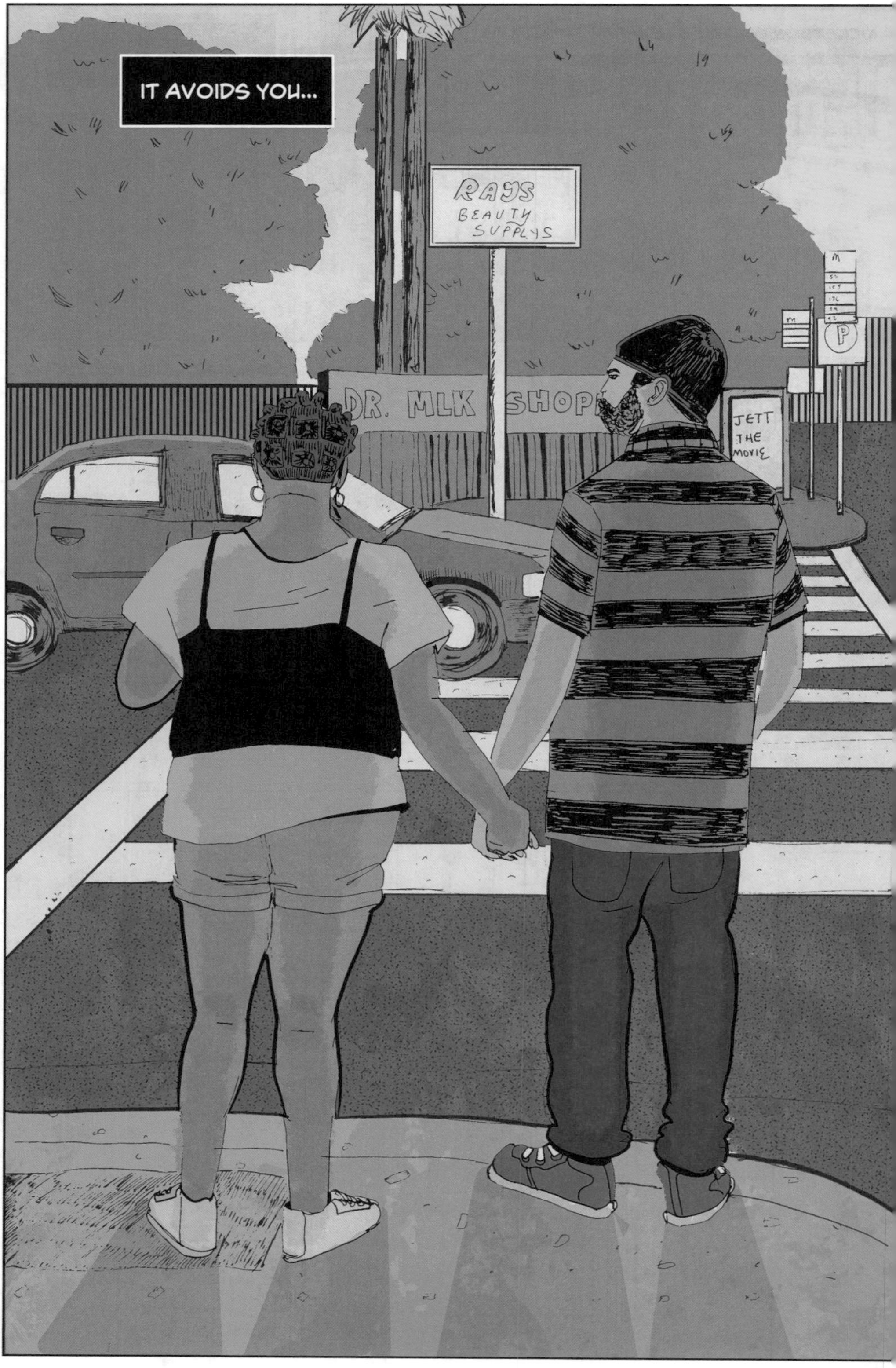
IT AVOIDS YOU...
RAYS
BEAUTY
SUPPLYS
DR. MLK SHOP
JETT
THE
MOVIE
P

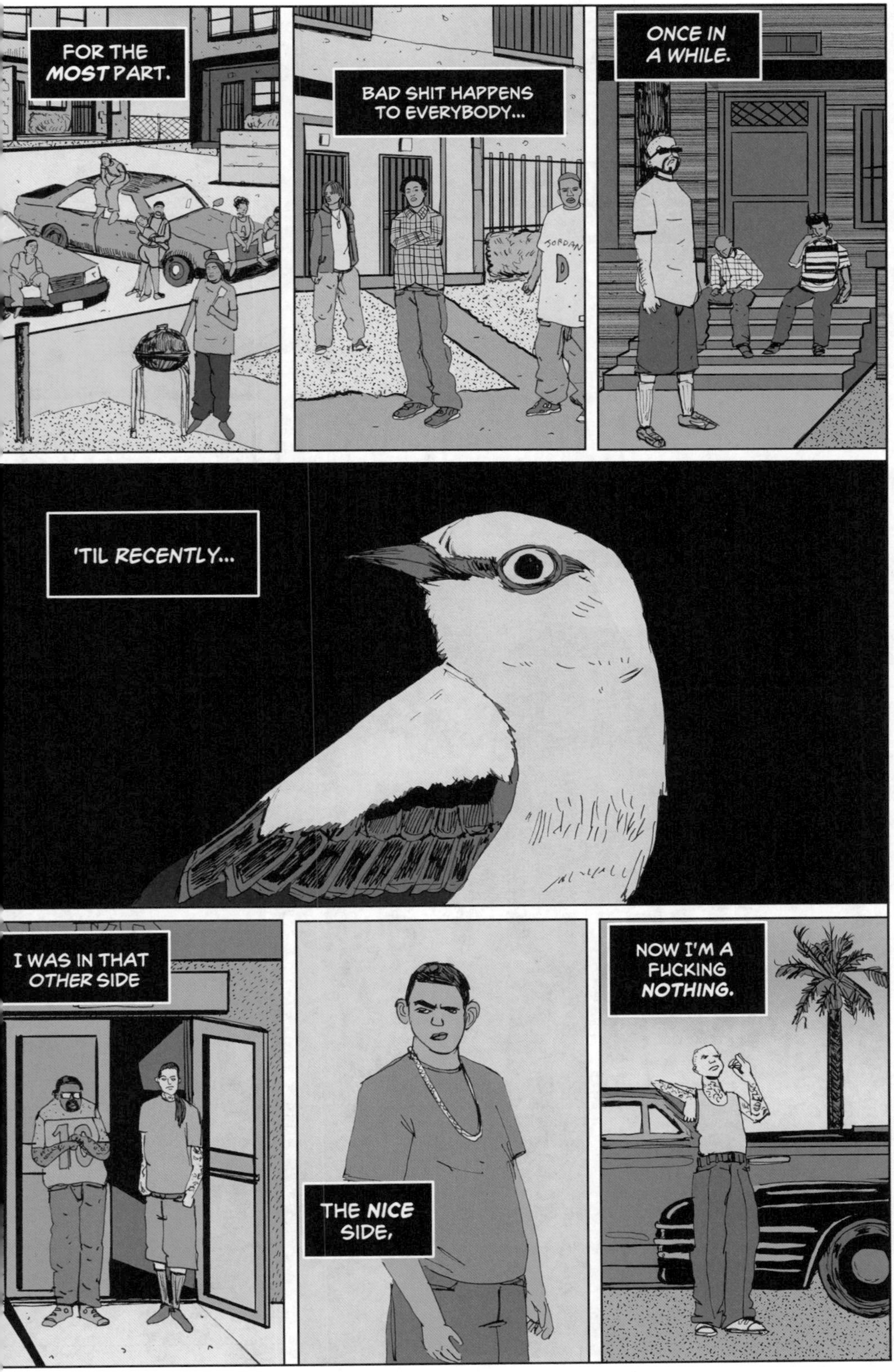
FOR THE MOST PART.
BAD SHIT HAPPENS TO EVERYBODY...
JORDAN
ONCE IN A WHILE.
'TIL RECENTLY...
I WAS IN THAT OTHER SIDE
THE NICE SIDE,
NOW I'M A FUCKING NOTHING.

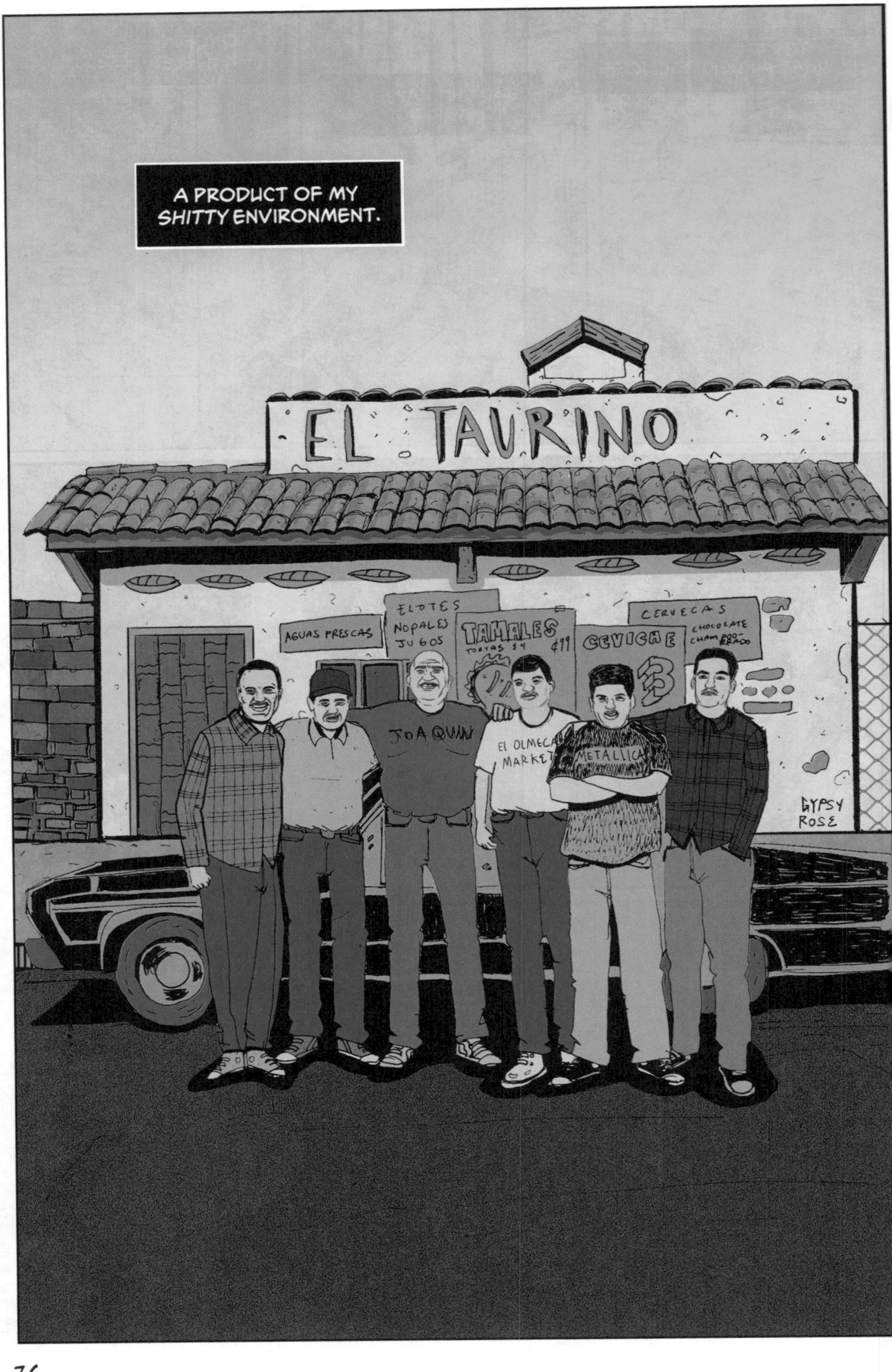

A PRODUCT OF MY SHITTY ENVIRONMENT.
EL TAURINO
AGUAS PRESCAS
ELOTES
NOPALES
JUGOS
TAMALES
TORTAS $4
¢99
CEVICHE
3
CERVECAS
CHOCOLATE
CHAMPOO-RRADO
JOAQUIN
EL OLMECA MARKET
METALLICA
GYPSY ROSE

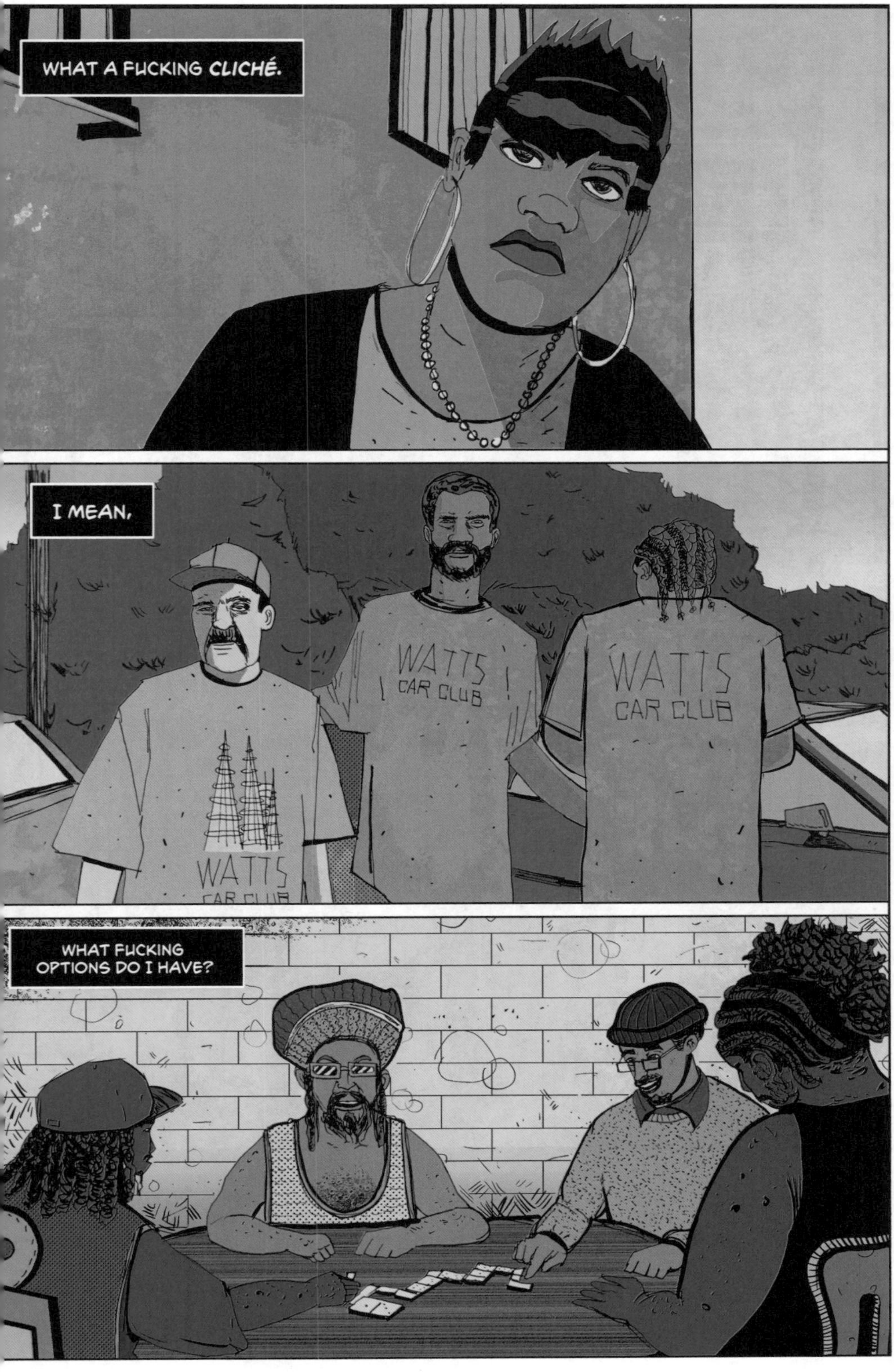
WHAT A FUCKING CLICHÉ.
I MEAN,
WATTS CAR CLUB
WATTS CAR CLUB
WHAT FUCKING OPTIONS DO I HAVE?

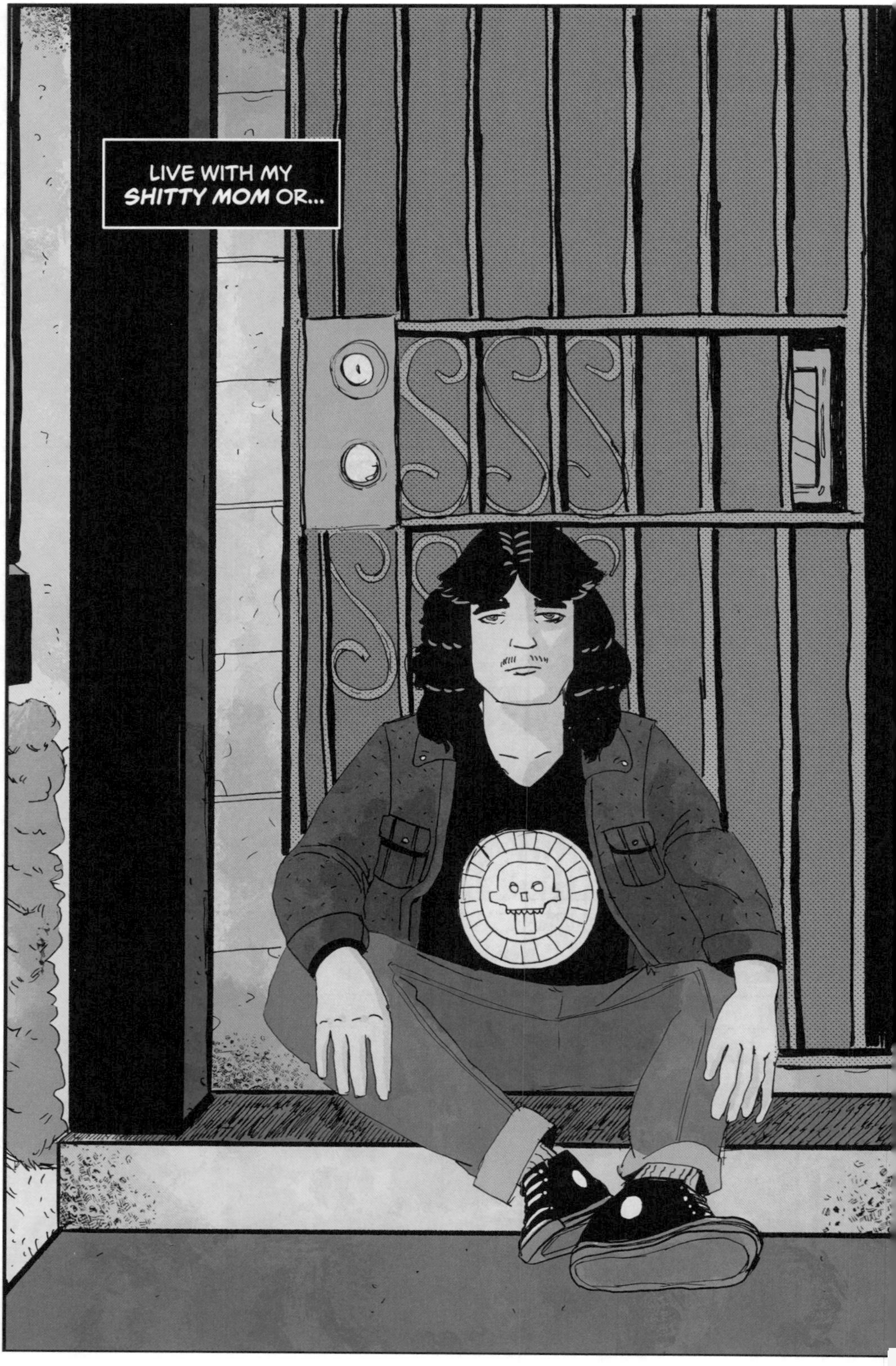
LIVE WITH MY SHITTY MOM OR...

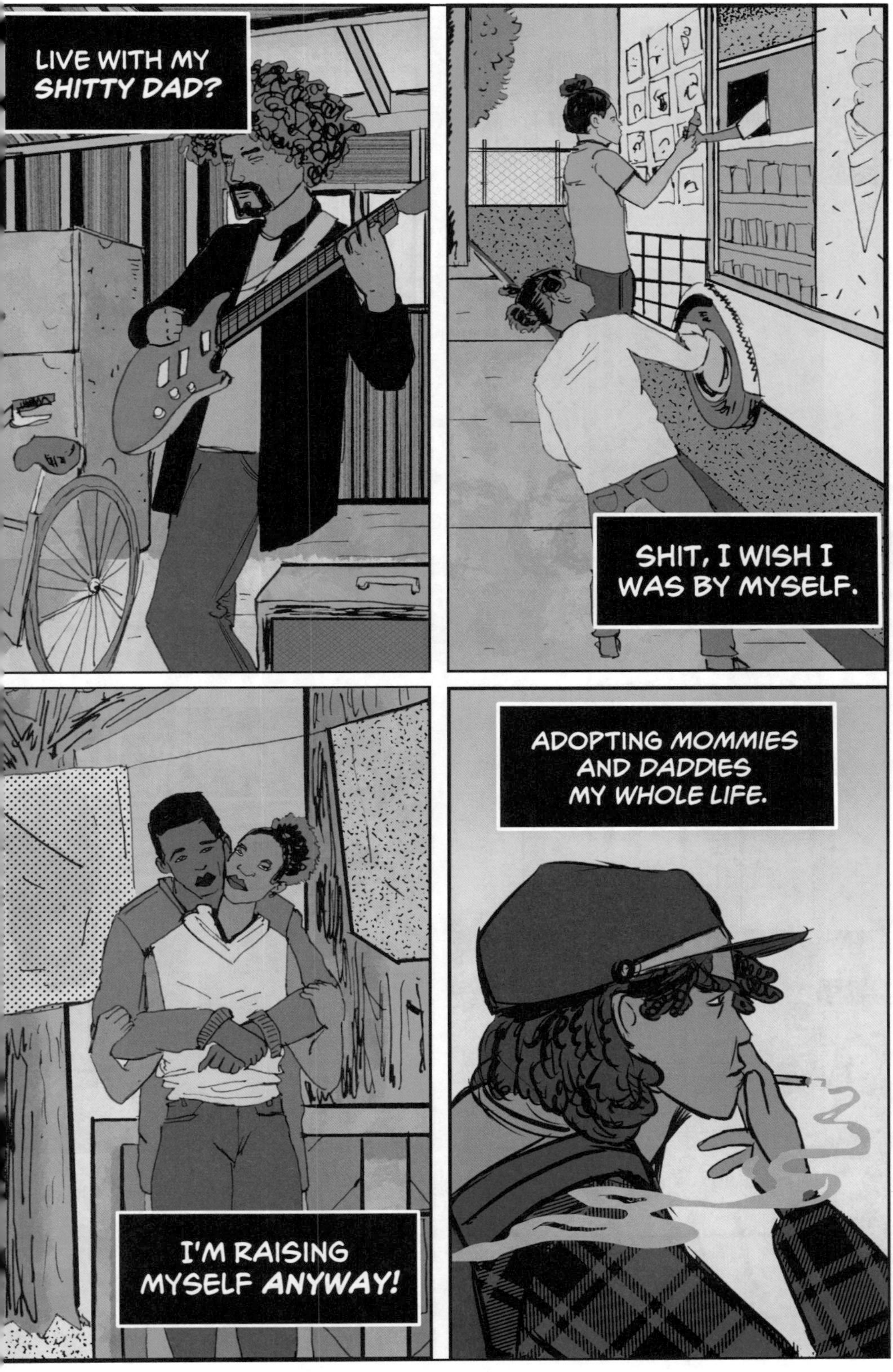
LIVE WITH MY SHITTY DAD?
SHIT, I WISH I WAS BY MYSELF.
I'M RAISING MYSELF ANYWAY!
ADOPTING MOMMIES AND DADDIES MY WHOLE LIFE.

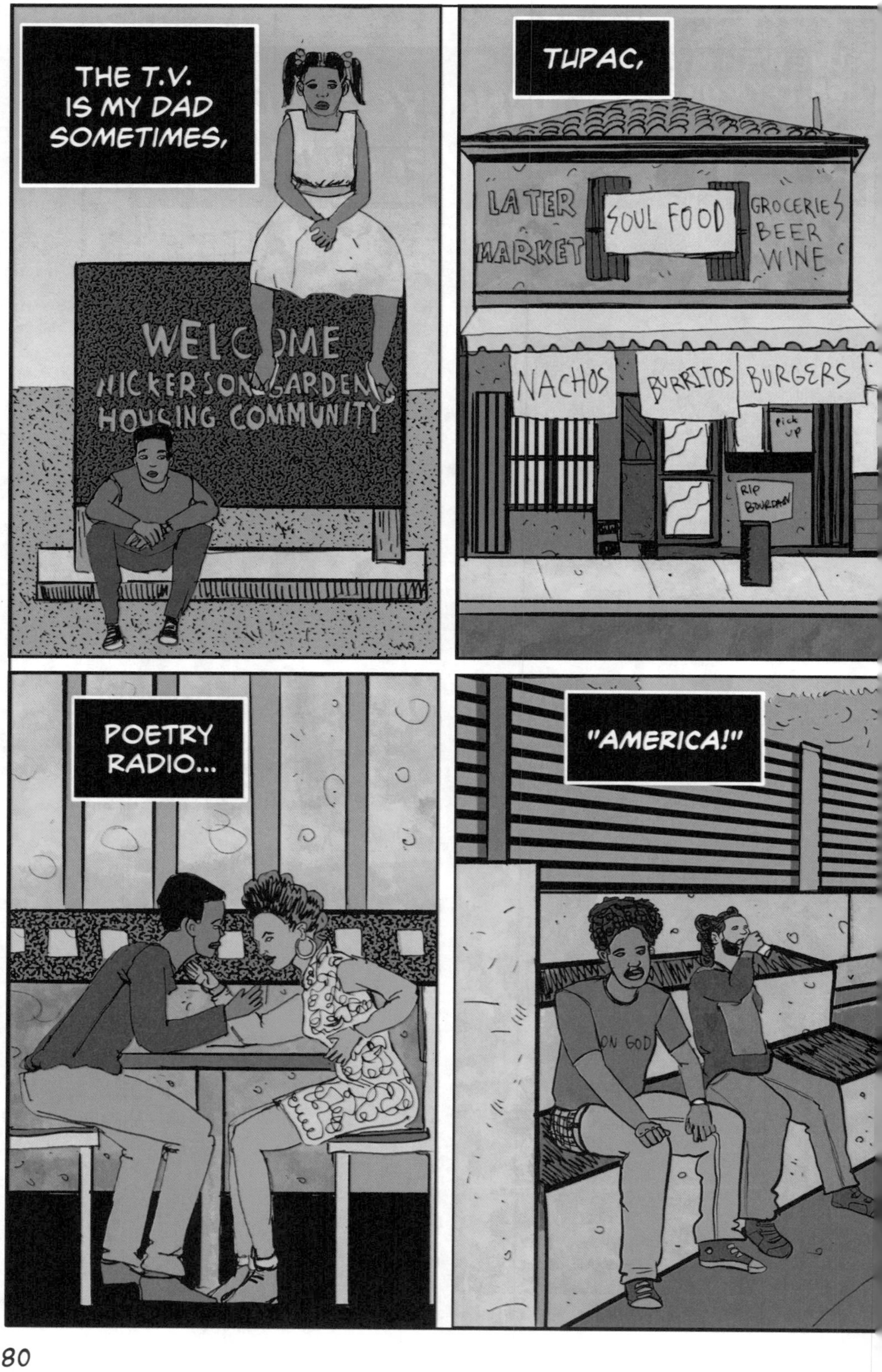

THE T.V. IS MY DAD SOMETIMES,
HOUSING COMMUNITY
TUPAC,
LATER MARKET
SOUL FOOD
GROCERIES BEER WINE
NACHOS
BURRITOS
BURGERS
PICK UP
RIP BOURDAIN
POETRY RADIO...
"AMERICA!"
ON GOD

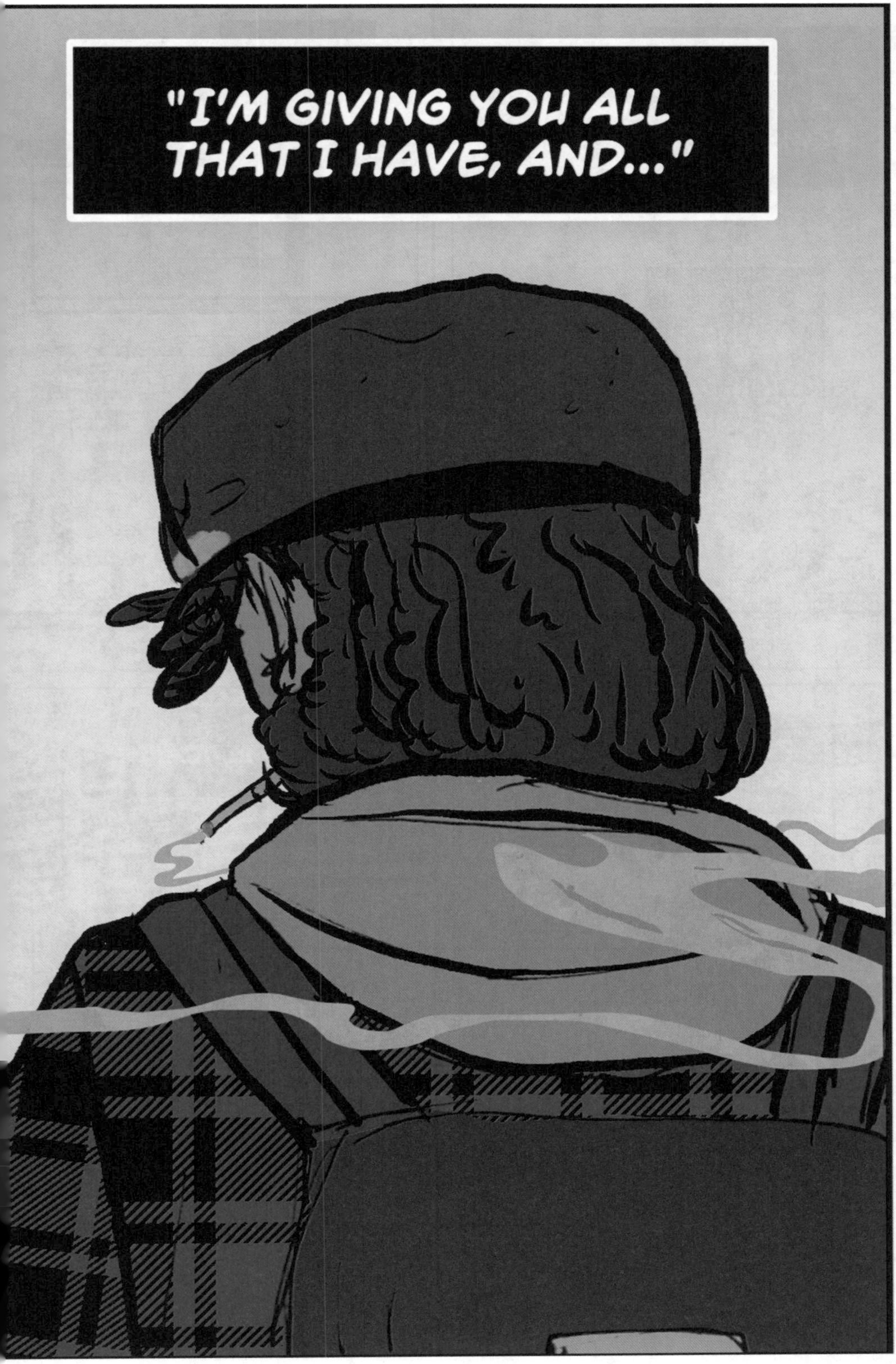
"I'M GIVING YOU ALL THAT I HAVE, AND..."

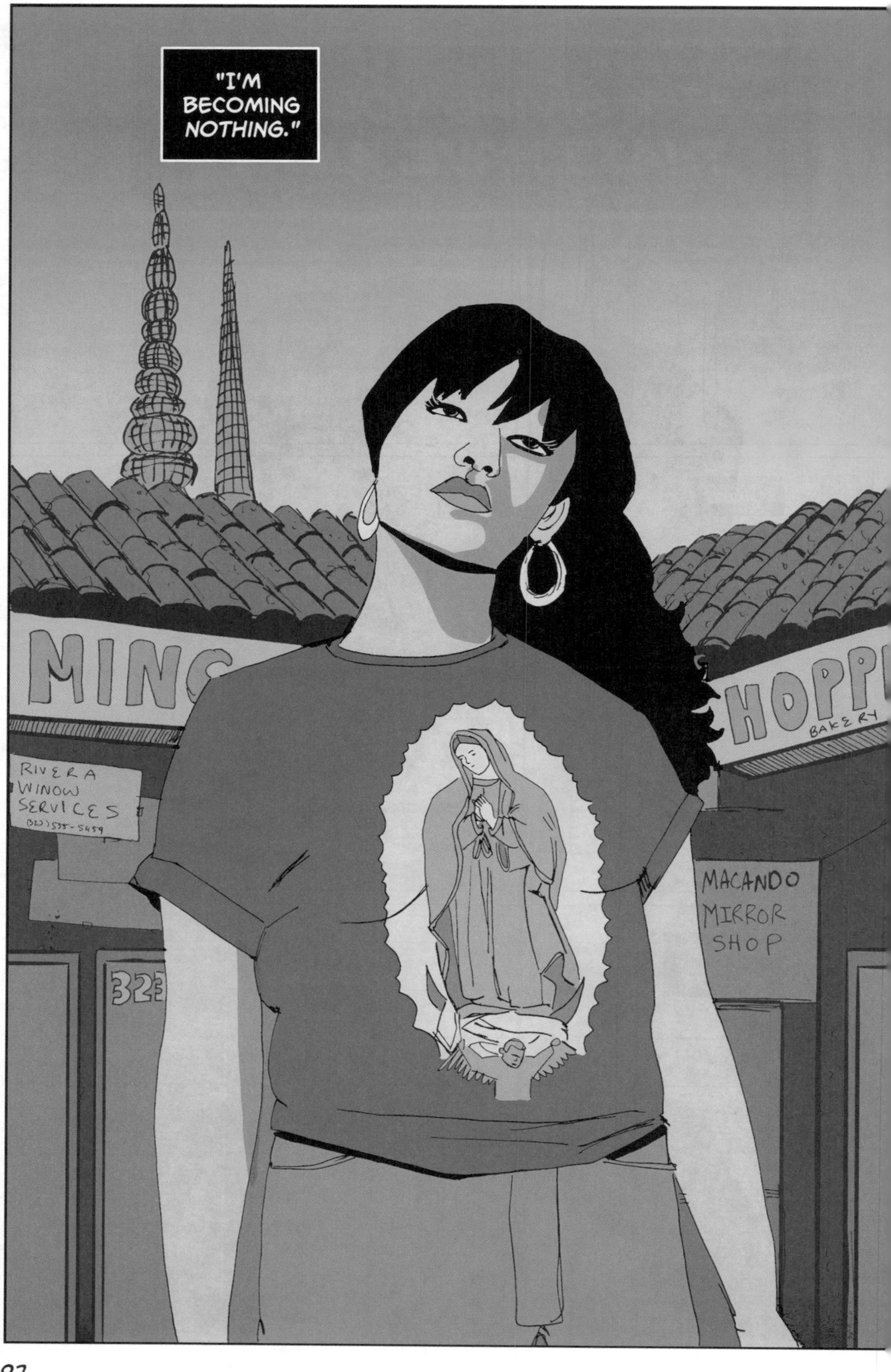
"I'M BECOMING NOTHING."
MING
RIVERA WINOW SERVICES
(323) 535-5459
323
HOPP
BAKERY
MACANDO MIRROR SHOP

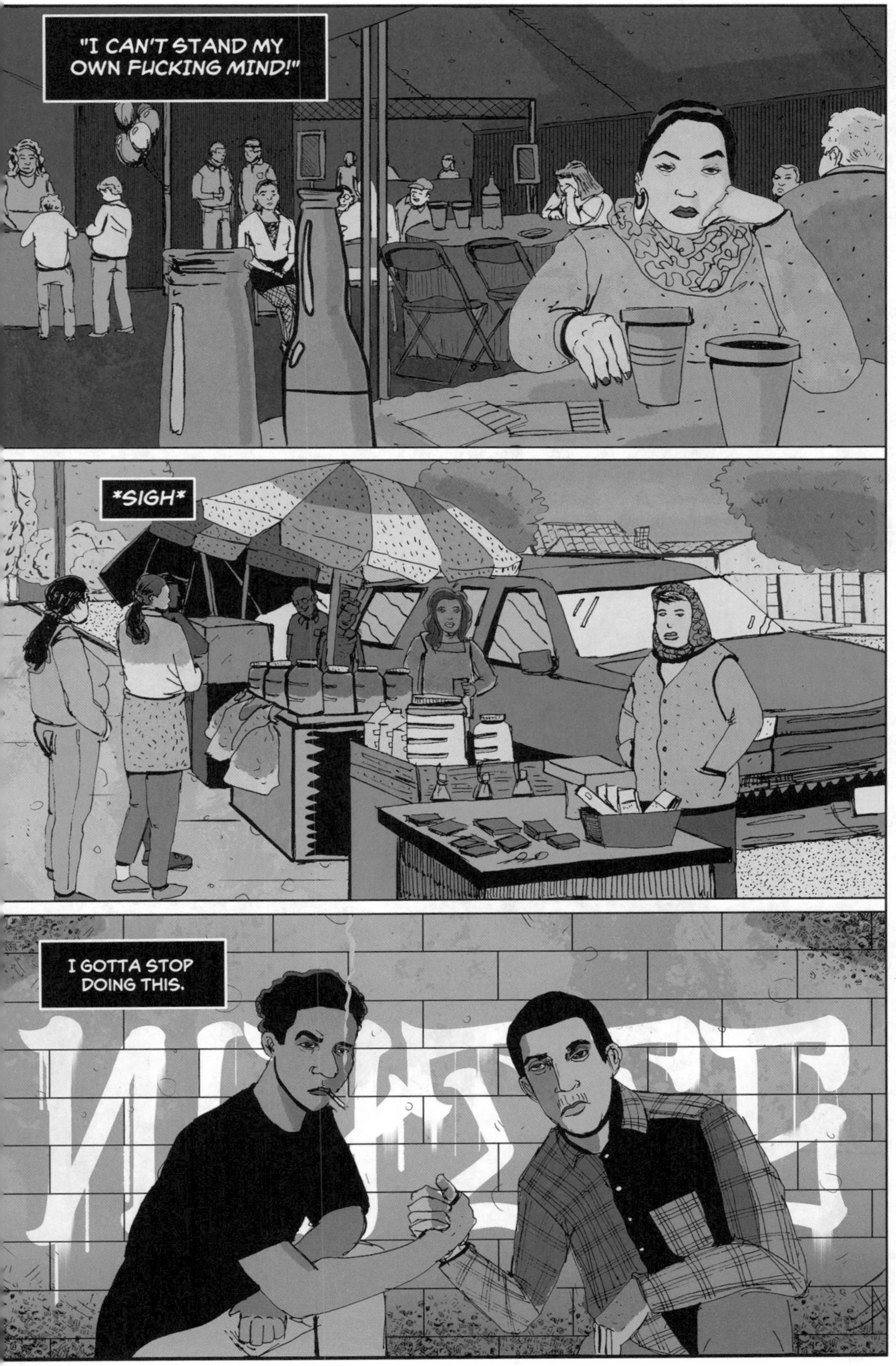
"I CAN'T STAND MY OWN FUCKING MIND!"
SIGH
I GOTTA STOP DOING THIS.

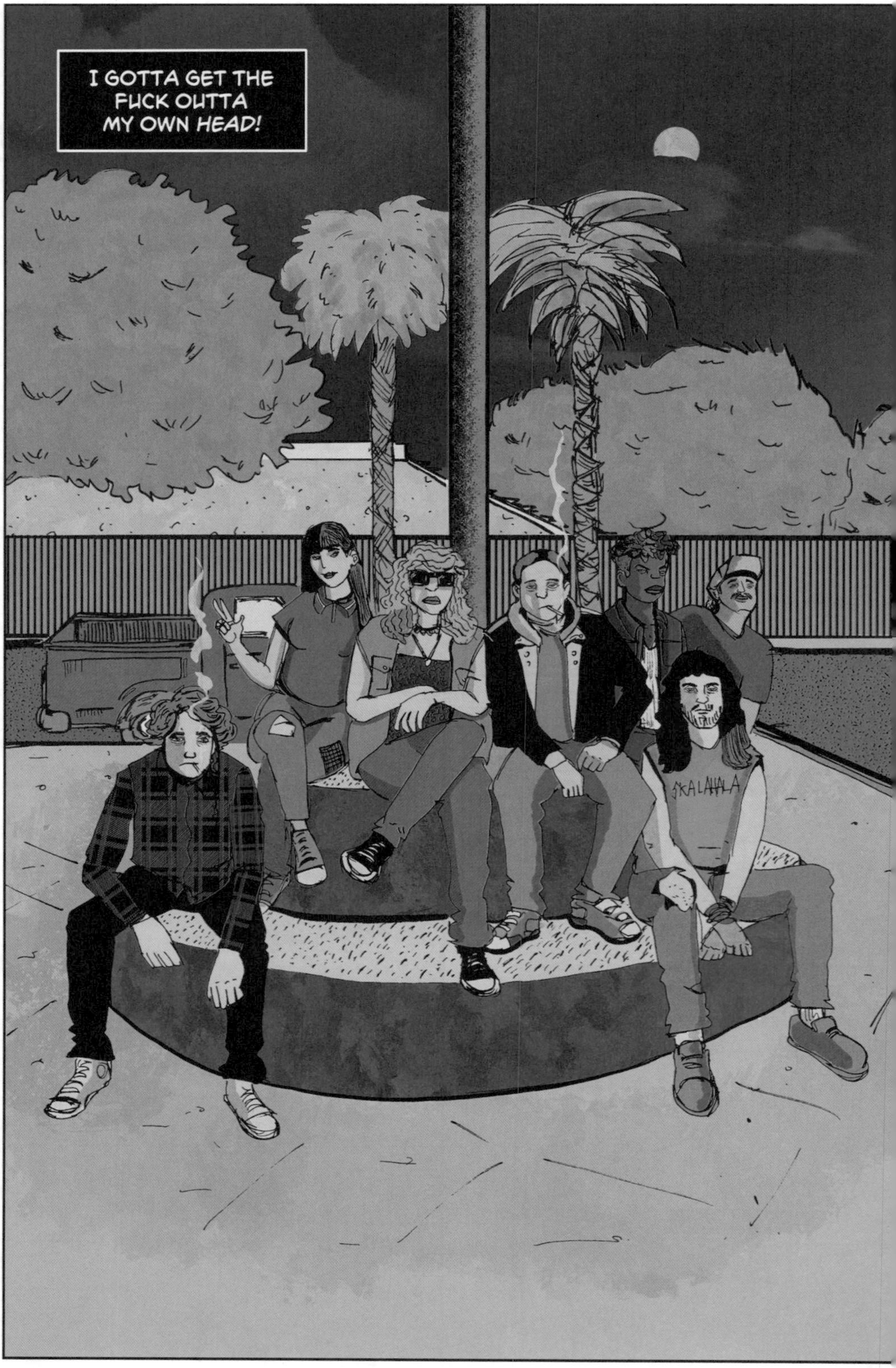
I GOTTA GET THE FUCK OUTTA MY OWN *HEAD!*
SKALAHALA

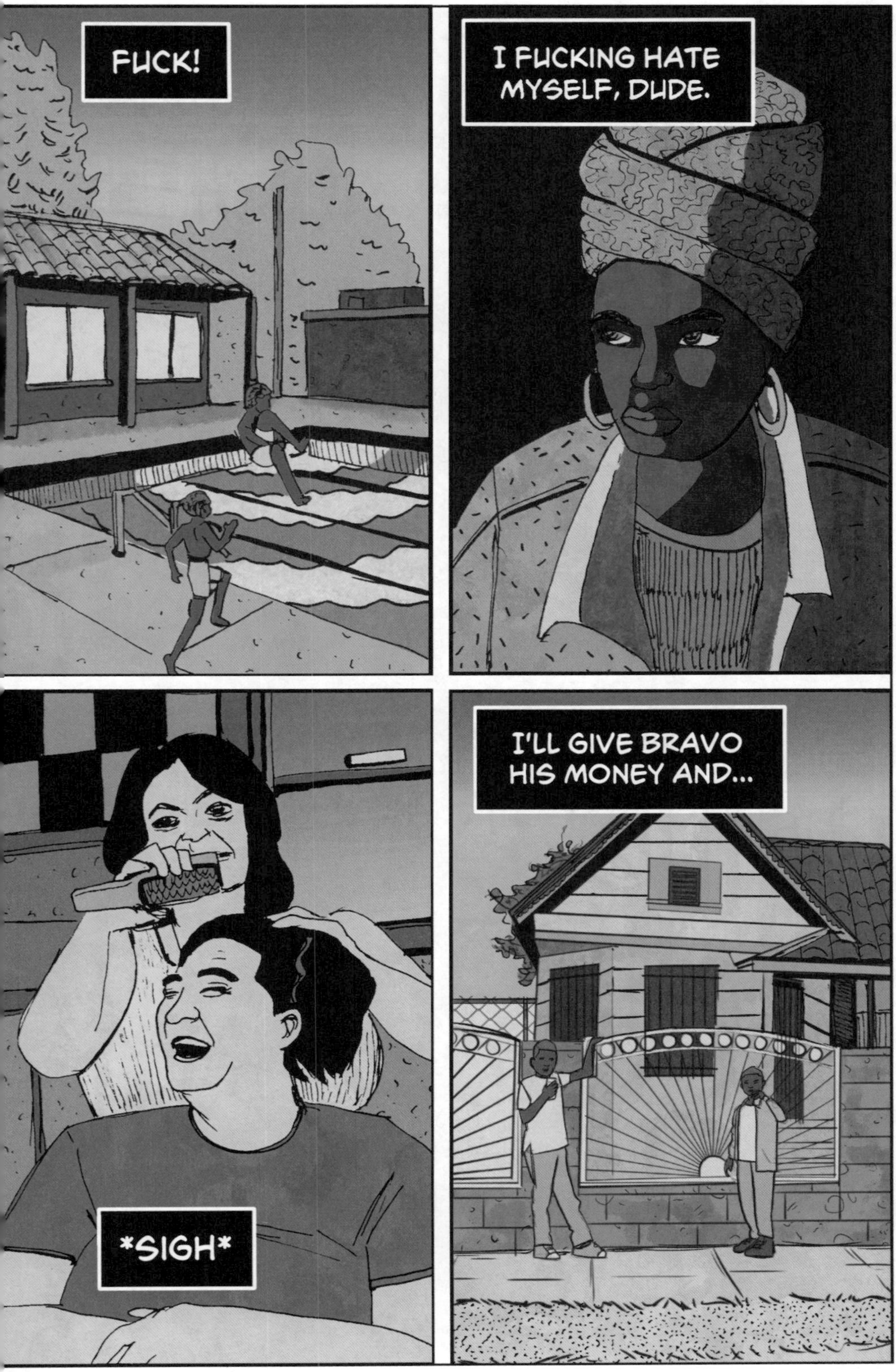
FUCK!
I FUCKING HATE MYSELF, DUDE.
SIGH
I'LL GIVE BRAVO HIS MONEY AND...

JUST SAY I CAN'T DO THIS SHIT ANYMORE, MAN.

IF HE GIVES ME FUCKING PROBLEMS,

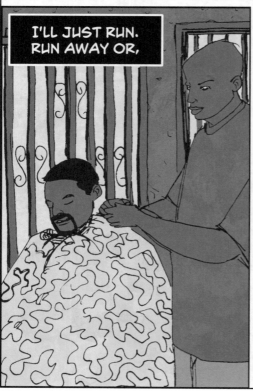

I'LL JUST RUN. RUN AWAY OR,

KILL 'EM OR SOMETHING.

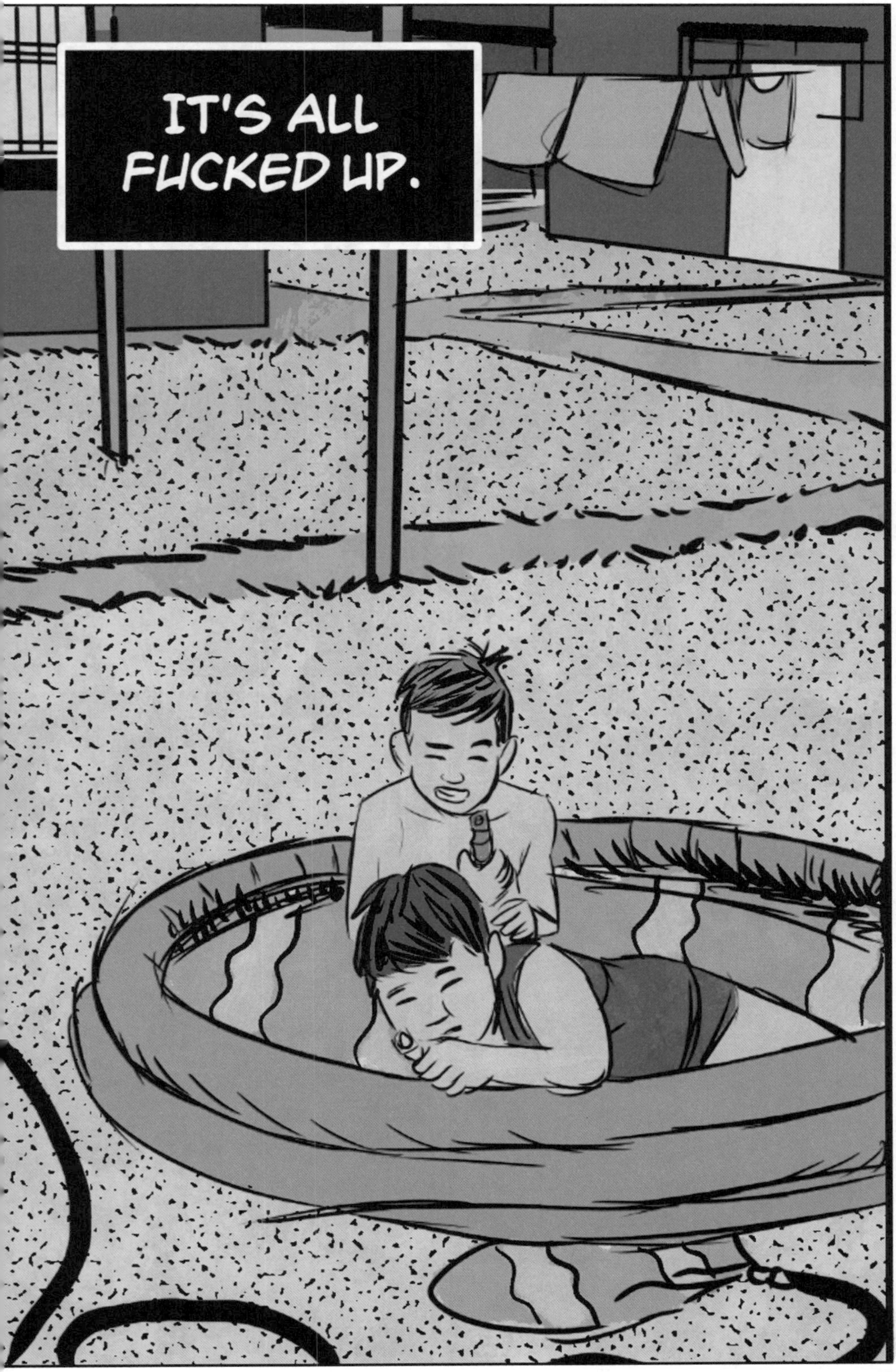
IT'S ALL FUCKED UP.

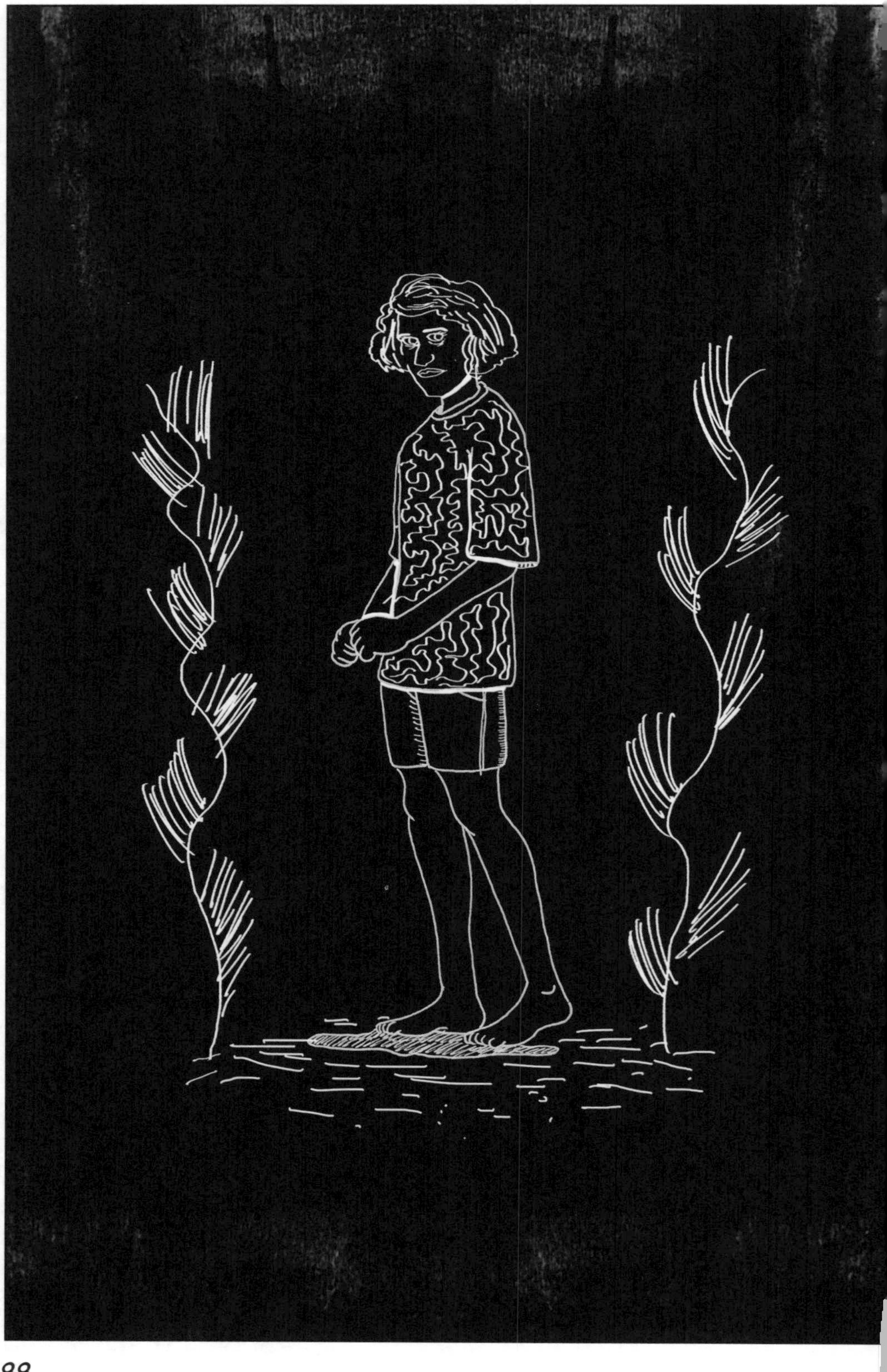

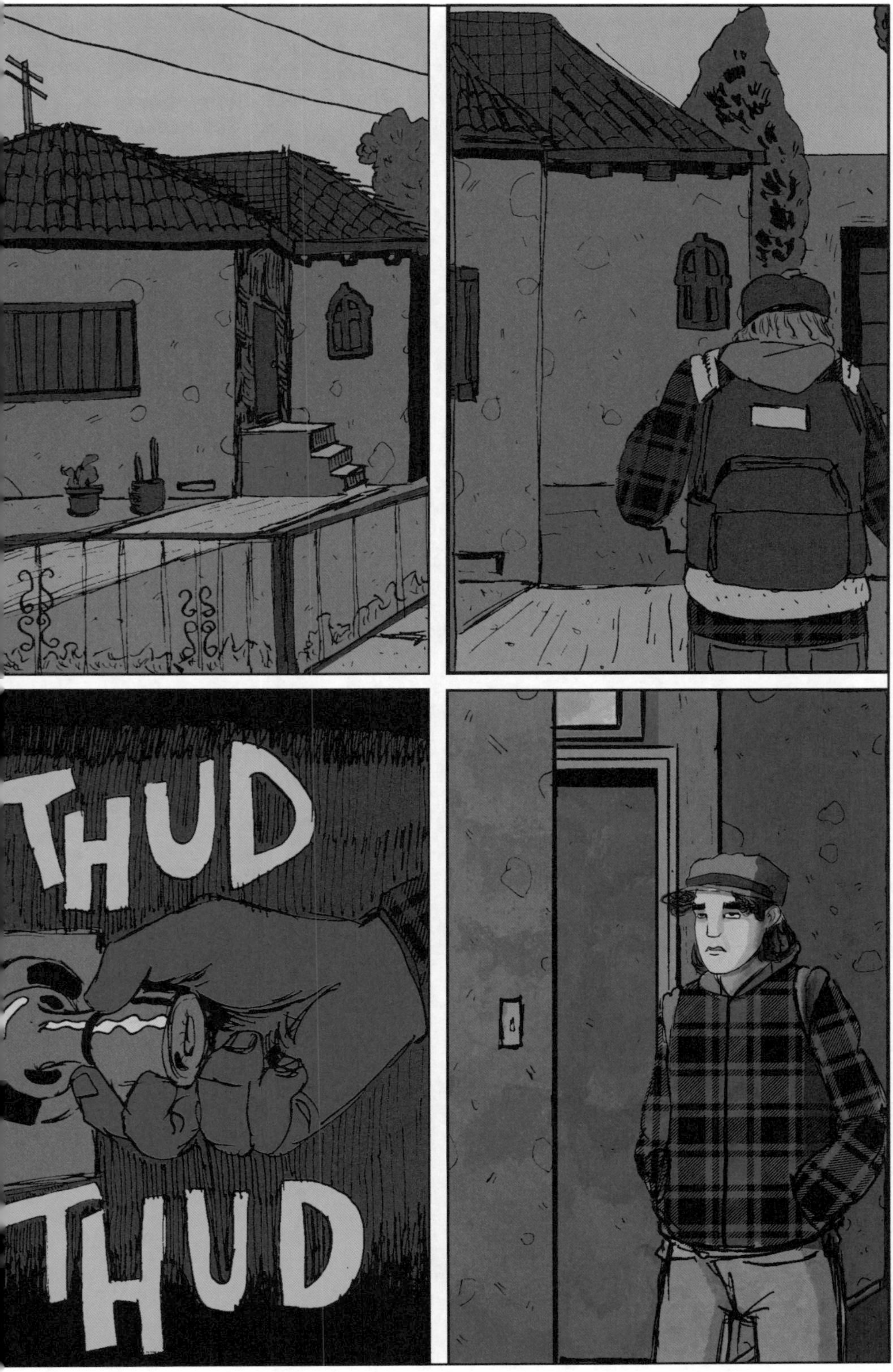
THUD
THUD

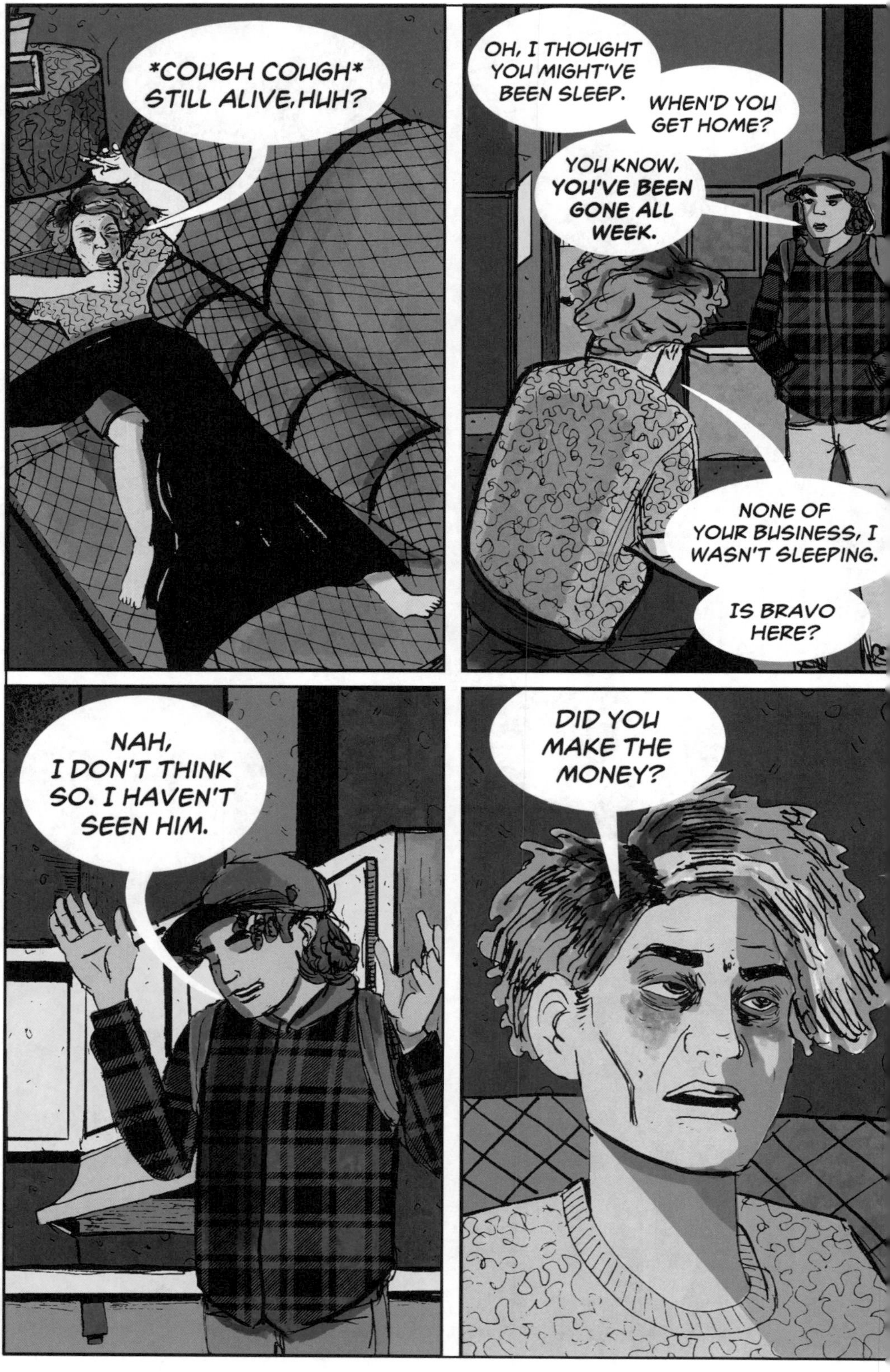
COUGH COUGH STILL ALIVE, HUH?
OH, I THOUGHT YOU MIGHT'VE BEEN SLEEP.
WHEN'D YOU GET HOME?
YOU KNOW, YOU'VE BEEN GONE ALL WEEK.
NONE OF YOUR BUSINESS, I WASN'T SLEEPING.
IS BRAVO HERE?
NAH, I DON'T THINK SO. I HAVEN'T SEEN HIM.
DID YOU MAKE THE MONEY?

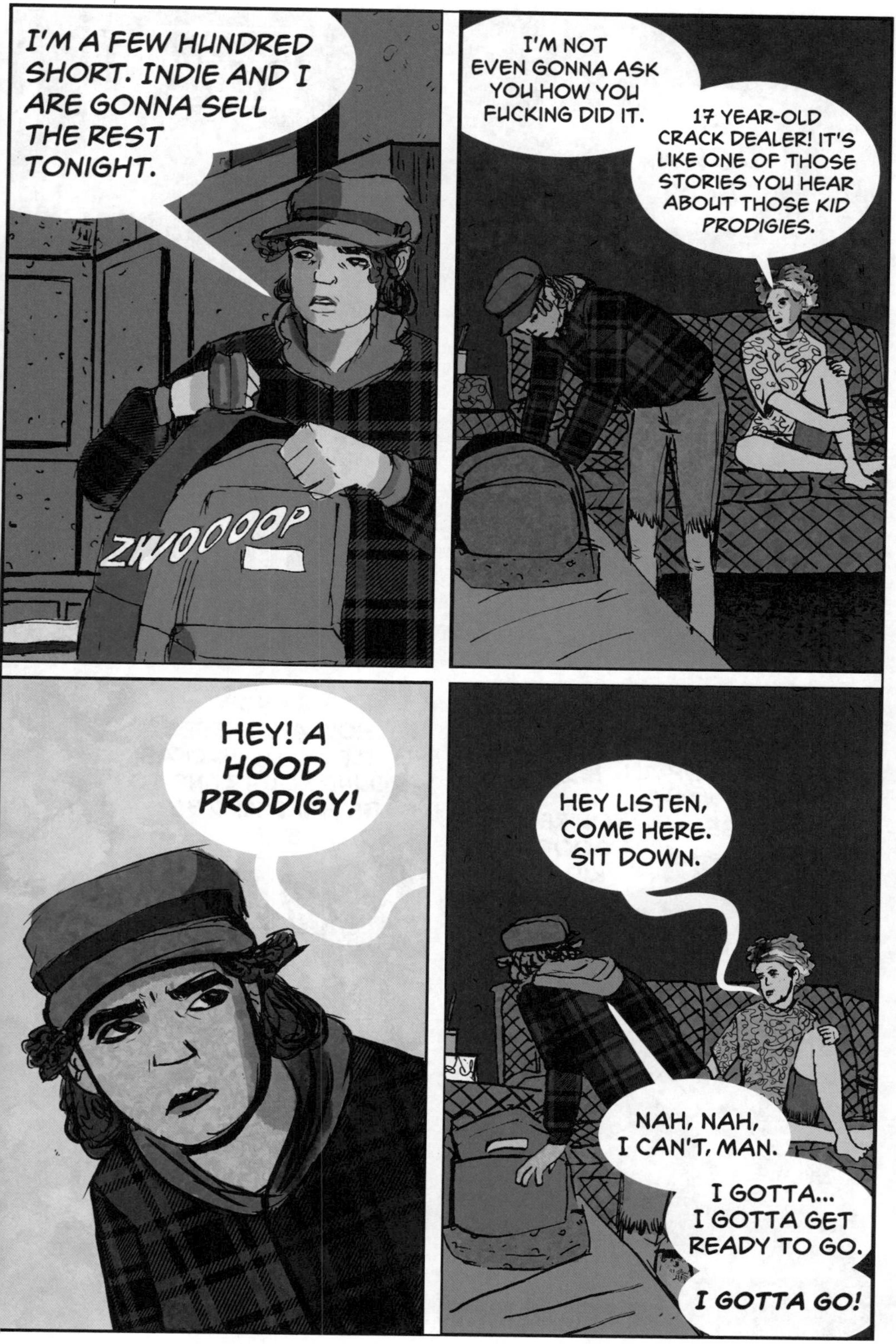
I'M A FEW HUNDRED SHORT. INDIE AND I ARE GONNA SELL THE REST TONIGHT.
ZWOOOOOP
I'M NOT EVEN GONNA ASK YOU HOW YOU FUCKING DID IT.
17 YEAR-OLD CRACK DEALER! IT'S LIKE ONE OF THOSE STORIES YOU HEAR ABOUT THOSE KID PRODIGIES.
HEY! A HOOD PRODIGY!
HEY LISTEN, COME HERE. SIT DOWN.
NAH, NAH, I CAN'T, MAN.
I GOTTA... I GOTTA GET READY TO GO.
I GOTTA GO!

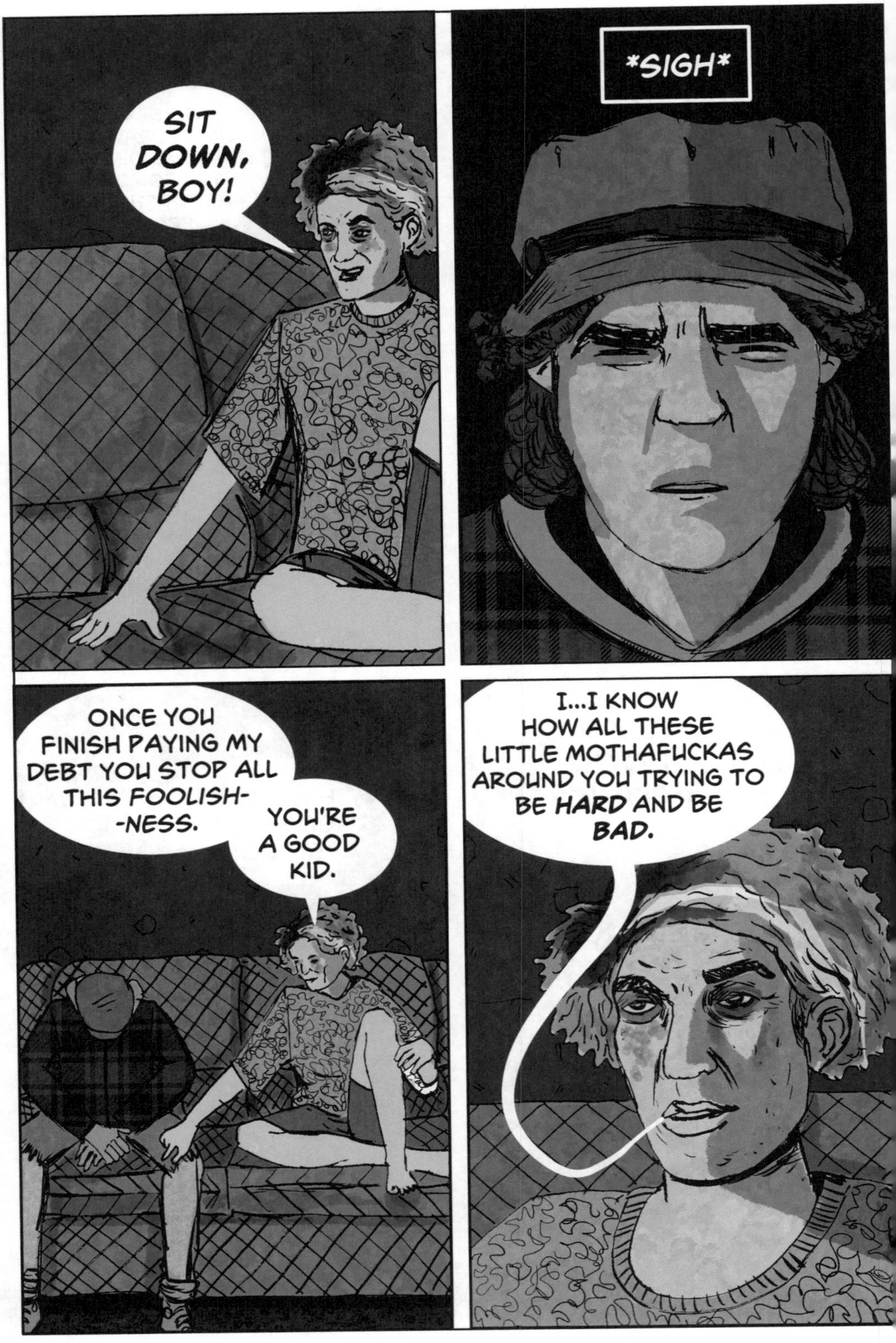
SIT DOWN, BOY!
SIGH
ONCE YOU FINISH PAYING MY DEBT YOU STOP ALL THIS FOOLISH- -NESS.
YOU'RE A GOOD KID.
I...I KNOW HOW ALL THESE LITTLE MOTHAFUCKAS AROUND YOU TRYING TO BE HARD AND BE BAD.

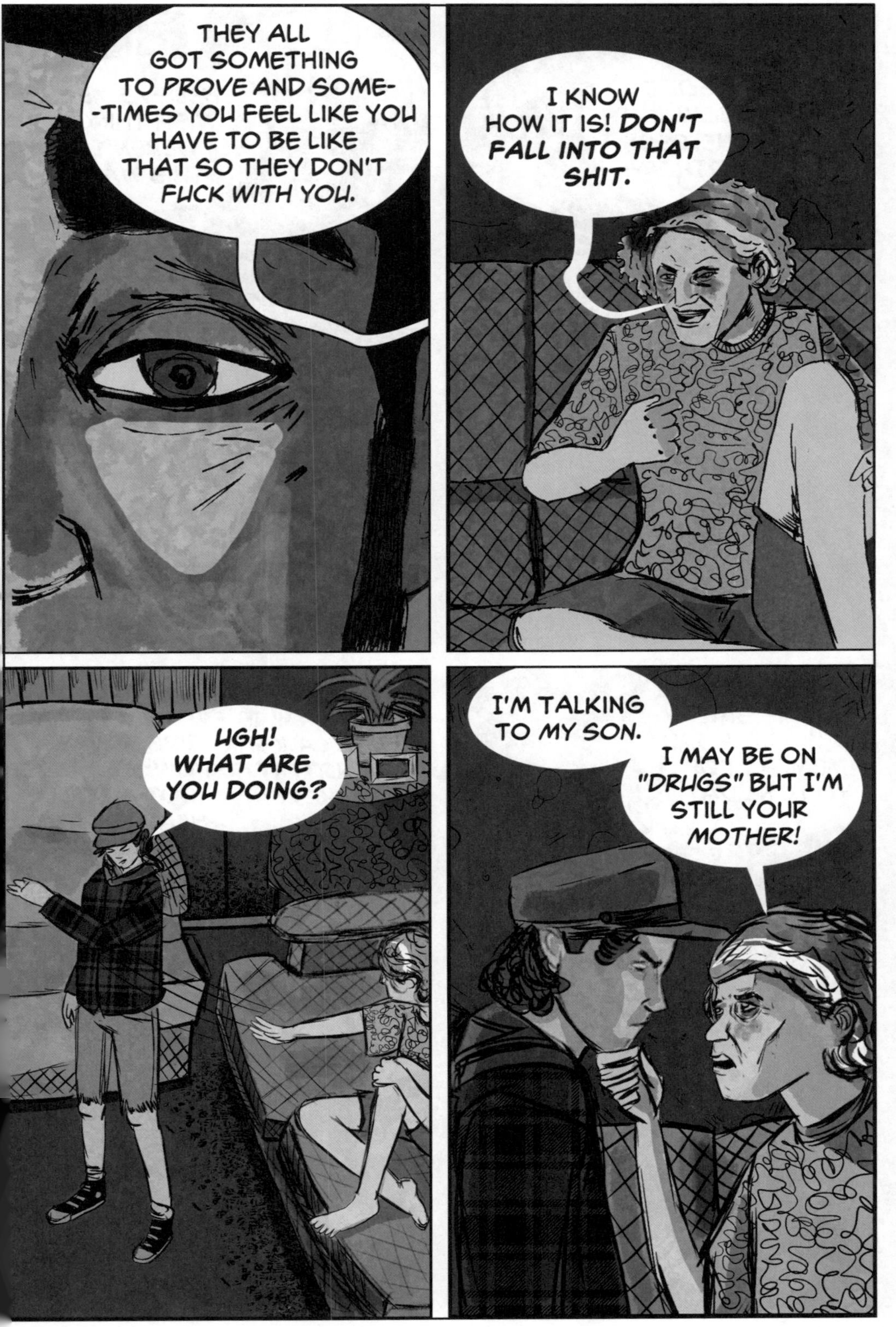
THEY ALL GOT SOMETHING TO PROVE AND SOME--TIMES YOU FEEL LIKE YOU HAVE TO BE LIKE THAT SO THEY DON'T FUCK WITH YOU.
I KNOW HOW IT IS! DON'T FALL INTO THAT SHIT.
UGH! WHAT ARE YOU DOING?
I'M TALKING TO MY SON.
I MAY BE ON "DRUGS" BUT I'M STILL YOUR MOTHER!

NOT A VERY GOOD ONE, I KNOW, BUT NONETHELESS YOUR *MOTHER*--

AND I LOVE YOU.

BELIEVE ME, I WISH THINGS WEREN'T THIS WAY.

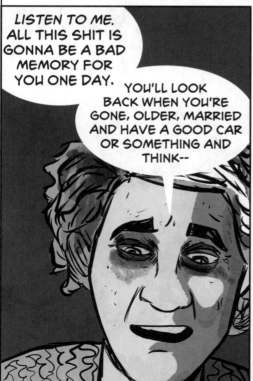

LISTEN TO ME. ALL THIS SHIT IS GONNA BE A BAD MEMORY FOR YOU ONE DAY.

YOU'LL LOOK BACK WHEN YOU'RE GONE, OLDER, MARRIED AND HAVE A GOOD CAR OR SOMETHING AND THINK--

"HOW THE FUCK WAS I EVER CAUGHT UP IN *THAT* RACKET?"

I'VE ALWAYS KNOWN IT. YOU'VE GOT A GOOD HEAD ON YOUR SHOULDERS.

YOU'RE JUST YOUNG. *DON'T KNOW NO BETTER.*

WHAT DO YOU *WANT* ME TO SAY?

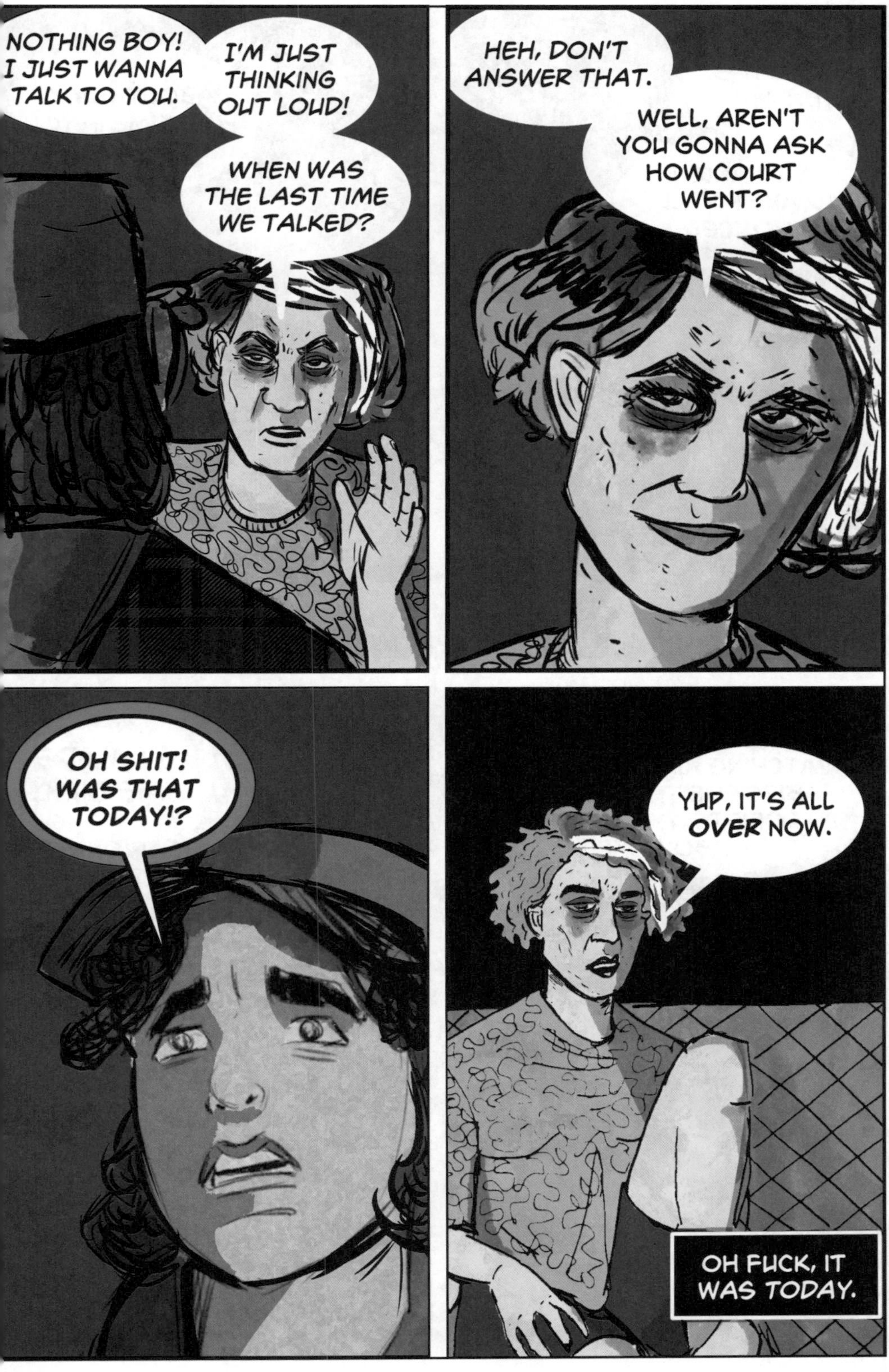
NOTHING BOY! I JUST WANNA TALK TO YOU.
I'M JUST THINKING OUT LOUD!
WHEN WAS THE LAST TIME WE TALKED?
HEH, DON'T ANSWER THAT.
WELL, AREN'T YOU GONNA ASK HOW COURT WENT?
OH SHIT! WAS THAT TODAY!?
YUP, IT'S ALL **OVER** NOW.
OH FUCK, IT WAS TODAY.

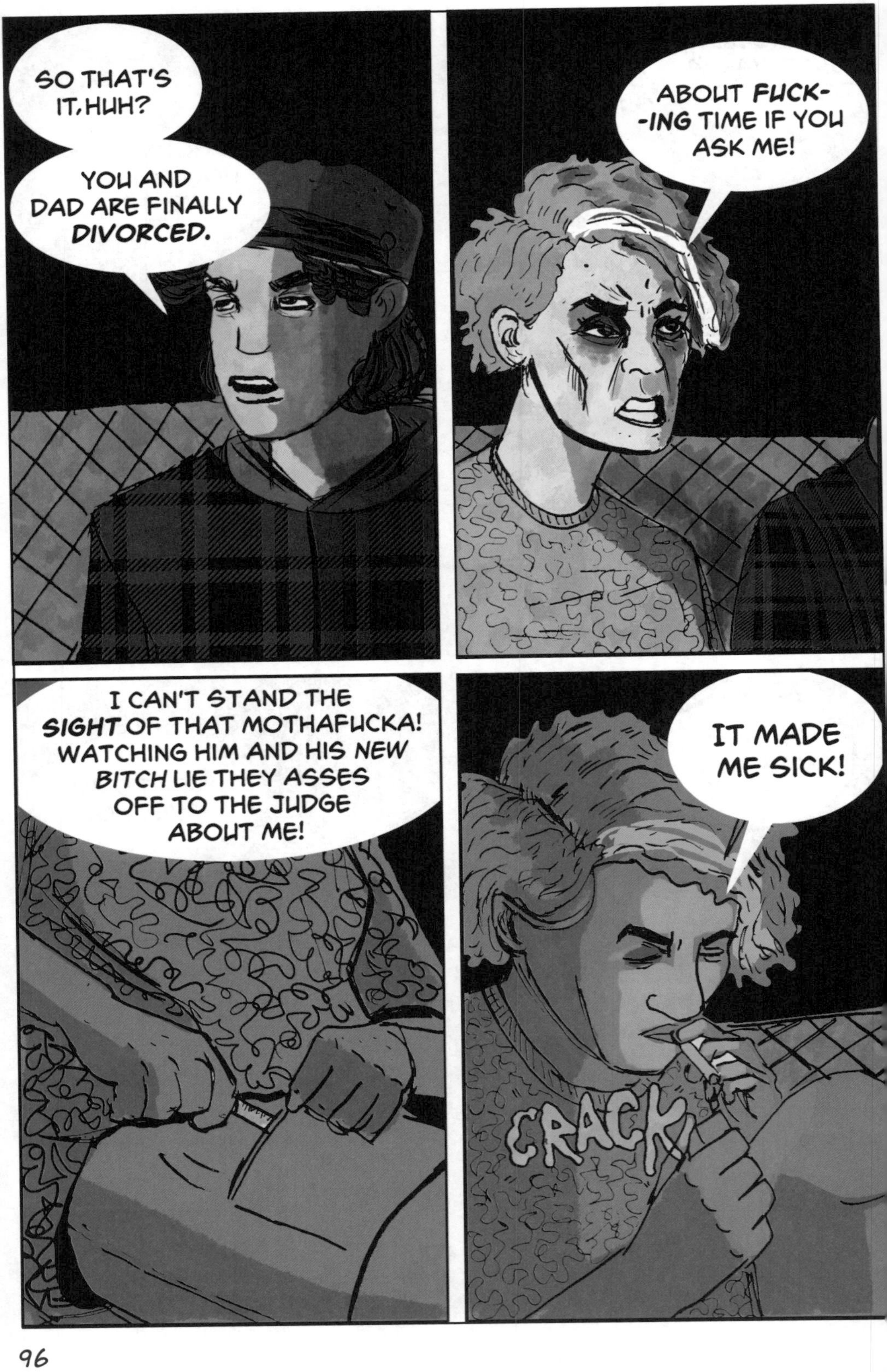
SO THAT'S IT, HUH?
YOU AND DAD ARE FINALLY DIVORCED.
ABOUT FUCK-ING TIME IF YOU ASK ME!
I CAN'T STAND THE SIGHT OF THAT MOTHAFUCKA! WATCHING HIM AND HIS NEW BITCH LIE THEY ASSES OFF TO THE JUDGE ABOUT ME!
IT MADE ME SICK!
CRACK

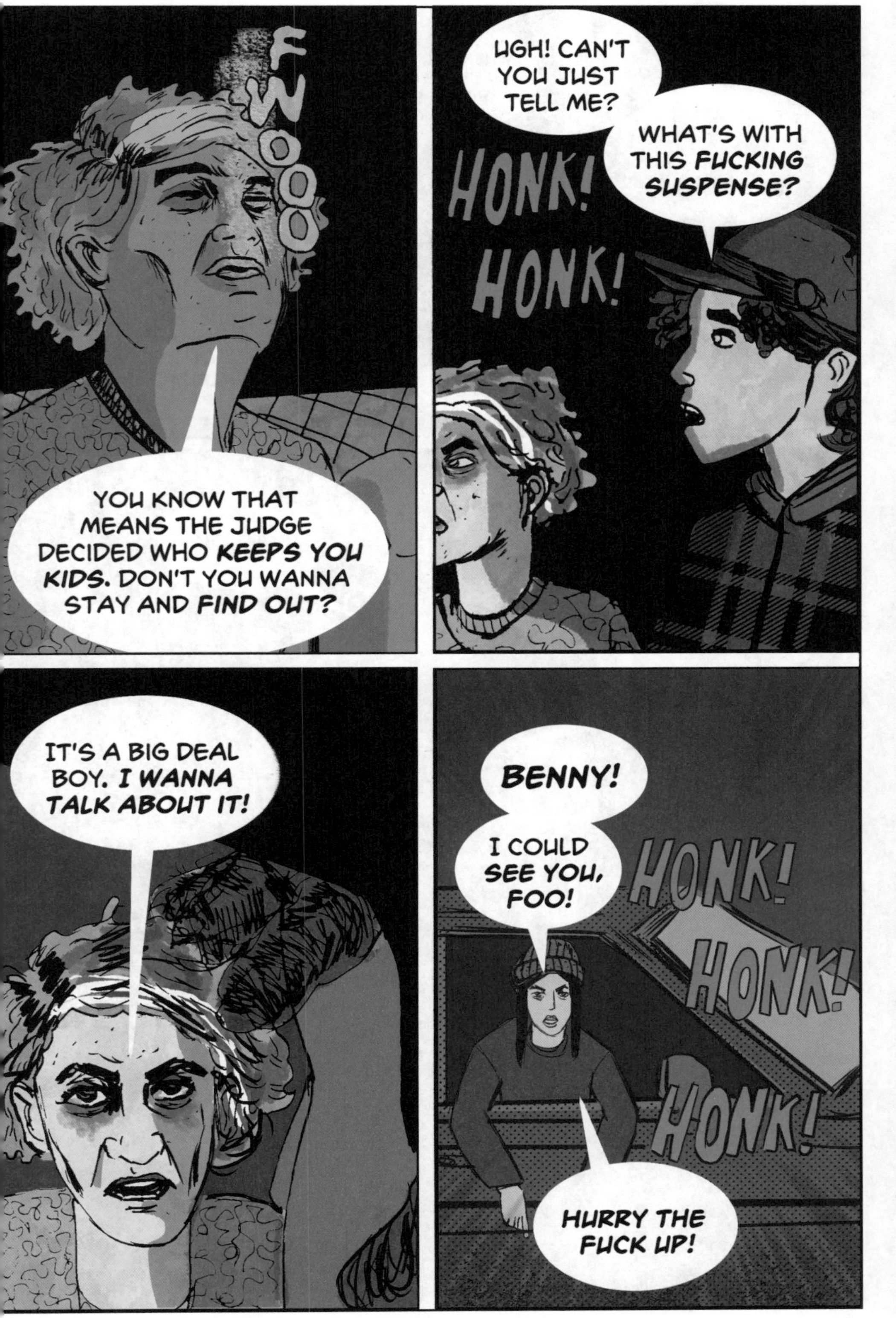
FWOOO
YOU KNOW THAT MEANS THE JUDGE DECIDED WHO KEEPS YOU KIDS. DON'T YOU WANNA STAY AND FIND OUT?
UGH! CAN'T YOU JUST TELL ME?
HONK! HONK!
WHAT'S WITH THIS FUCKING SUSPENSE?
IT'S A BIG DEAL BOY. I WANNA TALK ABOUT IT!
BENNY!
I COULD SEE YOU, FOO!
HONK! HONK! HONK!
HURRY THE FUCK UP!

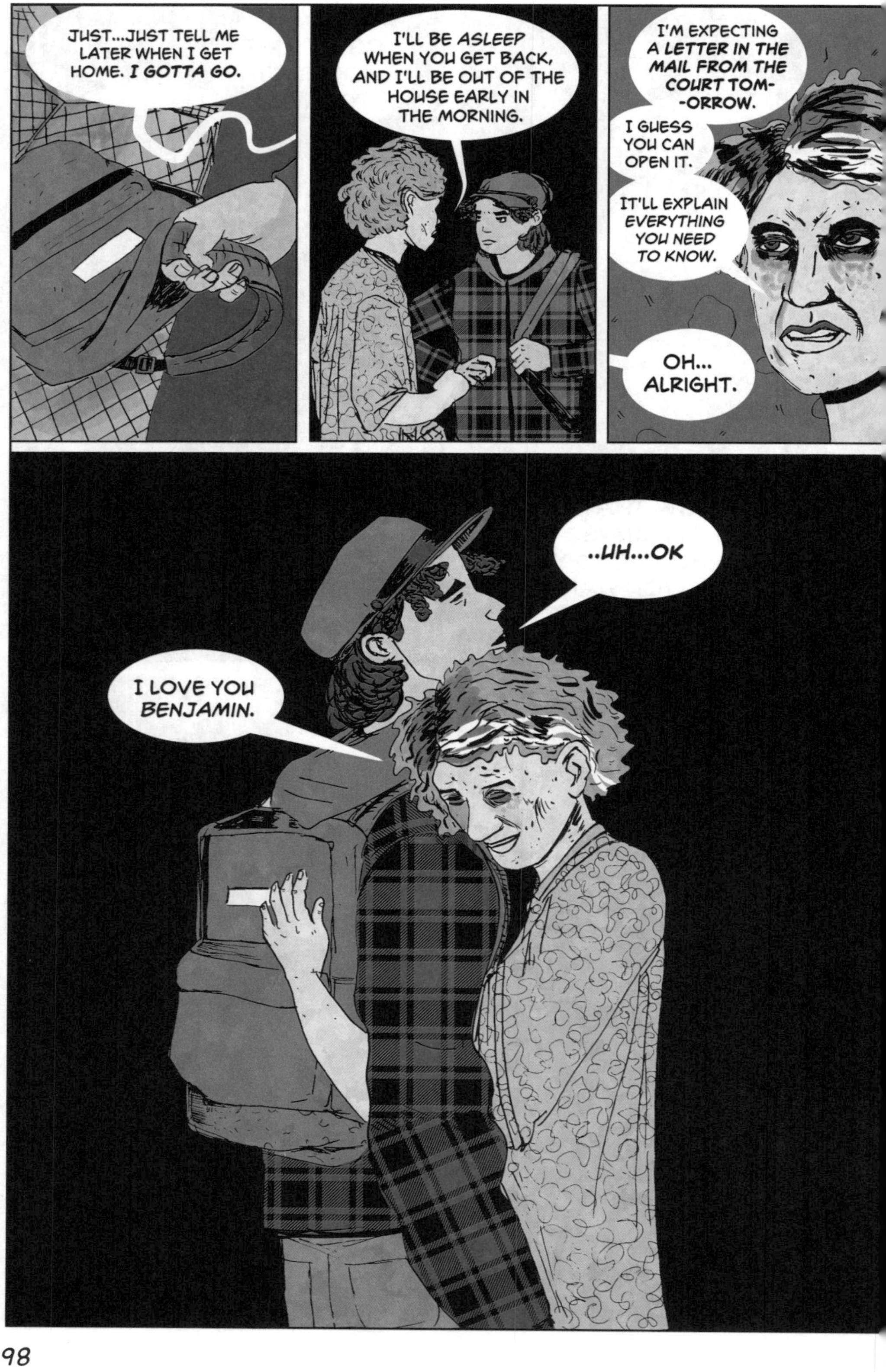
JUST...JUST TELL ME LATER WHEN I GET HOME. I GOTTA GO.
I'LL BE ASLEEP WHEN YOU GET BACK, AND I'LL BE OUT OF THE HOUSE EARLY IN THE MORNING.
I'M EXPECTING A LETTER IN THE MAIL FROM THE COURT TOM- -ORROW.
I GUESS YOU CAN OPEN IT.
IT'LL EXPLAIN EVERYTHING YOU NEED TO KNOW.
OH... ALRIGHT.
..UH...OK
I LOVE YOU BENJAMIN.

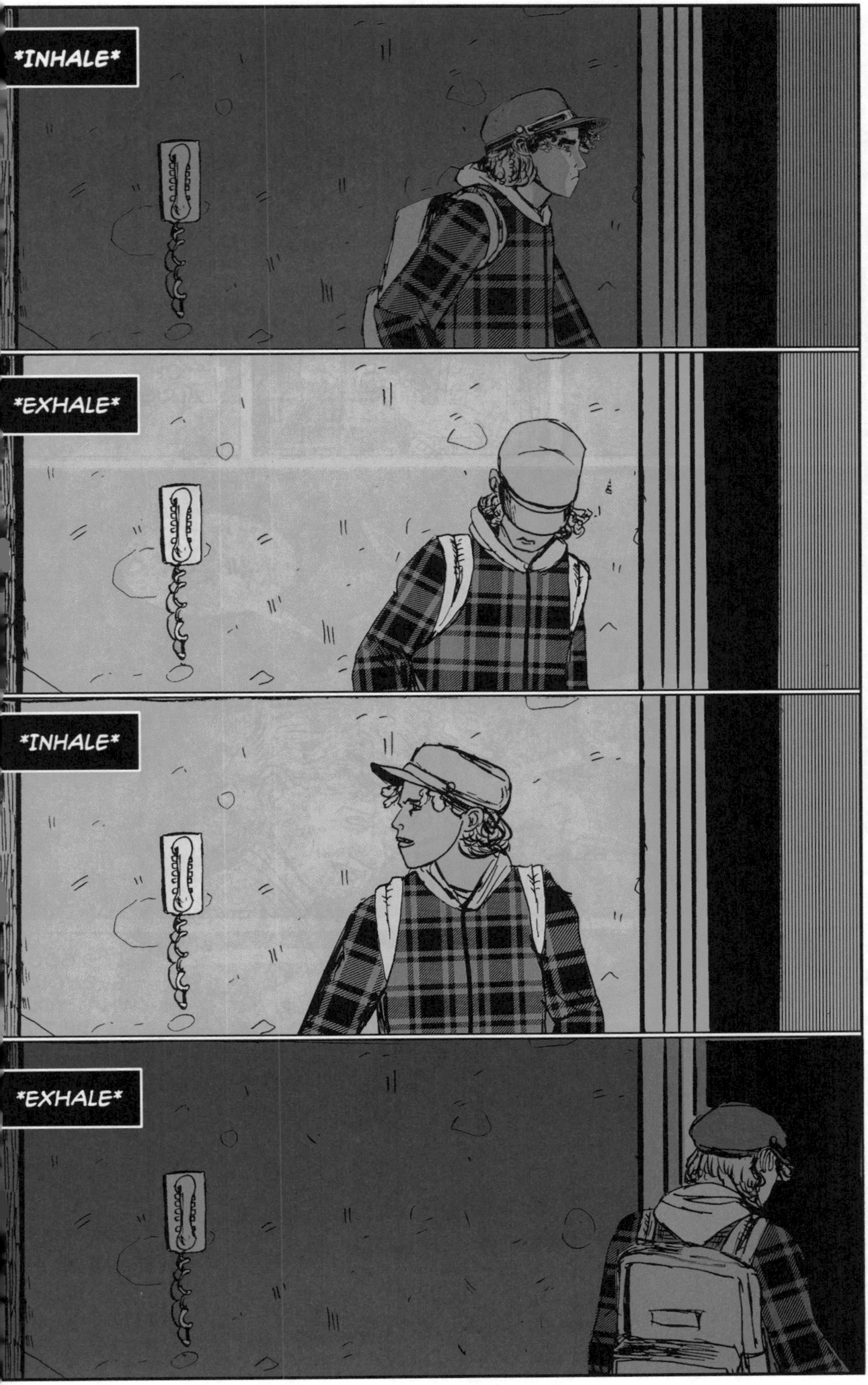
INHALE
EXHALE
INHALE
EXHALE

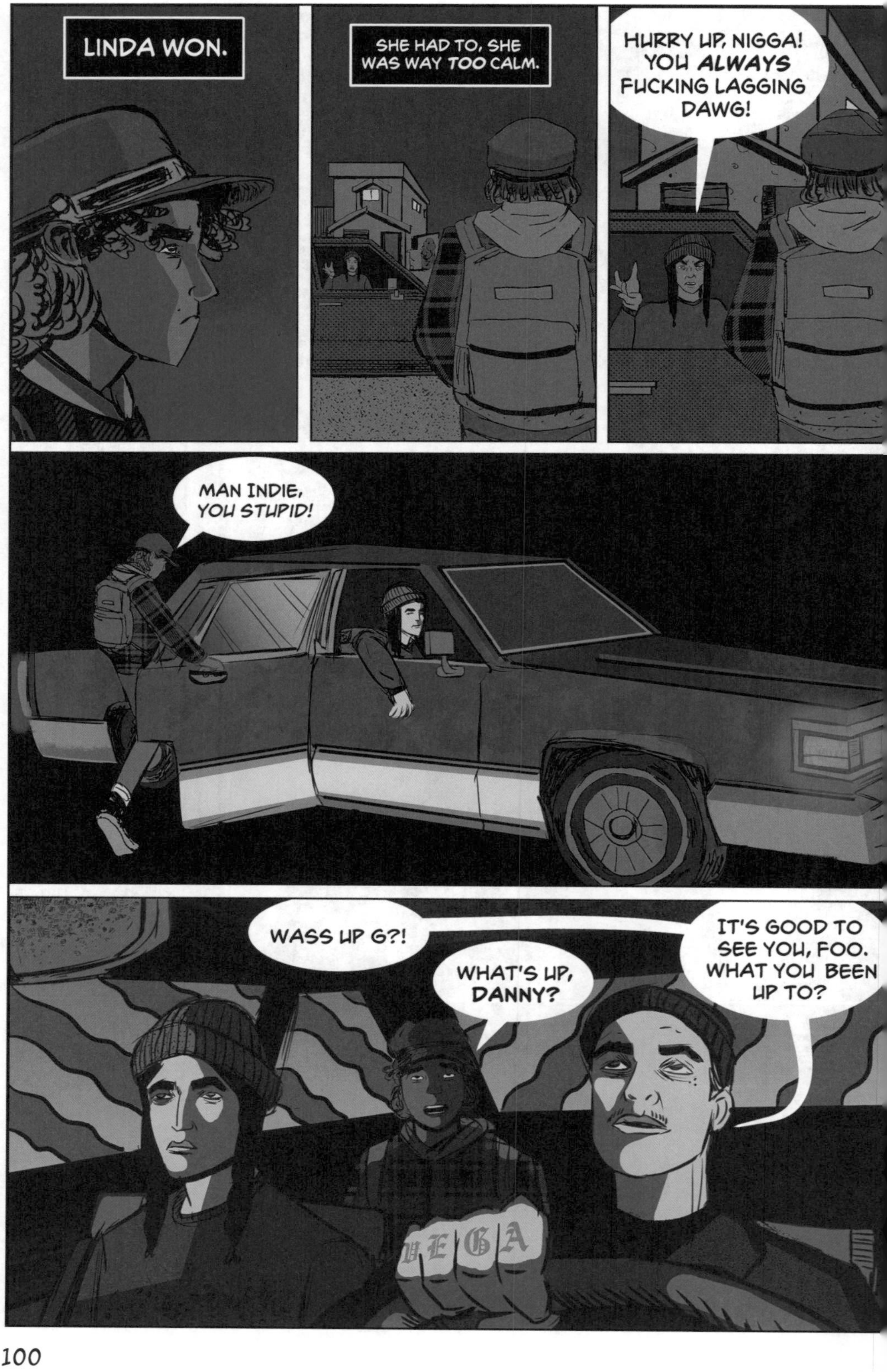
LINDA WON.
SHE HAD TO, SHE WAS WAY TOO CALM.
HURRY UP, NIGGA! YOU ALWAYS FUCKING LAGGING DAWG!
MAN INDIE, YOU STUPID!
WASS UP G?!
WHAT'S UP, DANNY?
IT'S GOOD TO SEE YOU, FOO. WHAT YOU BEEN UP TO?
VEGA

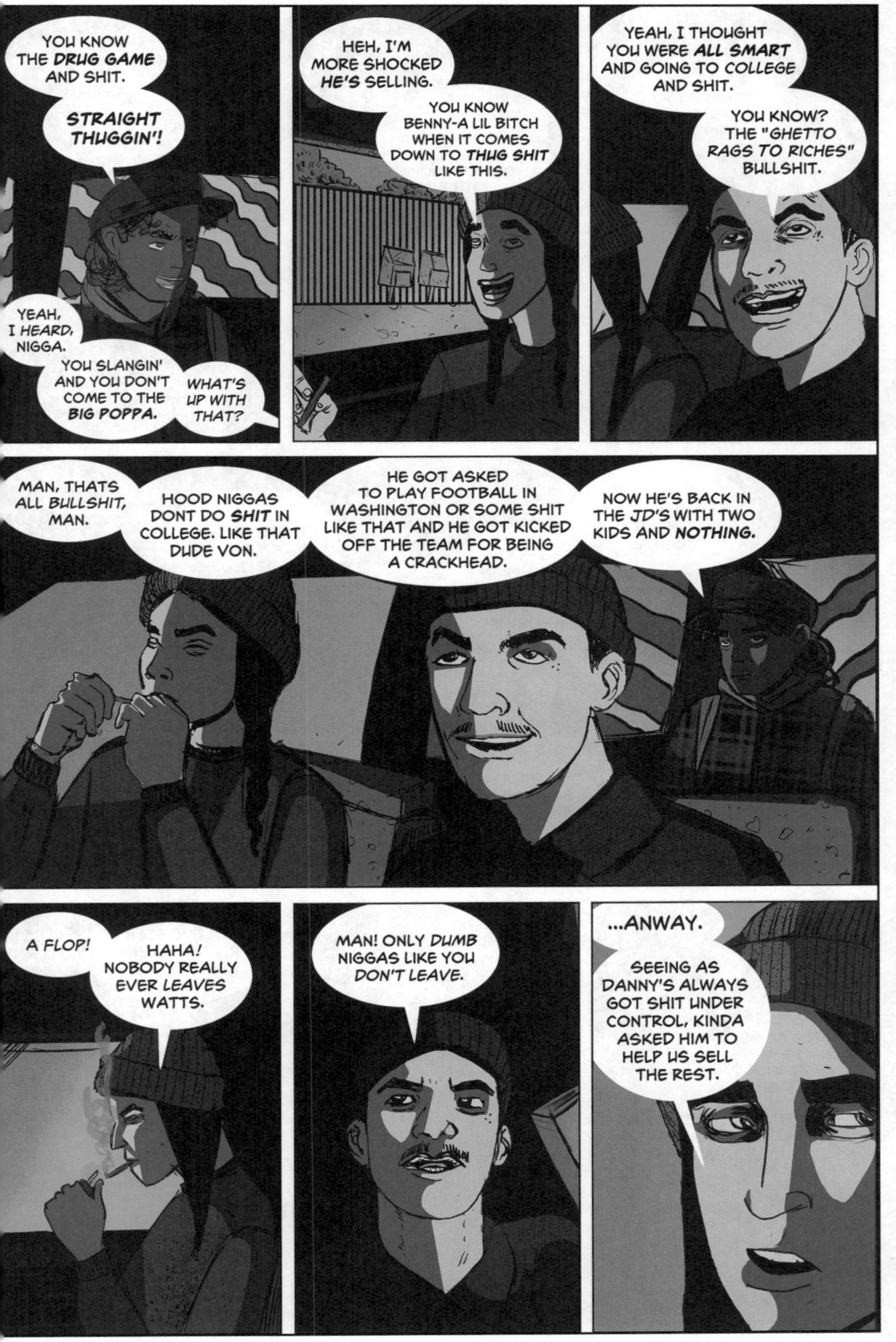
YOU KNOW THE DRUG GAME AND SHIT.
STRAIGHT THUGGIN'!
YEAH, I HEARD, NIGGA.
YOU SLANGIN' AND YOU DON'T COME TO THE BIG POPPA.
WHAT'S UP WITH THAT?
HEH, I'M MORE SHOCKED HE'S SELLING.
YOU KNOW BENNY-A LIL BITCH WHEN IT COMES DOWN TO THUG SHIT LIKE THIS.
YEAH, I THOUGHT YOU WERE ALL SMART AND GOING TO COLLEGE AND SHIT.
YOU KNOW? THE "GHETTO RAGS TO RICHES" BULLSHIT.
MAN, THATS ALL BULLSHIT, MAN.
HOOD NIGGAS DONT DO SHIT IN COLLEGE. LIKE THAT DUDE VON.
HE GOT ASKED TO PLAY FOOTBALL IN WASHINGTON OR SOME SHIT LIKE THAT AND HE GOT KICKED OFF THE TEAM FOR BEING A CRACKHEAD.
NOW HE'S BACK IN THE JD'S WITH TWO KIDS AND NOTHING.
A FLOP!
HAHA! NOBODY REALLY EVER LEAVES WATTS.
MAN! ONLY DUMB NIGGAS LIKE YOU DON'T LEAVE.
...ANWAY.
SEEING AS DANNY'S ALWAYS GOT SHIT UNDER CONTROL, KINDA ASKED HIM TO HELP US SELL THE REST.

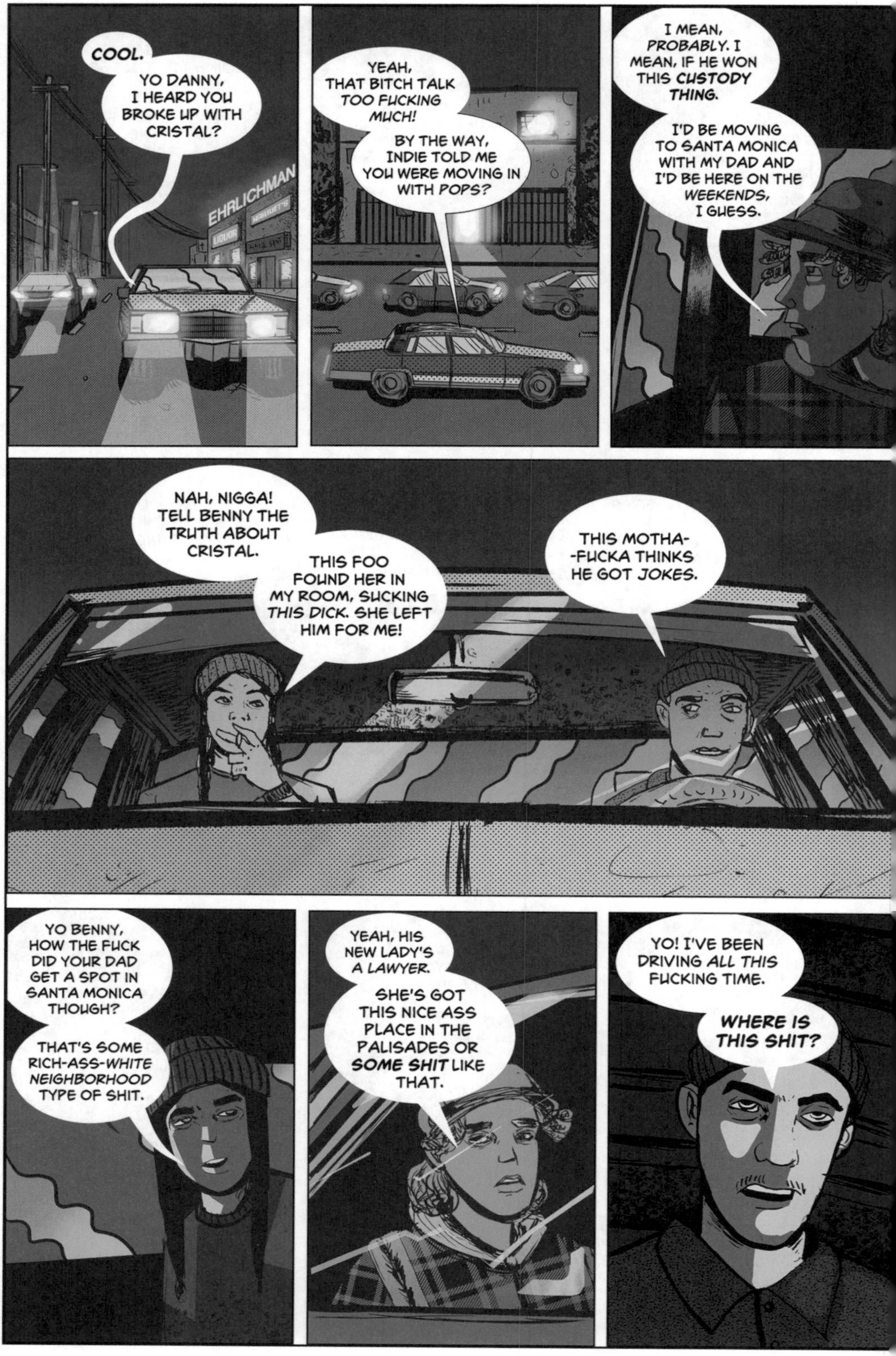
COOL.
YO DANNY, I HEARD YOU BROKE UP WITH CRISTAL?
EHRLICHMAN
LIQUOR
YEAH, THAT BITCH TALK TOO FUCKING MUCH!
BY THE WAY, INDIE TOLD ME YOU WERE MOVING IN WITH POPS?
I MEAN, PROBABLY. I MEAN, IF HE WON THIS CUSTODY THING.
I'D BE MOVING TO SANTA MONICA WITH MY DAD AND I'D BE HERE ON THE WEEKENDS, I GUESS.
NAH, NIGGA! TELL BENNY THE TRUTH ABOUT CRISTAL.
THIS FOO FOUND HER IN MY ROOM, SUCKING THIS DICK. SHE LEFT HIM FOR ME!
THIS MOTHA--FUCKA THINKS HE GOT JOKES.
YO BENNY, HOW THE FUCK DID YOUR DAD GET A SPOT IN SANTA MONICA THOUGH?
THAT'S SOME RICH-ASS-WHITE NEIGHBORHOOD TYPE OF SHIT.
YEAH, HIS NEW LADY'S A LAWYER.
SHE'S GOT THIS NICE ASS PLACE IN THE PALISADES OR SOME SHIT LIKE THAT.
YO! I'VE BEEN DRIVING ALL THIS FUCKING TIME.
WHERE IS THIS SHIT?

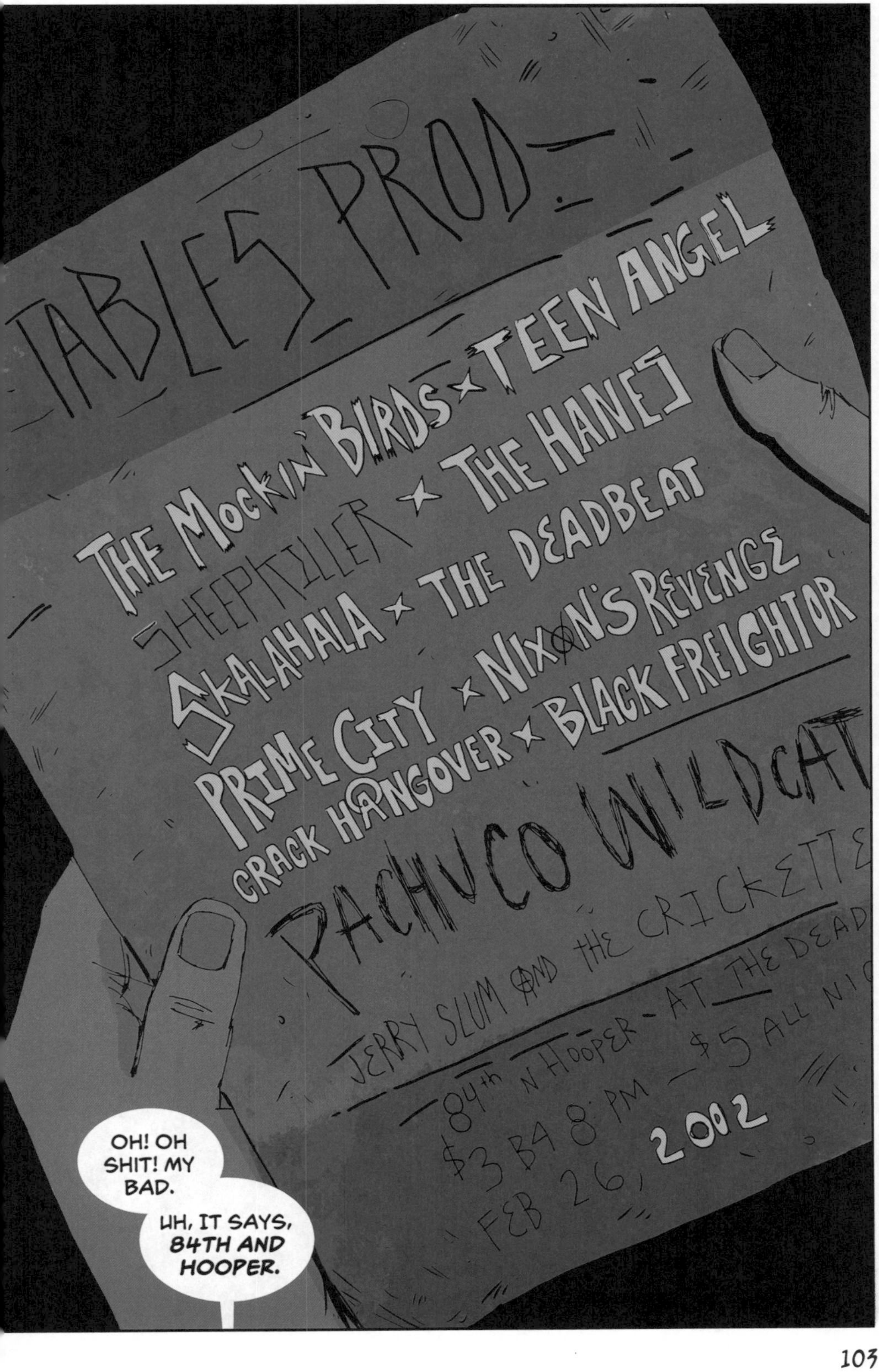
TABLES PROD
THE MOCKIN' BIRDS ★ TEEN ANGEL
SHEEPTELLER ★ THE HANES
SKALAHALA ★ THE DEADBEAT
PRIME CITY ★ NIXON'S REVENGE
CRACK HANGOVER ★ BLACK FREIGHTOR
PACHUCO WILDCAT
JERRY SLUM AND THE CRICKETTE
AT THE DEAD
84th N HOOPER
$5 ALL NI
$3 B4 8 PM
FEB 26, 2002
OH! OH SHIT! MY BAD.
UH, IT SAYS, 84TH AND HOOPER.

THE SHOW
84th ST. and Hooper Ave.

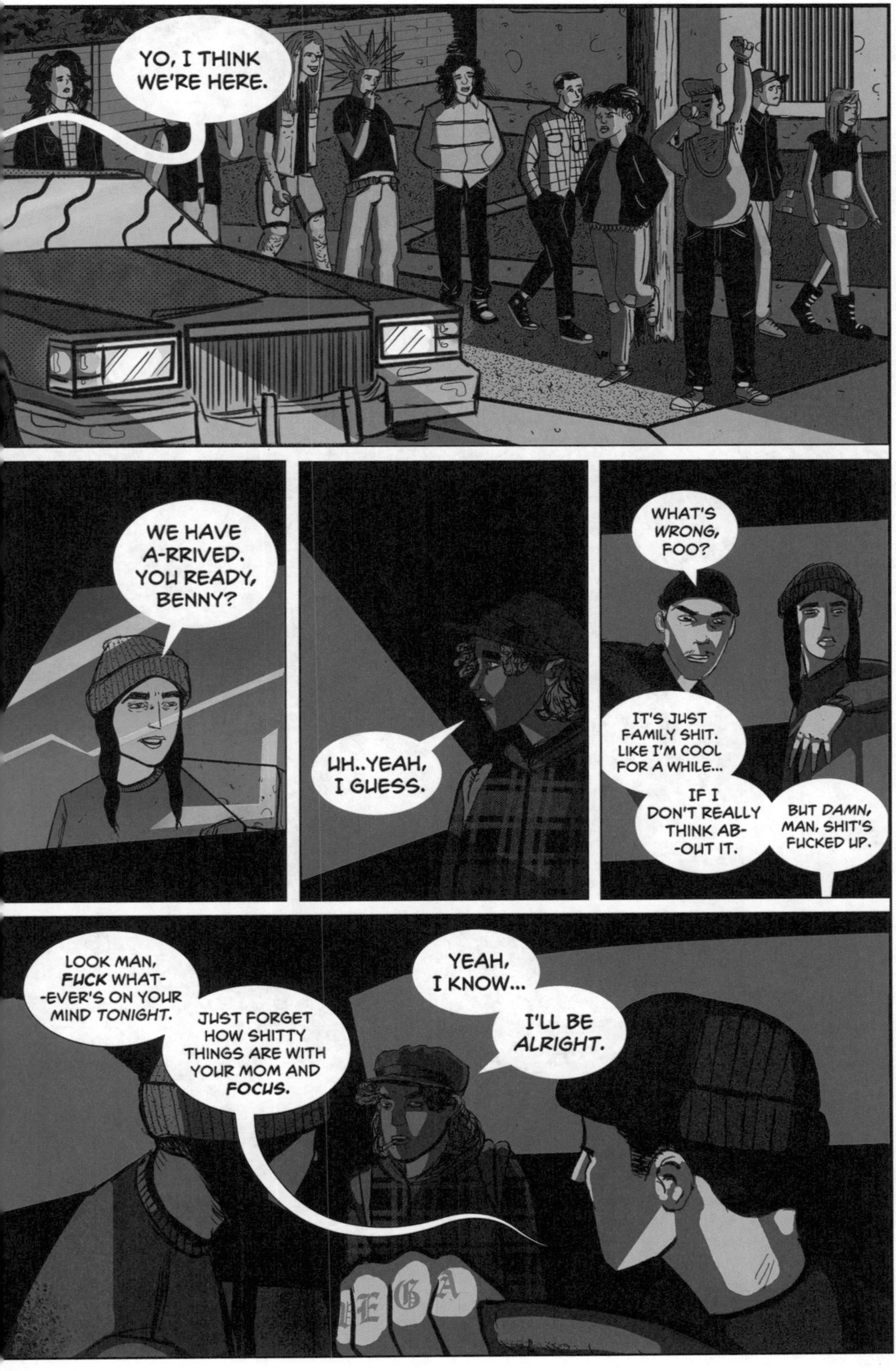
YO, I THINK WE'RE HERE.
WE HAVE A-RRIVED. YOU READY, BENNY?
UH..YEAH, I GUESS.
WHAT'S WRONG, FOO?
IT'S JUST FAMILY SHIT. LIKE I'M COOL FOR A WHILE...
IF I DON'T REALLY THINK AB- -OUT IT.
BUT *DAMN,* MAN, SHIT'S FUCKED UP.
LOOK MAN, **FUCK** WHAT- -EVER'S ON YOUR MIND *TONIGHT.*
JUST FORGET HOW SHITTY THINGS ARE WITH YOUR MOM AND **FOCUS.**
YEAH, I KNOW...
I'LL BE *ALRIGHT.*
VEGA

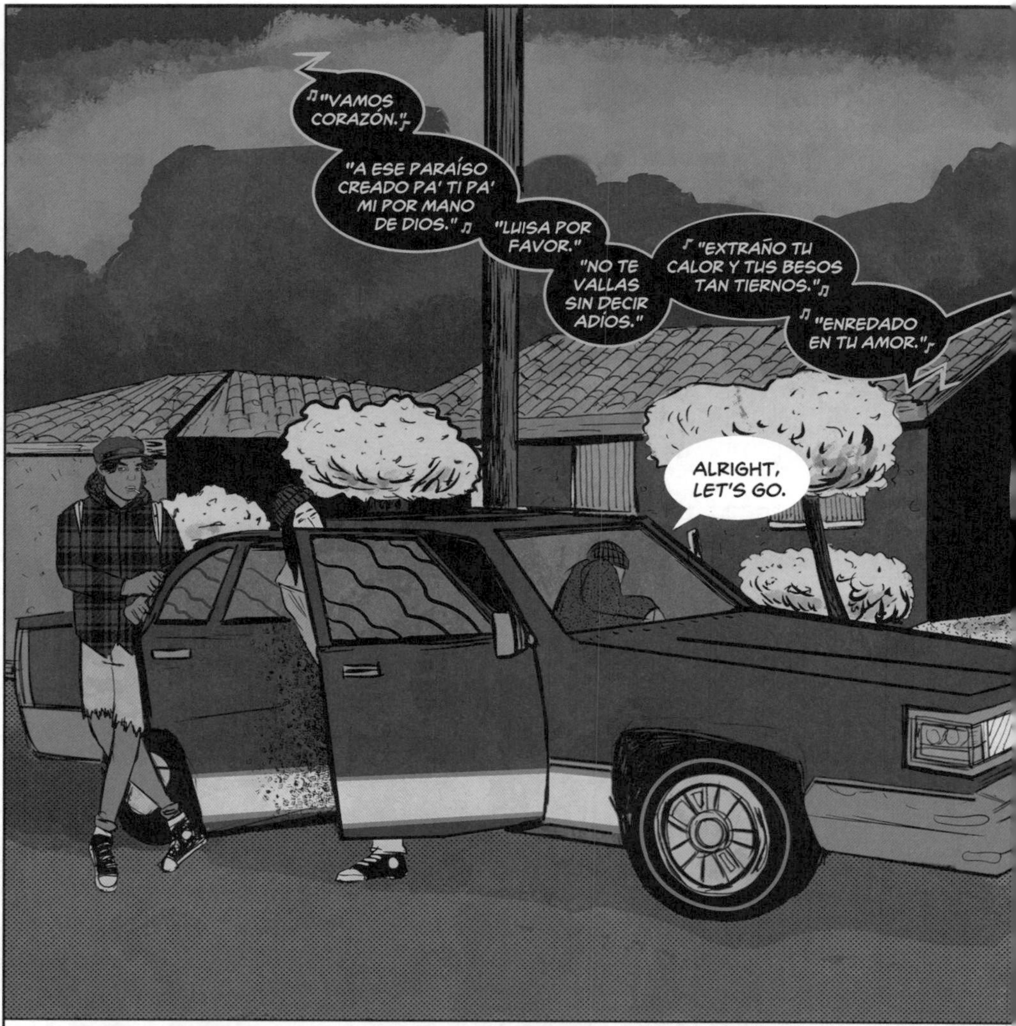
"VAMOS CORAZÓN."
"A ESE PARAÍSO CREADO PA' TI PA' MI POR MANO DE DIOS."
"LUISA POR FAVOR."
"NO TE VALLAS SIN DECIR ADÍOS."
"EXTRAÑO TU CALOR Y TUS BESOS TAN TIERNOS."
"ENREDADO EN TU AMOR."
ALRIGHT, LET'S GO.

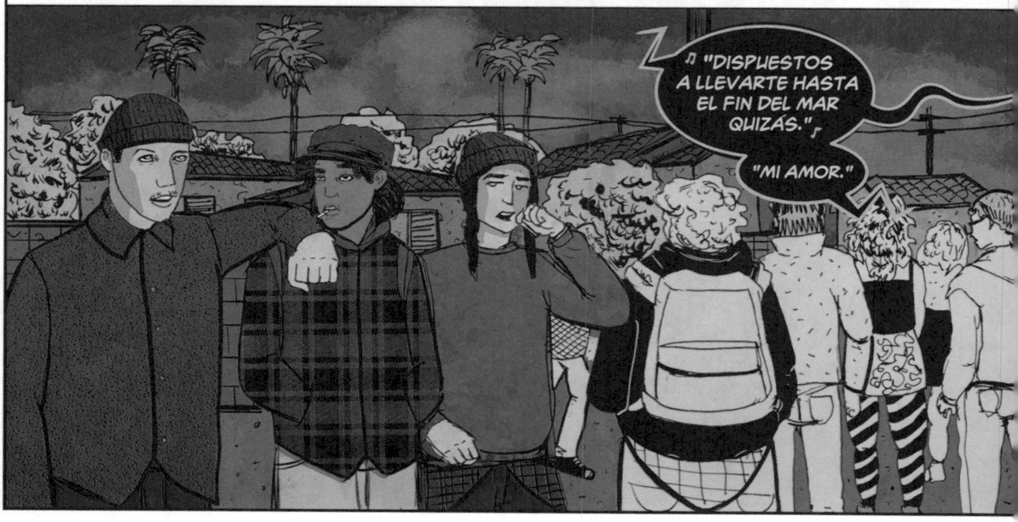
"DISPUESTOS A LLEVARTE HASTA EL FIN DEL MAR QUIZÁS."
"MI AMOR."

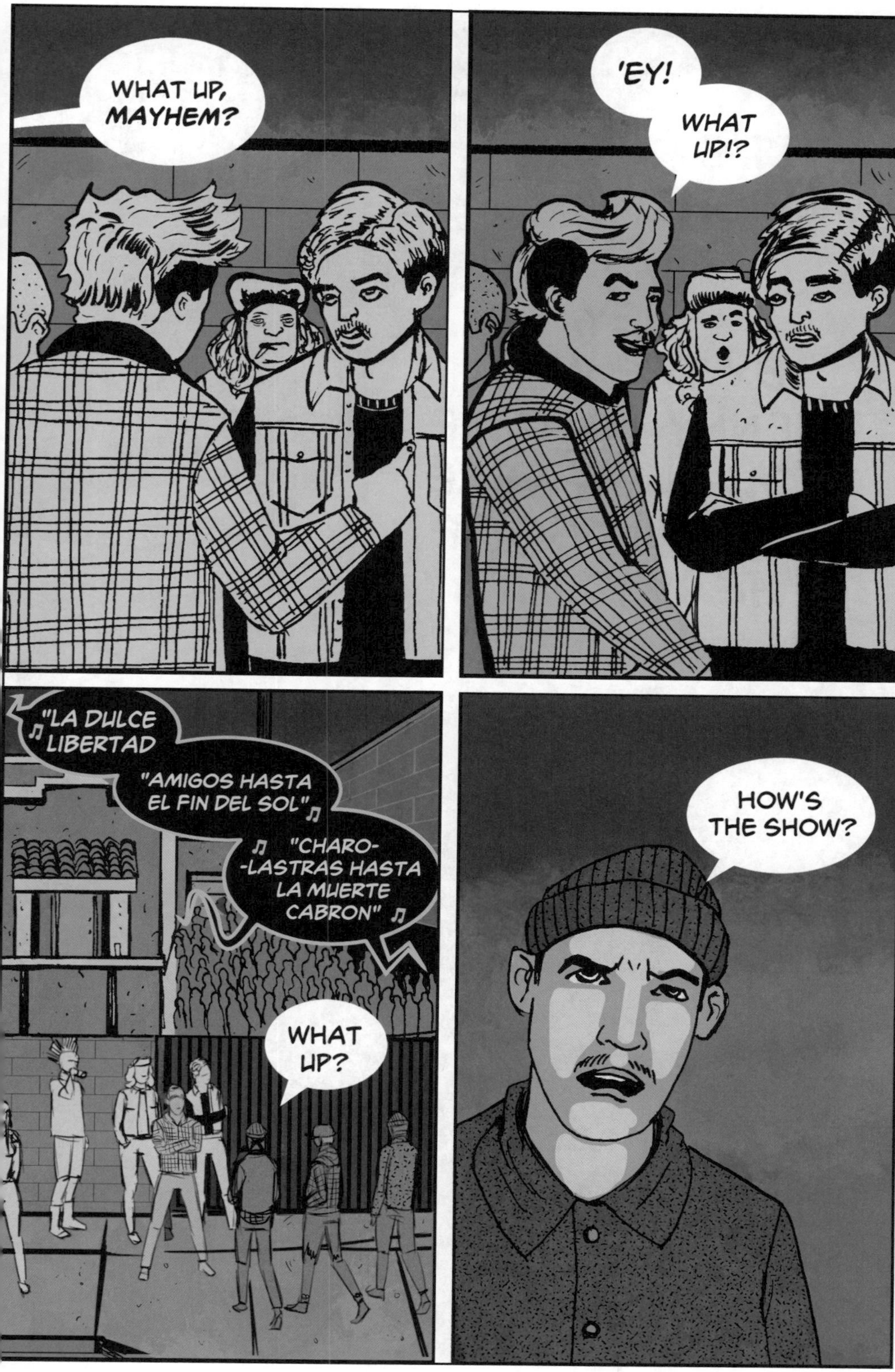
WHAT UP, MAYHEM?
'EY!
WHAT UP!?
♫ "LA DULCE LIBERTAD
"AMIGOS HASTA EL FIN DEL SOL" ♫
♫ "CHARO- -LASTRAS HASTA LA MUERTE CABRON" ♫
WHAT UP?
HOW'S THE SHOW?

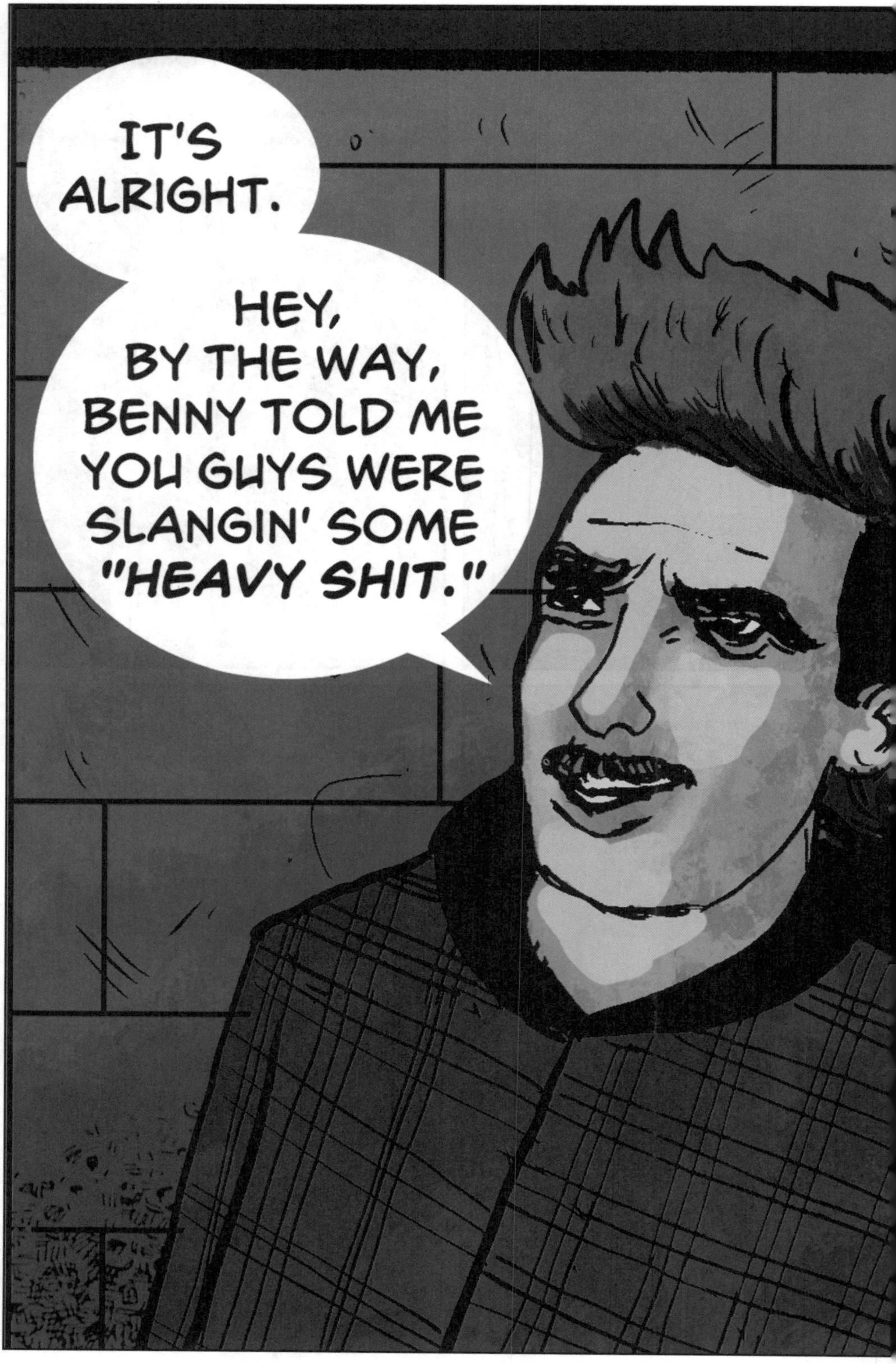
IT'S ALRIGHT.
HEY, BY THE WAY, BENNY TOLD ME YOU GUYS WERE SLANGIN' SOME "HEAVY SHIT."

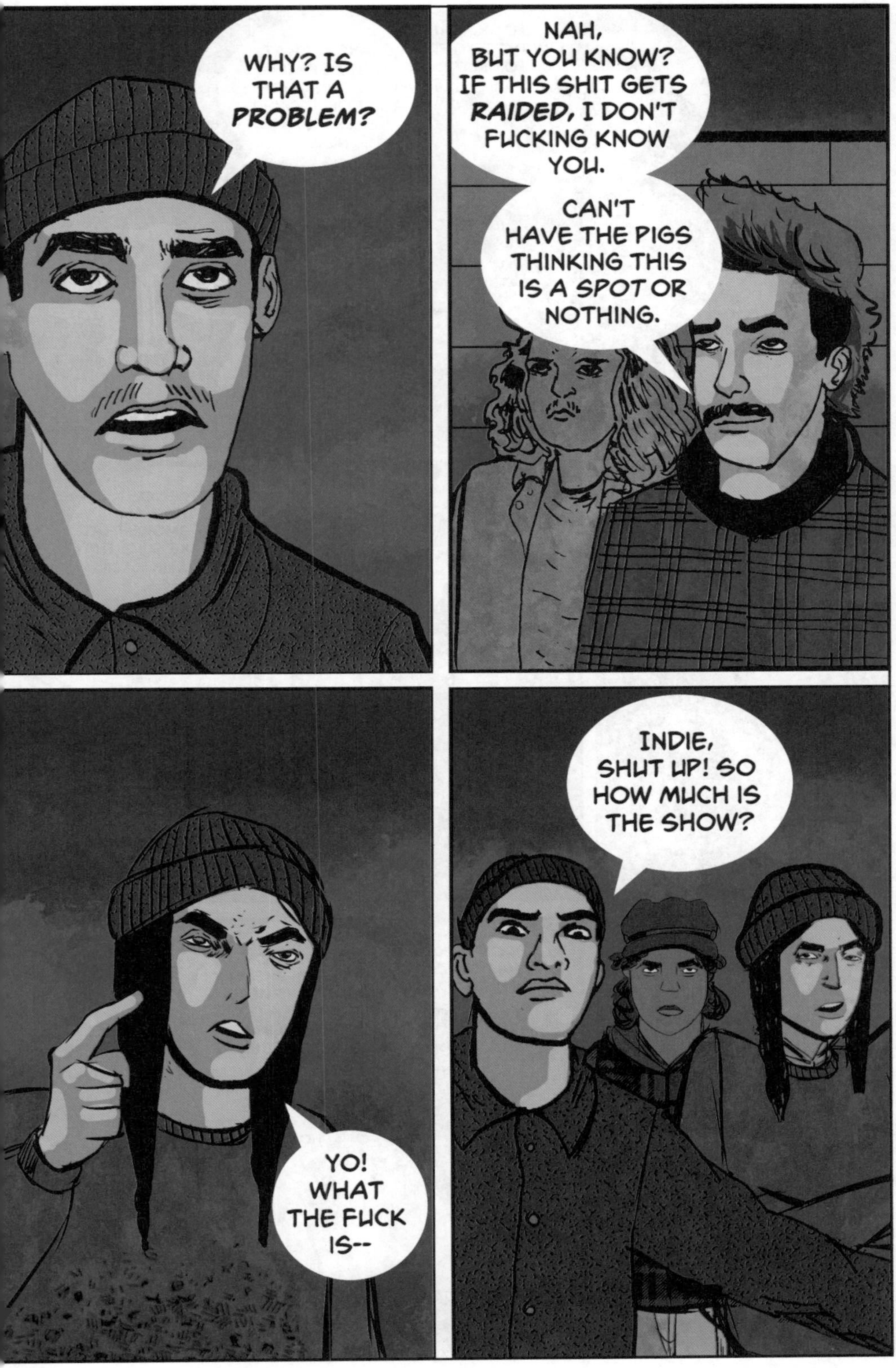
WHY? IS THAT A *PROBLEM?*
NAH, BUT YOU KNOW? IF THIS SHIT GETS *RAIDED,* I DON'T FUCKING KNOW YOU.
CAN'T HAVE THE PIGS THINKING THIS IS A *SPOT* OR NOTHING.
YO! WHAT THE FUCK IS--
INDIE, SHUT UP! SO HOW MUCH IS THE SHOW?

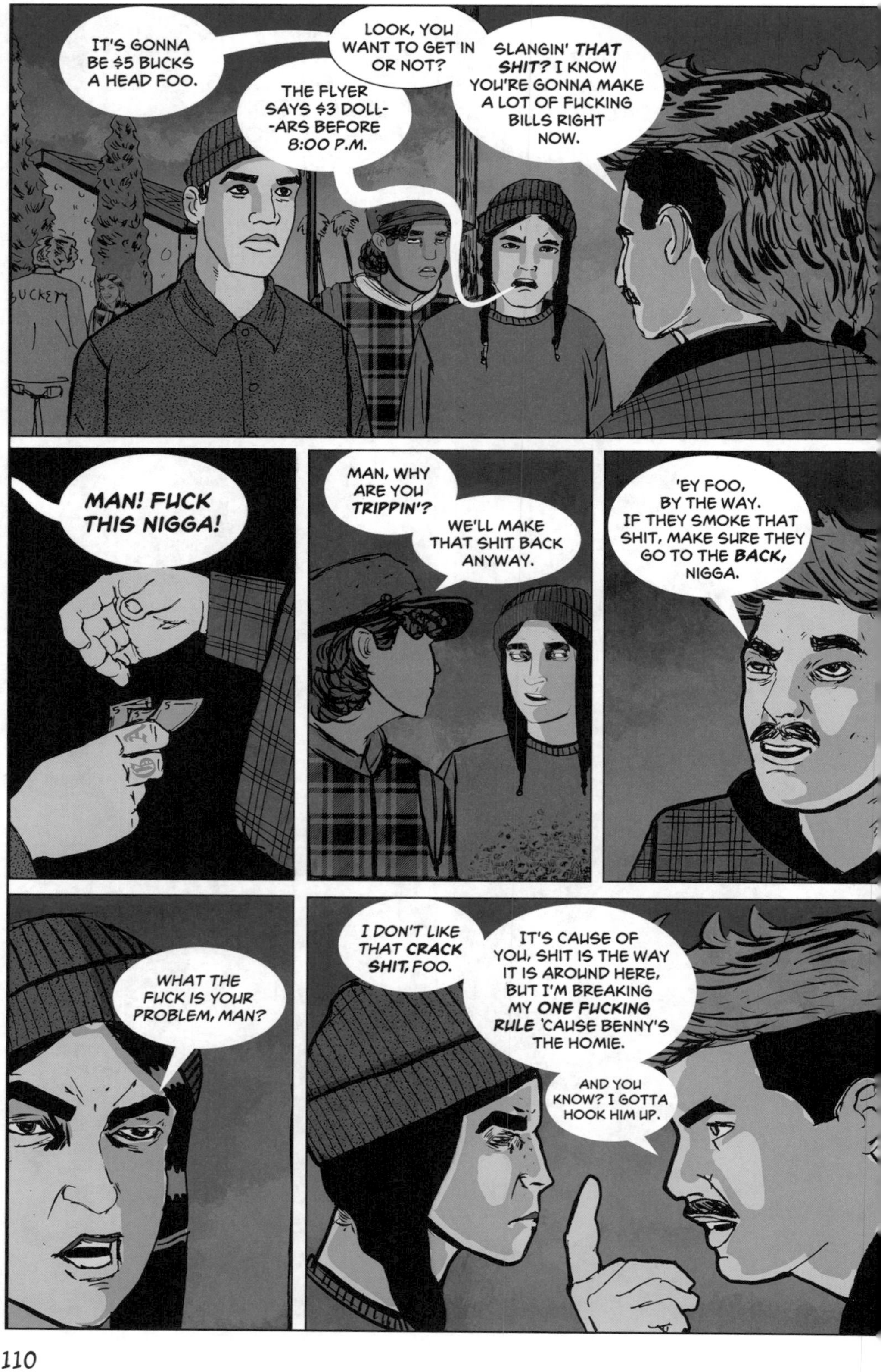
IT'S GONNA BE $5 BUCKS A HEAD FOO.
THE FLYER SAYS $3 DOLL- -ARS BEFORE 8:00 P.M.
LOOK, YOU WANT TO GET IN OR NOT?
SLANGIN' THAT SHIT? I KNOW YOU'RE GONNA MAKE A LOT OF FUCKING BILLS RIGHT NOW.
BUCKET
MAN! FUCK THIS NIGGA!
MAN, WHY ARE YOU TRIPPIN'?
WE'LL MAKE THAT SHIT BACK ANYWAY.
'EY FOO, BY THE WAY. IF THEY SMOKE THAT SHIT, MAKE SURE THEY GO TO THE BACK, NIGGA.
WHAT THE FUCK IS YOUR PROBLEM, MAN?
I DON'T LIKE THAT CRACK SHIT, FOO.
IT'S CAUSE OF YOU, SHIT IS THE WAY IT IS AROUND HERE, BUT I'M BREAKING MY ONE FUCKING RULE 'CAUSE BENNY'S THE HOMIE.
AND YOU KNOW? I GOTTA HOOK HIM UP.

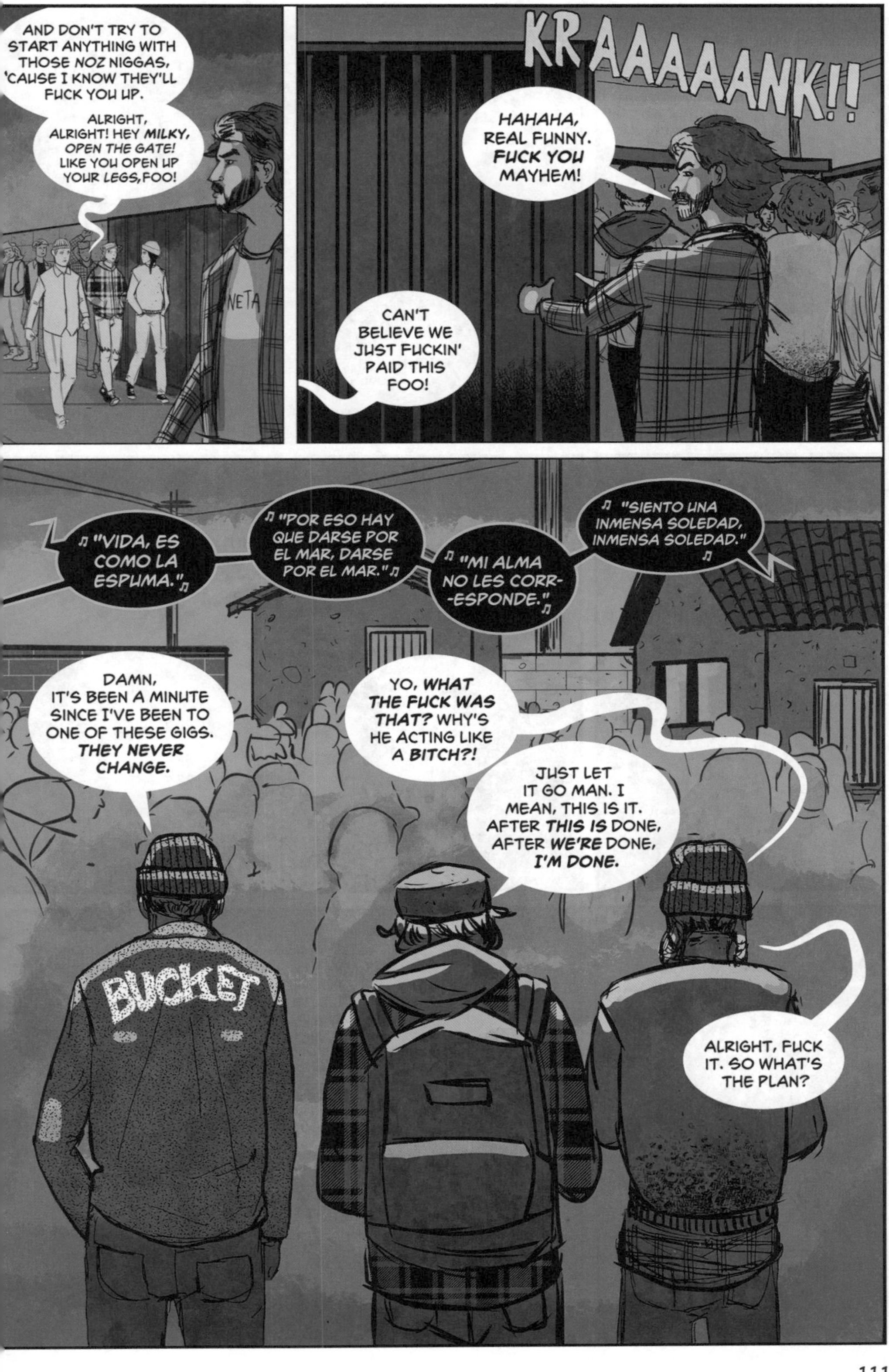
AND DON'T TRY TO START ANYTHING WITH THOSE NOZ NIGGAS, 'CAUSE I KNOW THEY'LL FUCK YOU UP.
ALRIGHT, ALRIGHT! HEY MILKY, OPEN THE GATE! LIKE YOU OPEN UP YOUR LEGS, FOO!
NETA
KRAAAAAANK!!
HAHAHA, REAL FUNNY. FUCK YOU MAYHEM!
CAN'T BELIEVE WE JUST FUCKIN' PAID THIS FOO!
♫ "VIDA, ES COMO LA ESPUMA." ♫
♫ "POR ESO HAY QUE DARSE POR EL MAR, DARSE POR EL MAR." ♫
♫ "MI ALMA NO LES CORR-ESPONDE." ♫
♫ "SIENTO UNA INMENSA SOLEDAD, INMENSA SOLEDAD." ♫
DAMN, IT'S BEEN A MINUTE SINCE I'VE BEEN TO ONE OF THESE GIGS. THEY NEVER CHANGE.
YO, WHAT THE FUCK WAS THAT? WHY'S HE ACTING LIKE A BITCH?!
JUST LET IT GO MAN. I MEAN, THIS IS IT. AFTER THIS IS DONE, AFTER WE'RE DONE, I'M DONE.
BUCKET
ALRIGHT, FUCK IT. SO WHAT'S THE PLAN?

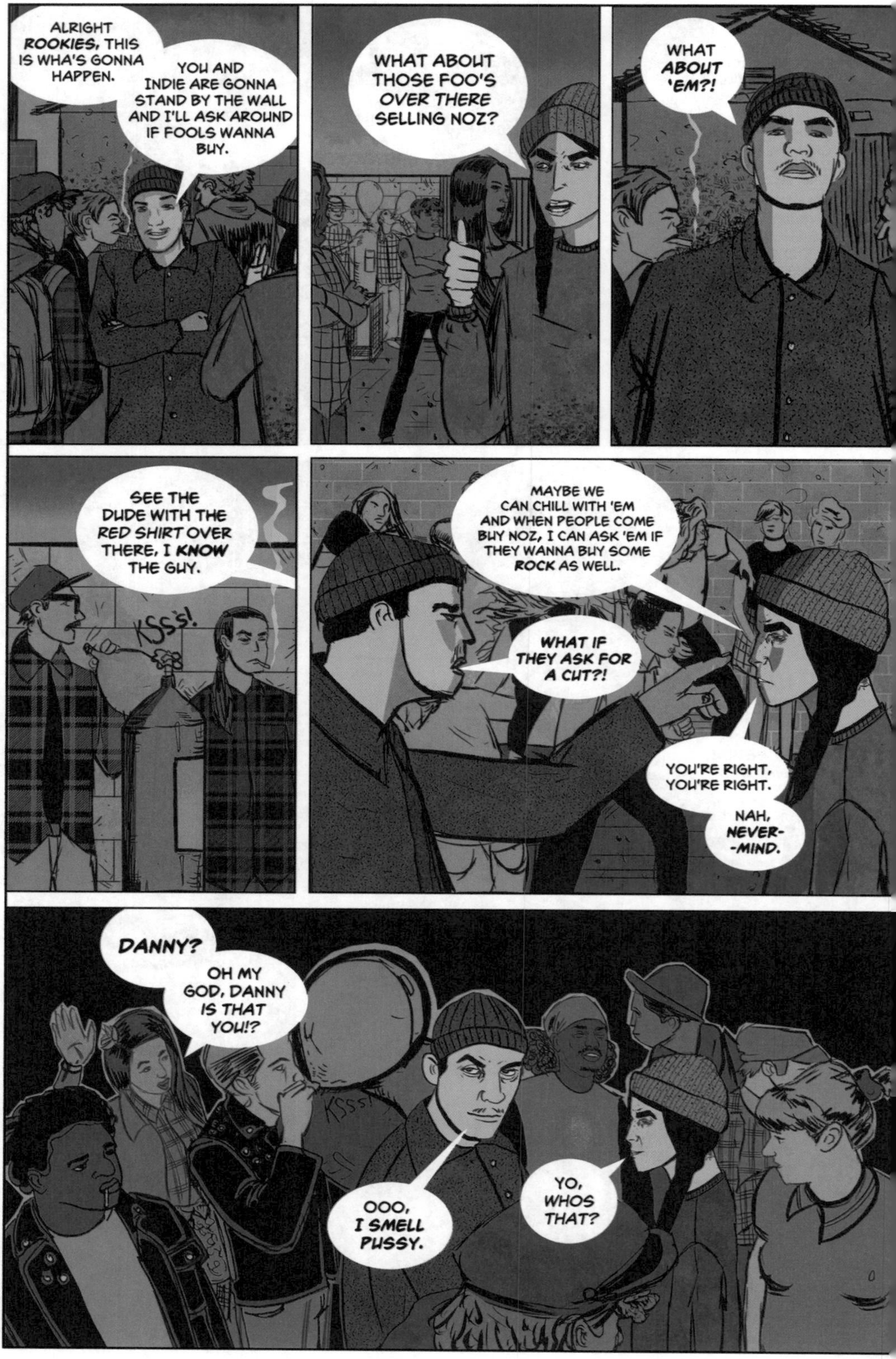
ALRIGHT ROOKIES, THIS IS WHA'S GONNA HAPPEN.
YOU AND INDIE ARE GONNA STAND BY THE WALL AND I'LL ASK AROUND IF FOOLS WANNA BUY.
WHAT ABOUT THOSE FOO'S OVER THERE SELLING NOZ?
WHAT ABOUT 'EM?!
SEE THE DUDE WITH THE RED SHIRT OVER THERE, I KNOW THE GUY.
KSSS!
MAYBE WE CAN CHILL WITH 'EM AND WHEN PEOPLE COME BUY NOZ, I CAN ASK 'EM IF THEY WANNA BUY SOME ROCK AS WELL.
WHAT IF THEY ASK FOR A CUT?!
YOU'RE RIGHT, YOU'RE RIGHT.
NAH, NEVER-MIND.
DANNY?
OH MY GOD, DANNY IS THAT YOU!?
KSSS!
OOO, I SMELL PUSSY.
YO, WHOS THAT?

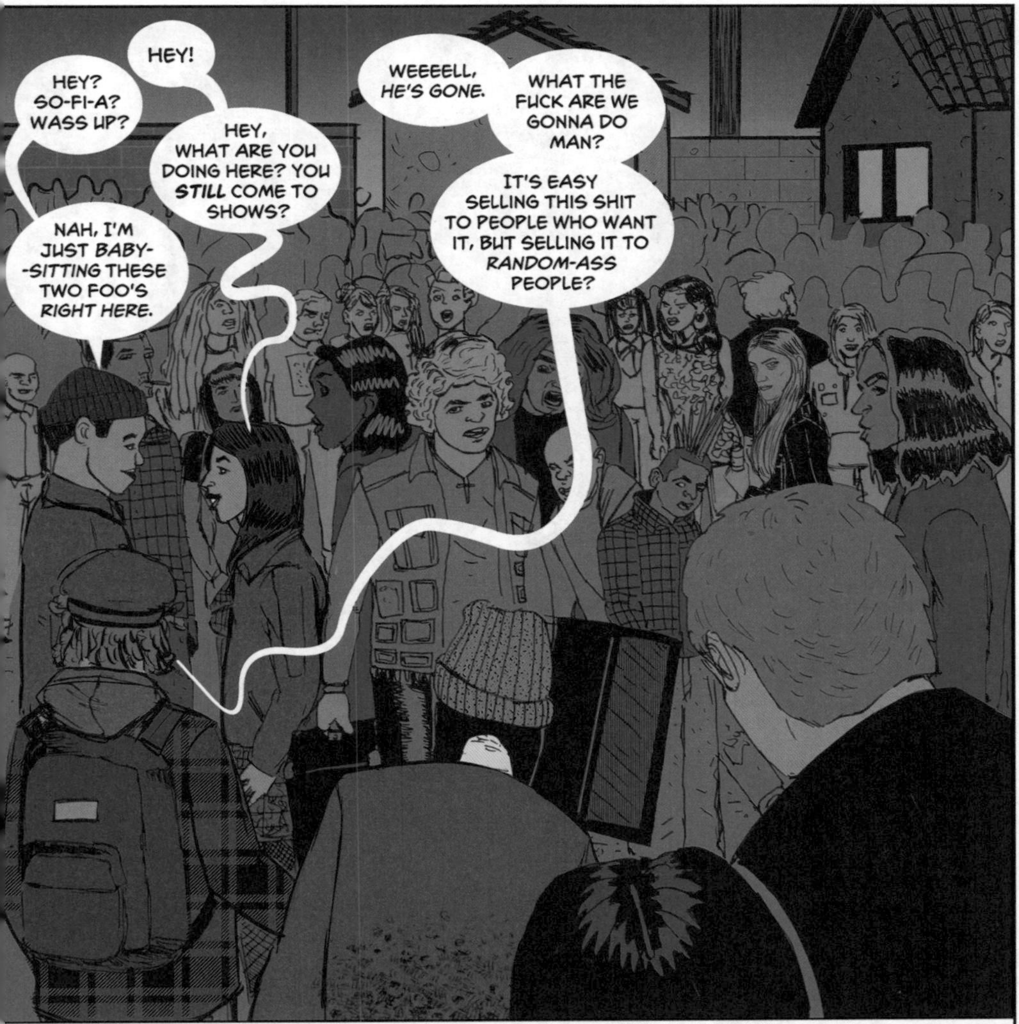
HEY? SO-FI-A? WASS UP?
HEY!
HEY, WHAT ARE YOU DOING HERE? YOU STILL COME TO SHOWS?
NAH, I'M JUST BABY--SITTING THESE TWO FOO'S RIGHT HERE.
WEEEELL, HE'S GONE.
WHAT THE FUCK ARE WE GONNA DO MAN?
IT'S EASY SELLING THIS SHIT TO PEOPLE WHO WANT IT, BUT SELLING IT TO RANDOM-ASS PEOPLE?

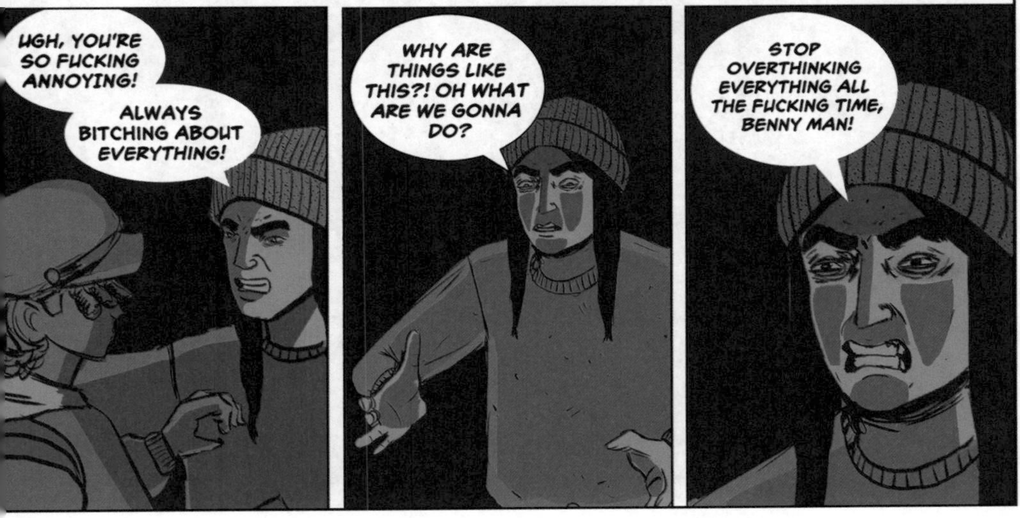
UGH, YOU'RE SO FUCKING ANNOYING!
ALWAYS BITCHING ABOUT EVERYTHING!
WHY ARE THINGS LIKE THIS?! OH WHAT ARE WE GONNA DO?
STOP OVERTHINKING EVERYTHING ALL THE FUCKING TIME, BENNY MAN!

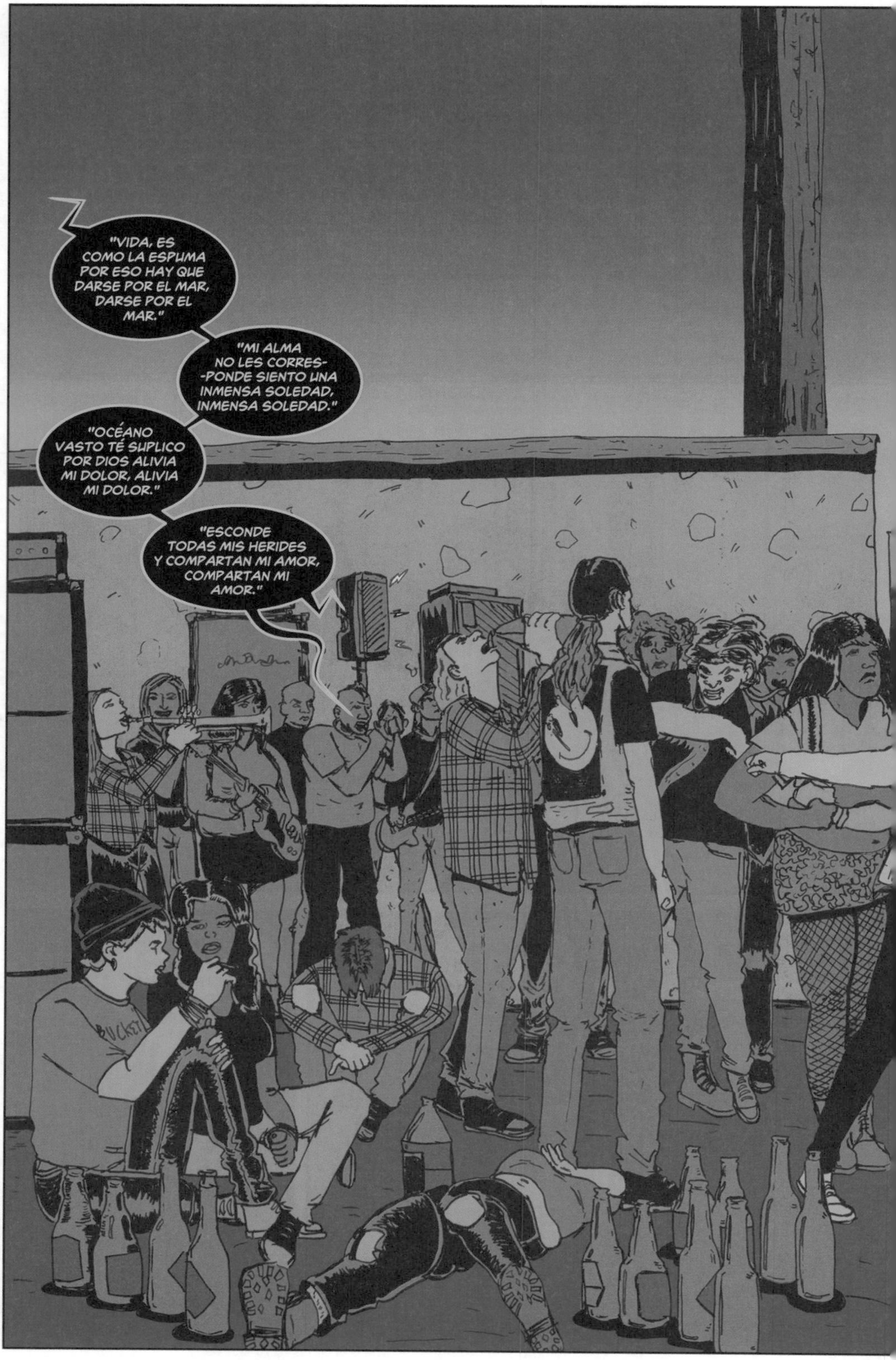
"VIDA, ES COMO LA ESPUMA POR ESO HAY QUE DARSE POR EL MAR, DARSE POR EL MAR."
"MI ALMA NO LES CORRES-PONDE SIENTO UNA INMENSA SOLEDAD, INMENSA SOLEDAD."
"OCÉANO VASTO TÉ SUPLICO POR DIOS ALIVIA MI DOLOR, ALIVIA MI DOLOR."
"ESCONDE TODAS MIS HERIDES Y COMPARTAN MI AMOR, COMPARTAN MI AMOR."
BUCKET

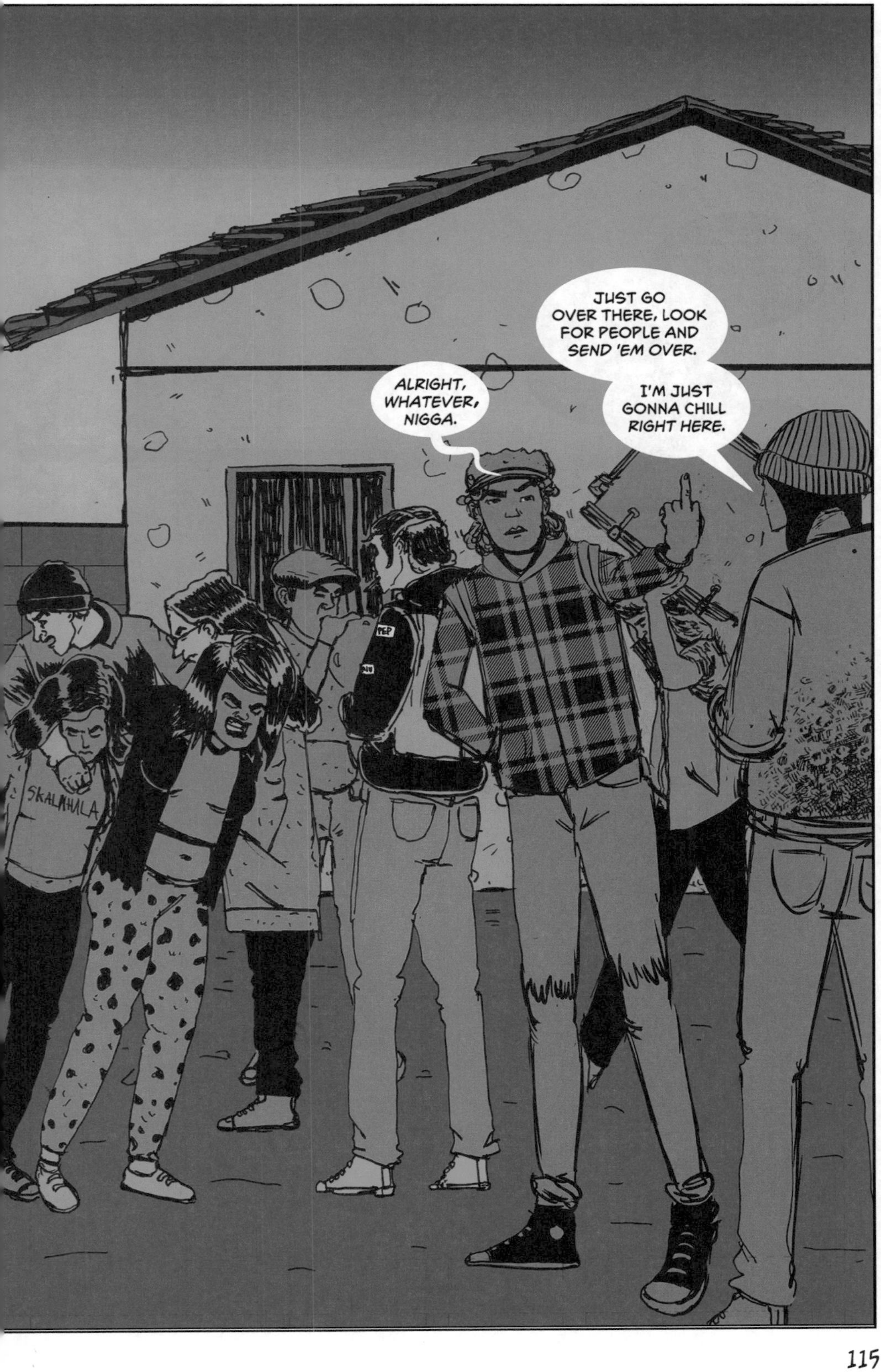
JUST GO OVER THERE, LOOK FOR PEOPLE AND SEND 'EM OVER.
I'M JUST GONNA CHILL RIGHT HERE.
ALRIGHT, WHATEVER, NIGGA.
SKALHALA

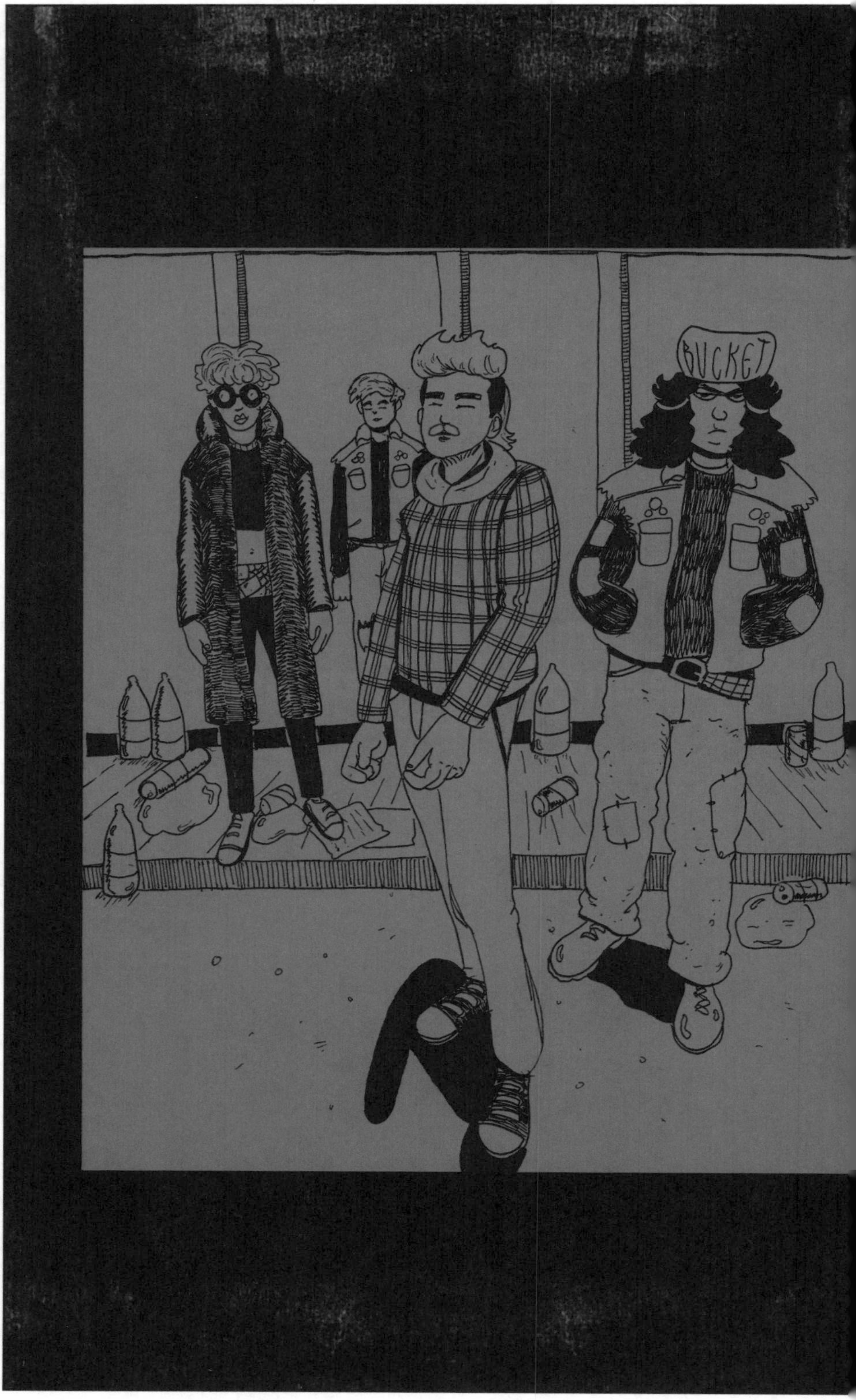
BUCKET

Meanwhile, Outside
THE SHOW

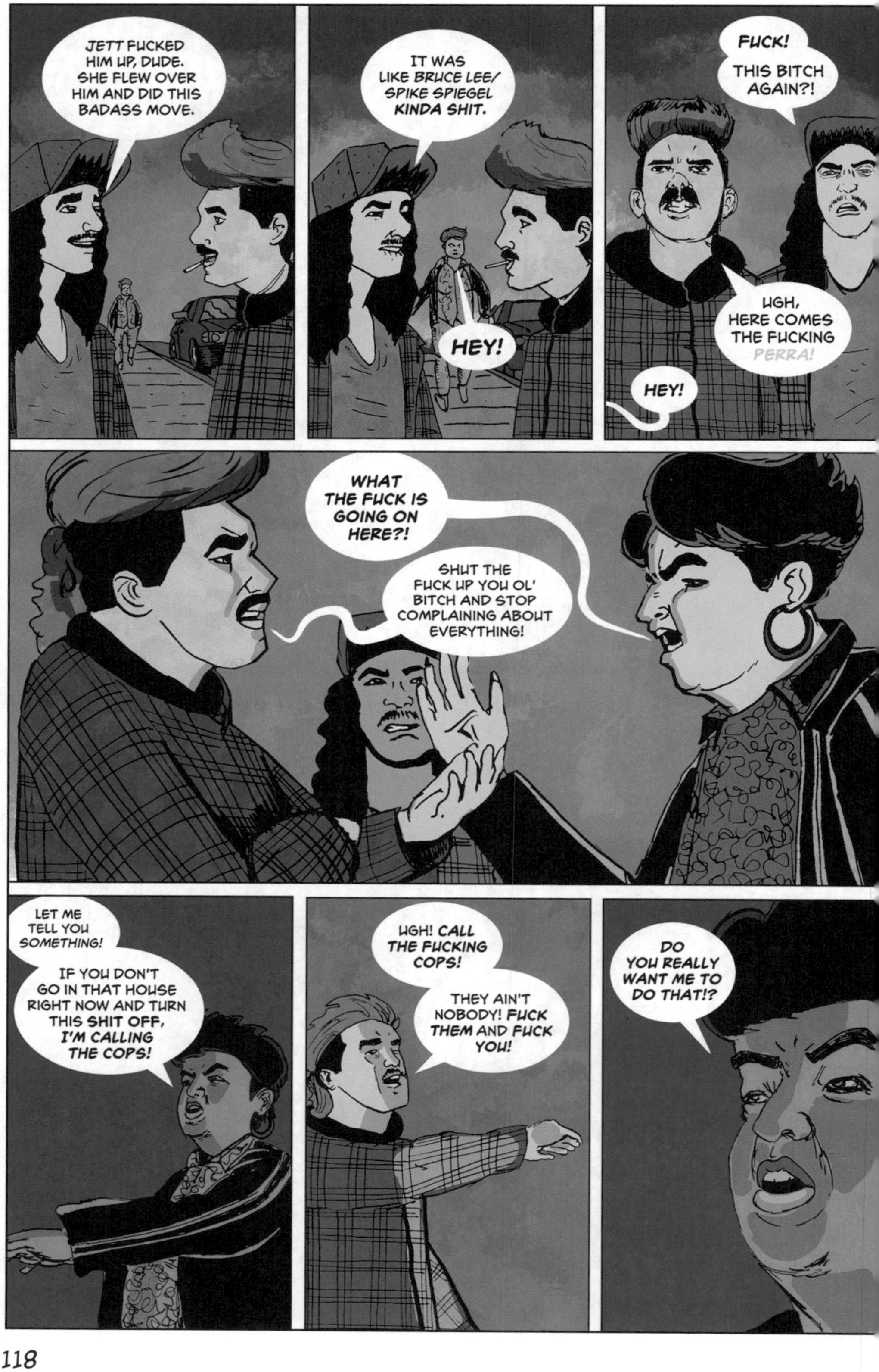

JETT FUCKED HIM UP, DUDE. SHE FLEW OVER HIM AND DID THIS BADASS MOVE.
IT WAS LIKE BRUCE LEE/ SPIKE SPIEGEL KINDA SHIT.
HEY!
FUCK!
THIS BITCH AGAIN?!
UGH, HERE COMES THE FUCKING PERRA!
HEY!
WHAT THE FUCK IS GOING ON HERE?!
SHUT THE FUCK UP YOU OL' BITCH AND STOP COMPLAINING ABOUT EVERYTHING!
LET ME TELL YOU SOMETHING!
IF YOU DON'T GO IN THAT HOUSE RIGHT NOW AND TURN THIS SHIT OFF, I'M CALLING THE COPS!
UGH! CALL THE FUCKING COPS!
THEY AIN'T NOBODY! FUCK THEM AND FUCK YOU!
DO YOU REALLY WANT ME TO DO THAT!?

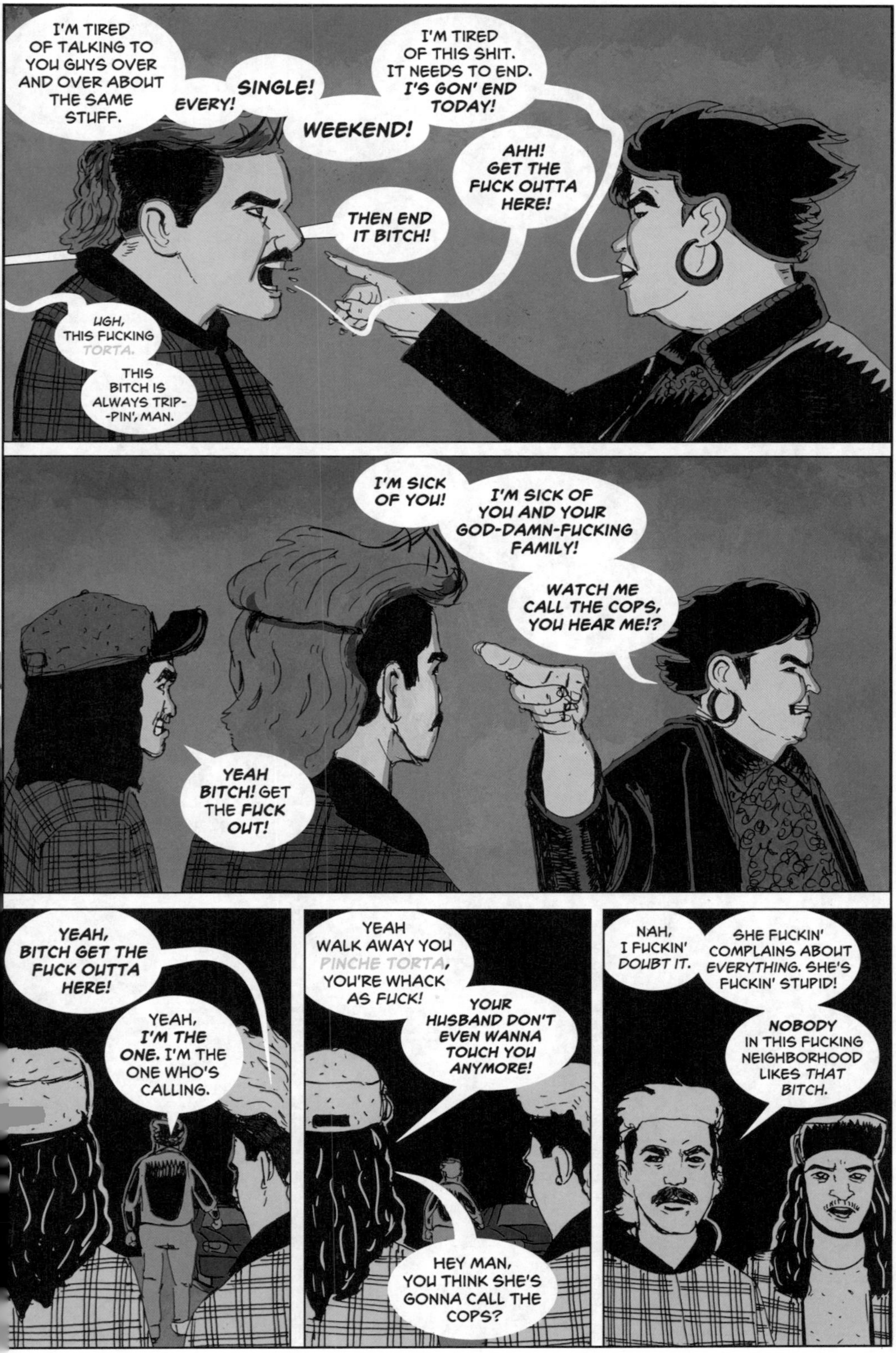
I'M TIRED OF TALKING TO YOU GUYS OVER AND OVER ABOUT THE SAME STUFF.
EVERY!
SINGLE!
WEEKEND!
I'M TIRED OF THIS SHIT. IT NEEDS TO END. I'S GON' END TODAY!
AHH! GET THE FUCK OUTTA HERE!
THEN END IT BITCH!
UGH, THIS FUCKING TORTA.
THIS BITCH IS ALWAYS TRIP-PIN', MAN.
I'M SICK OF YOU!
I'M SICK OF YOU AND YOUR GOD-DAMN-FUCKING FAMILY!
WATCH ME CALL THE COPS, YOU HEAR ME!?
YEAH BITCH! GET THE FUCK OUT!
YEAH, BITCH GET THE FUCK OUTTA HERE!
YEAH, I'M THE ONE. I'M THE ONE WHO'S CALLING.
YEAH WALK AWAY YOU PINCHE TORTA, YOU'RE WHACK AS FUCK!
YOUR HUSBAND DON'T EVEN WANNA TOUCH YOU ANYMORE!
HEY MAN, YOU THINK SHE'S GONNA CALL THE COPS?
NAH, I FUCKIN' DOUBT IT.
SHE FUCKIN' COMPLAINS ABOUT EVERYTHING. SHE'S FUCKIN' STUPID!
NOBODY IN THIS FUCKING NEIGHBORHOOD LIKES THAT BITCH.

Back Inside
THE SHOW

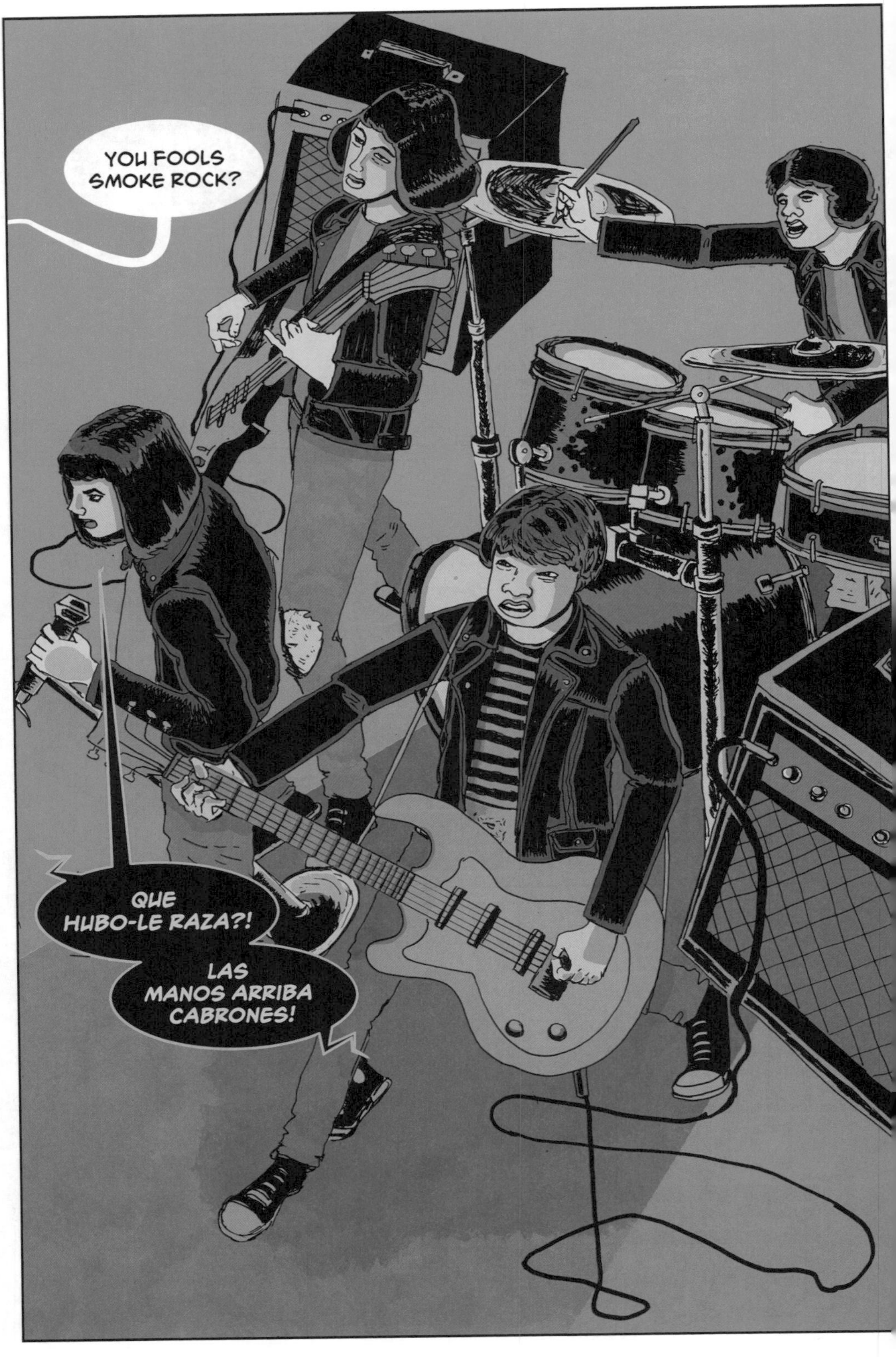
YOU FOOLS SMOKE ROCK?
QUE HUBO-LE RAZA?!
LAS MANOS ARRIBA CABRONES!

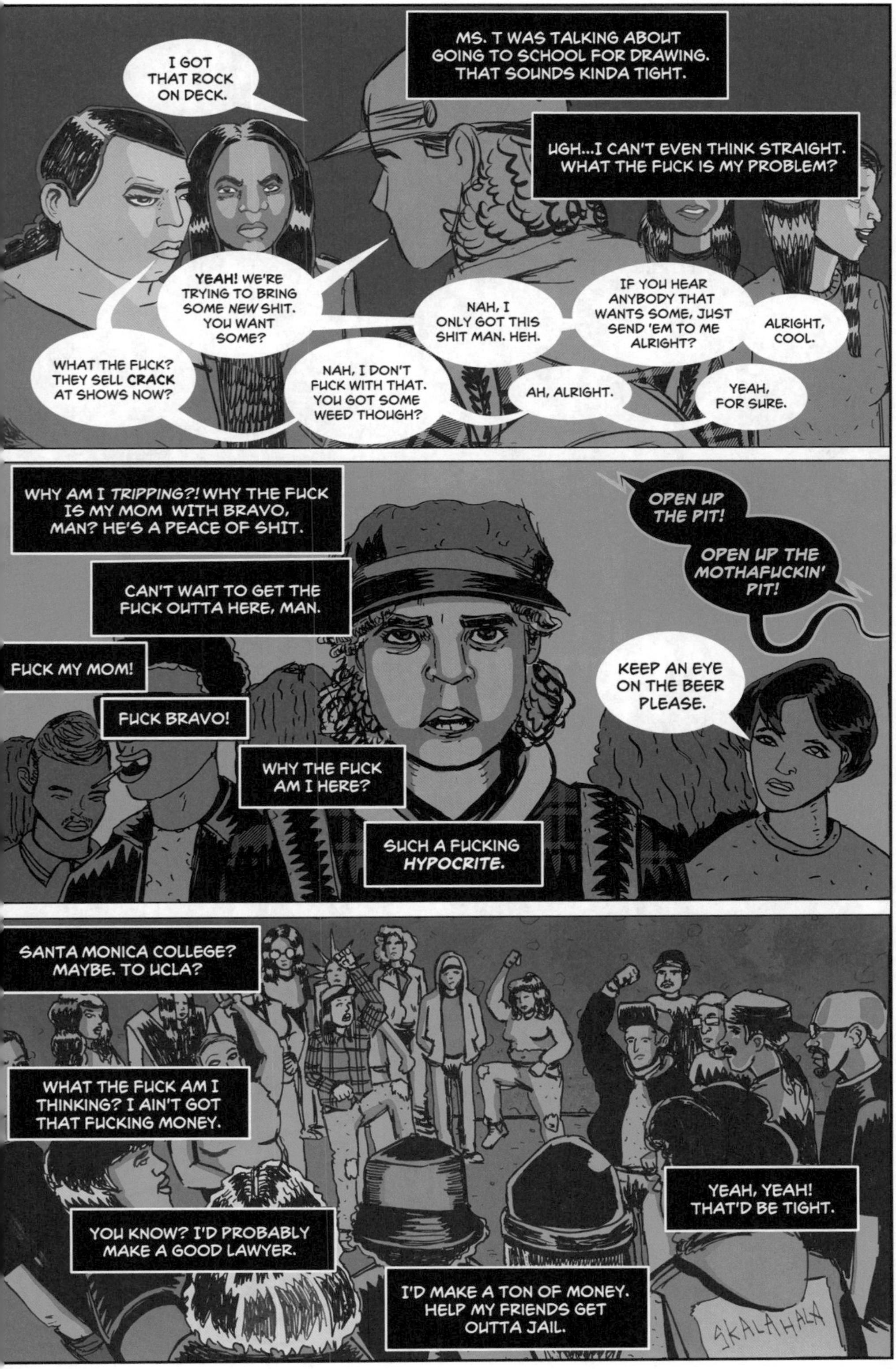

MS. T WAS TALKING ABOUT GOING TO SCHOOL FOR DRAWING. THAT SOUNDS KINDA TIGHT.
I GOT THAT ROCK ON DECK.
UGH...I CAN'T EVEN THINK STRAIGHT. WHAT THE FUCK IS MY PROBLEM?
YEAH! WE'RE TRYING TO BRING SOME *NEW* SHIT. YOU WANT SOME?
WHAT THE FUCK? THEY SELL **CRACK** AT SHOWS NOW?
NAH, I DON'T FUCK WITH THAT. YOU GOT SOME WEED THOUGH?
NAH, I ONLY GOT THIS SHIT MAN. HEH.
AH, ALRIGHT.
IF YOU HEAR ANYBODY THAT WANTS SOME, JUST SEND 'EM TO ME ALRIGHT?
YEAH, FOR SURE.
ALRIGHT, COOL.
WHY AM I *TRIPPING?!* WHY THE FUCK IS MY MOM WITH BRAVO, MAN? HE'S A PEACE OF SHIT.
CAN'T WAIT TO GET THE FUCK OUTTA HERE, MAN.
OPEN UP THE PIT!
OPEN UP THE MOTHAFUCKIN' PIT!
FUCK MY MOM!
FUCK BRAVO!
WHY THE FUCK AM I HERE?
KEEP AN EYE ON THE BEER PLEASE.
SUCH A FUCKING *HYPOCRITE.*
SANTA MONICA COLLEGE? MAYBE. TO UCLA?
WHAT THE FUCK AM I THINKING? I AIN'T GOT THAT FUCKING MONEY.
YOU KNOW? I'D PROBABLY MAKE A GOOD LAWYER.
YEAH, YEAH! THAT'D BE TIGHT.
I'D MAKE A TON OF MONEY. HELP MY FRIENDS GET OUTTA JAIL.
SKALAHALA

Meanwhile, Outside
THE SHOW

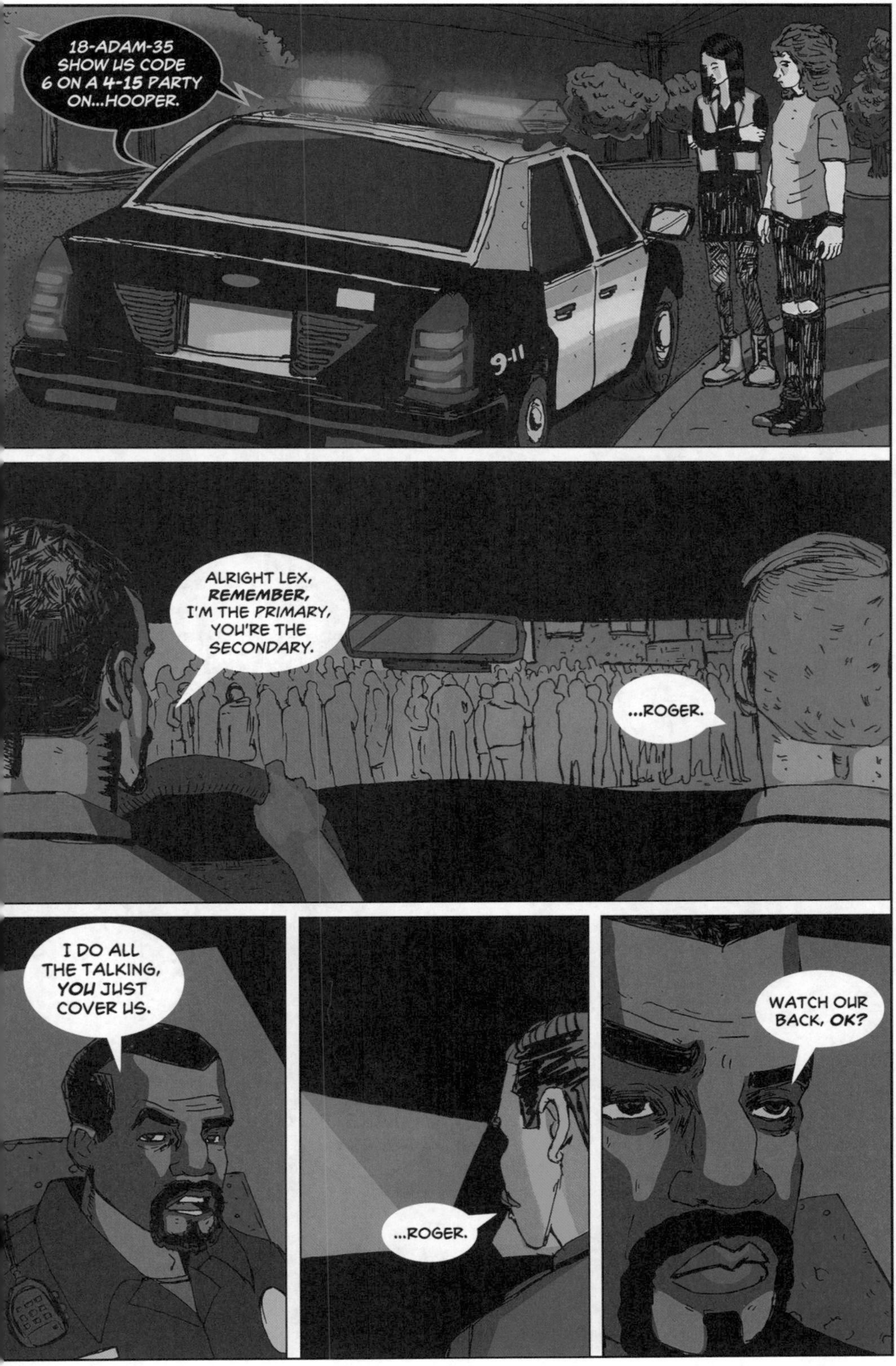

18-ADAM-35 SHOW US CODE 6 ON A 4-15 PARTY ON...HOOPER.
ALRIGHT LEX, REMEMBER, I'M THE PRIMARY, YOU'RE THE SECONDARY.
...ROGER.
I DO ALL THE TALKING, YOU JUST COVER US.
...ROGER.
WATCH OUR BACK, OK?

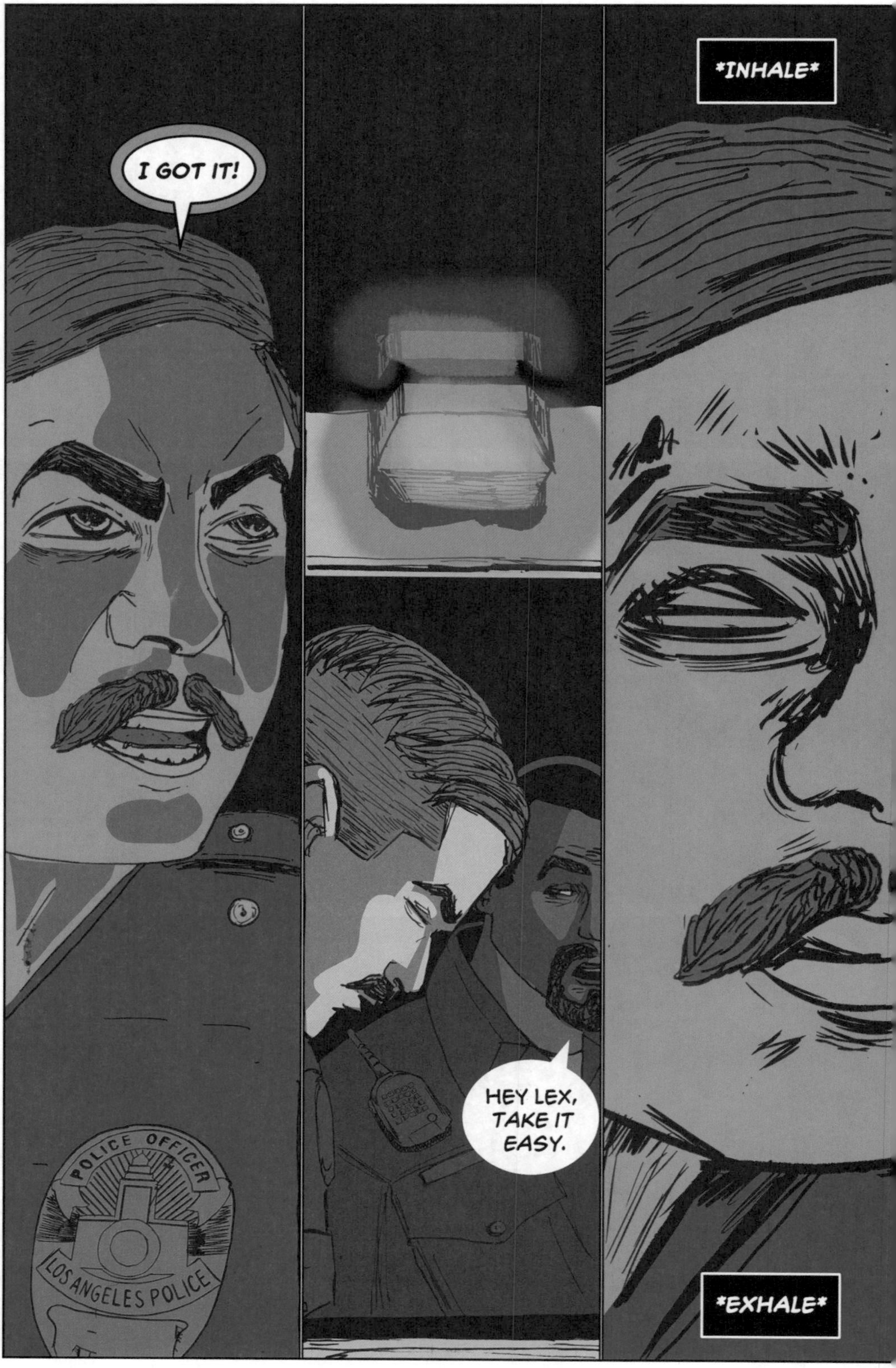
I GOT IT!
POLICE OFFICER
LOS ANGELES POLICE
HEY LEX, TAKE IT EASY.
INHALE
EXHALE

Back Inside
THE SHOW

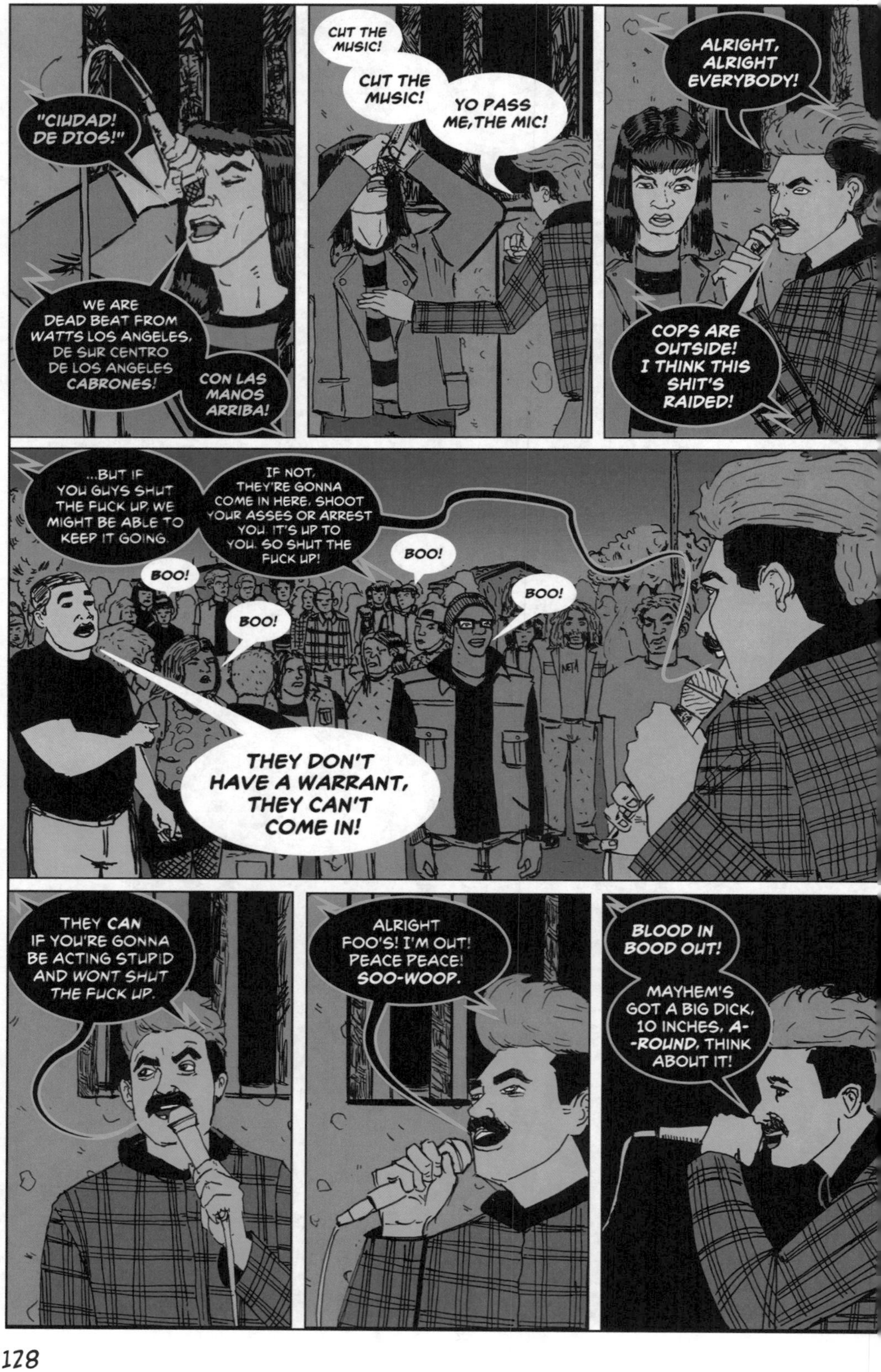
"CIUDAD! DE DIOS!"
WE ARE DEAD BEAT FROM WATTS LOS ANGELES, DE SUR CENTRO DE LOS ANGELES CABRONES!
CON LAS MANOS ARRIBA!
CUT THE MUSIC!
CUT THE MUSIC!
YO PASS ME, THE MIC!
ALRIGHT, ALRIGHT EVERYBODY!
COPS ARE OUTSIDE! I THINK THIS SHIT'S RAIDED!
...BUT IF YOU GUYS SHUT THE FUCK UP, WE MIGHT BE ABLE TO KEEP IT GOING.
IF NOT, THEY'RE GONNA COME IN HERE, SHOOT YOUR ASSES OR ARREST YOU. IT'S UP TO YOU. SO SHUT THE FUCK UP!
BOO!
BOO!
BOO!
BOO!
THEY DON'T HAVE A WARRANT, THEY CAN'T COME IN!
THEY CAN IF YOU'RE GONNA BE ACTING STUPID AND WONT SHUT THE FUCK UP.
ALRIGHT FOO'S! I'M OUT! PEACE PEACE! SOO-WOOP.
BLOOD IN BOOD OUT!
MAYHEM'S GOT A BIG DICK, 10 INCHES, A- -ROUND, THINK ABOUT IT!

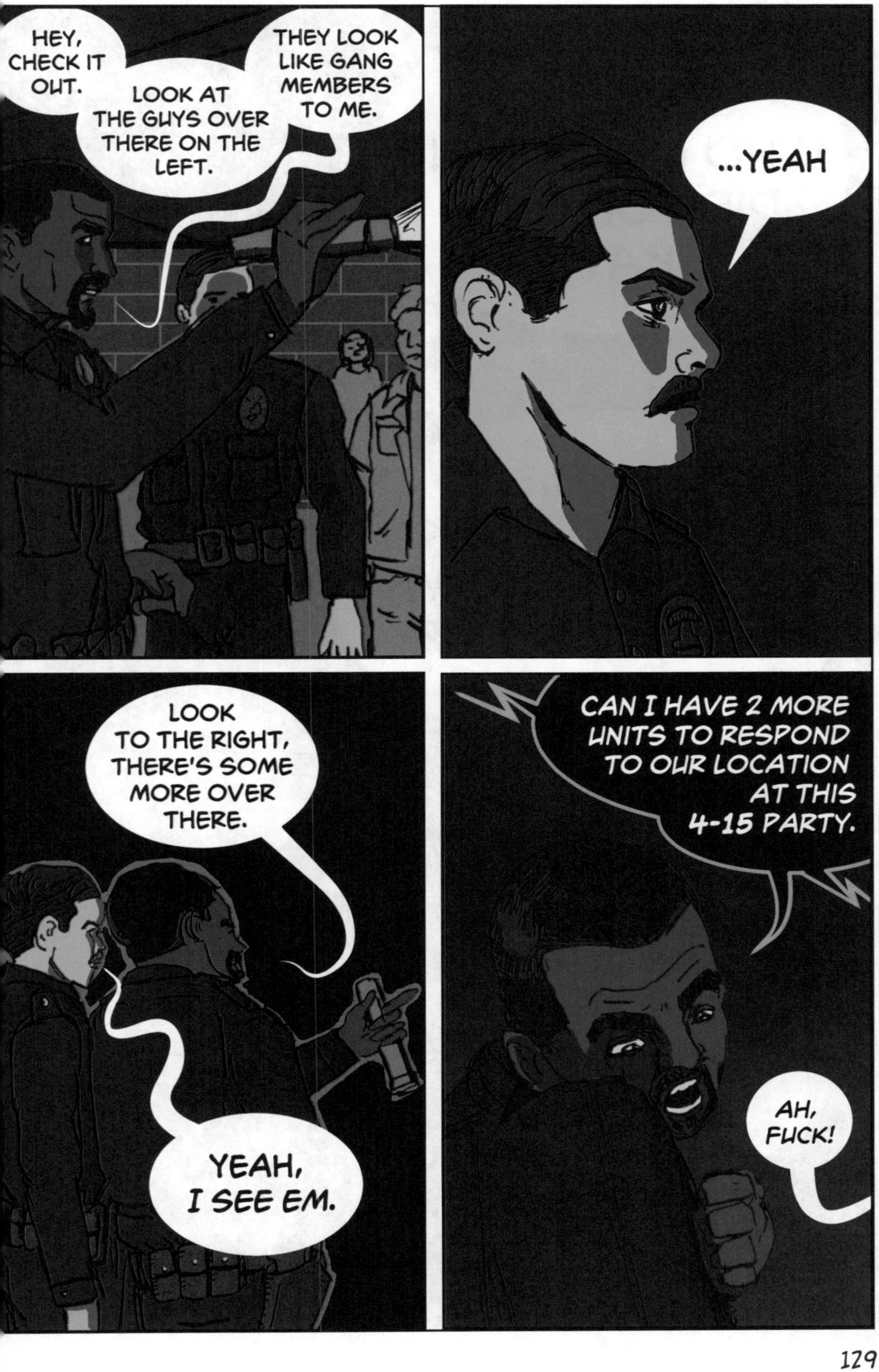
HEY, CHECK IT OUT.
LOOK AT THE GUYS OVER THERE ON THE LEFT.
THEY LOOK LIKE GANG MEMBERS TO ME.
...YEAH
LOOK TO THE RIGHT, THERE'S SOME MORE OVER THERE.
YEAH, I SEE EM.
CAN I HAVE 2 MORE UNITS TO RESPOND TO OUR LOCATION AT THIS 4-15 PARTY.
AH, FUCK!

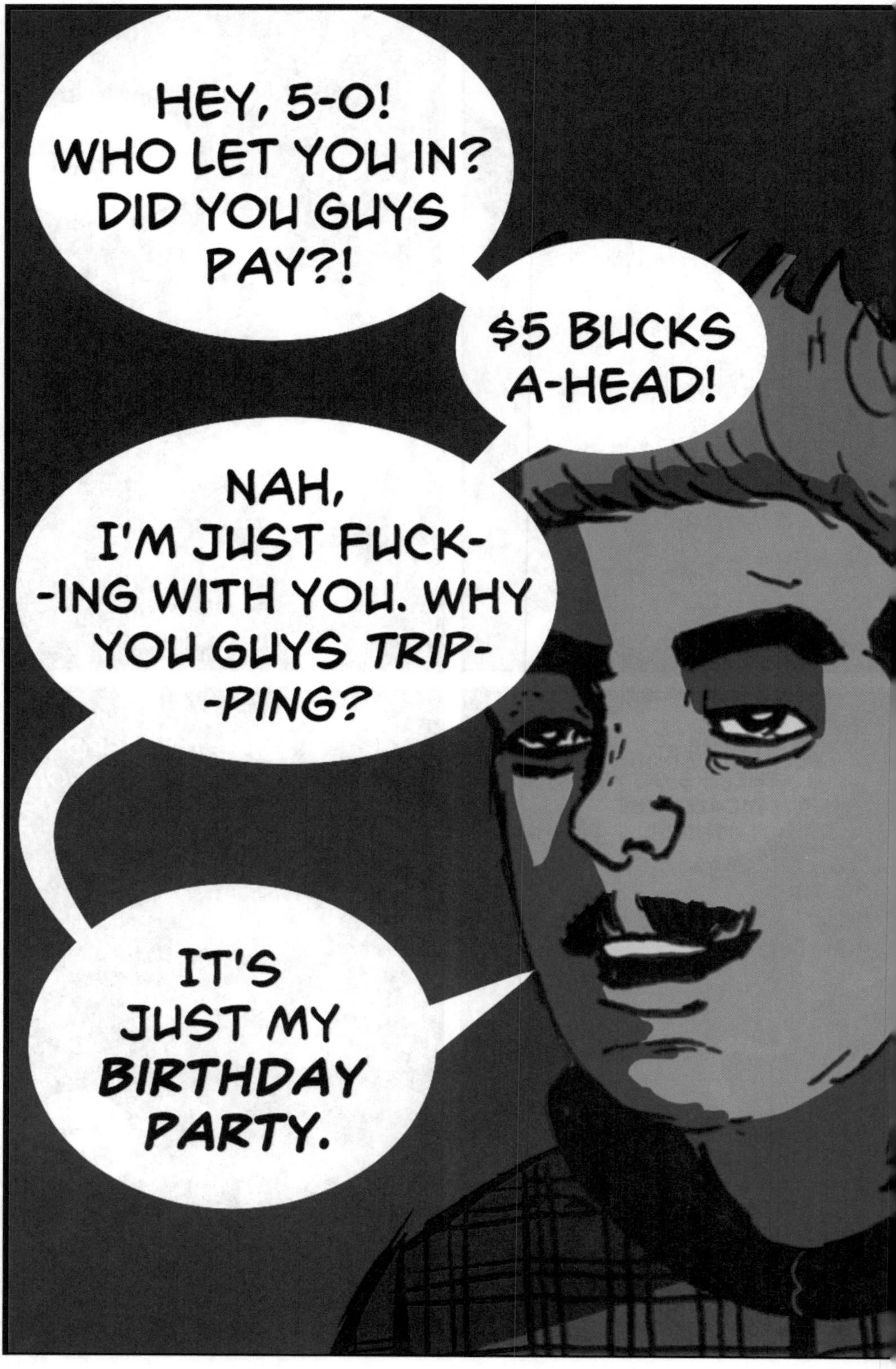
HEY, 5-O! WHO LET YOU IN? DID YOU GUYS PAY?!
$5 BUCKS A-HEAD!
NAH, I'M JUST FUCK-ING WITH YOU. WHY YOU GUYS TRIP-PING?
IT'S JUST MY BIRTHDAY PARTY.

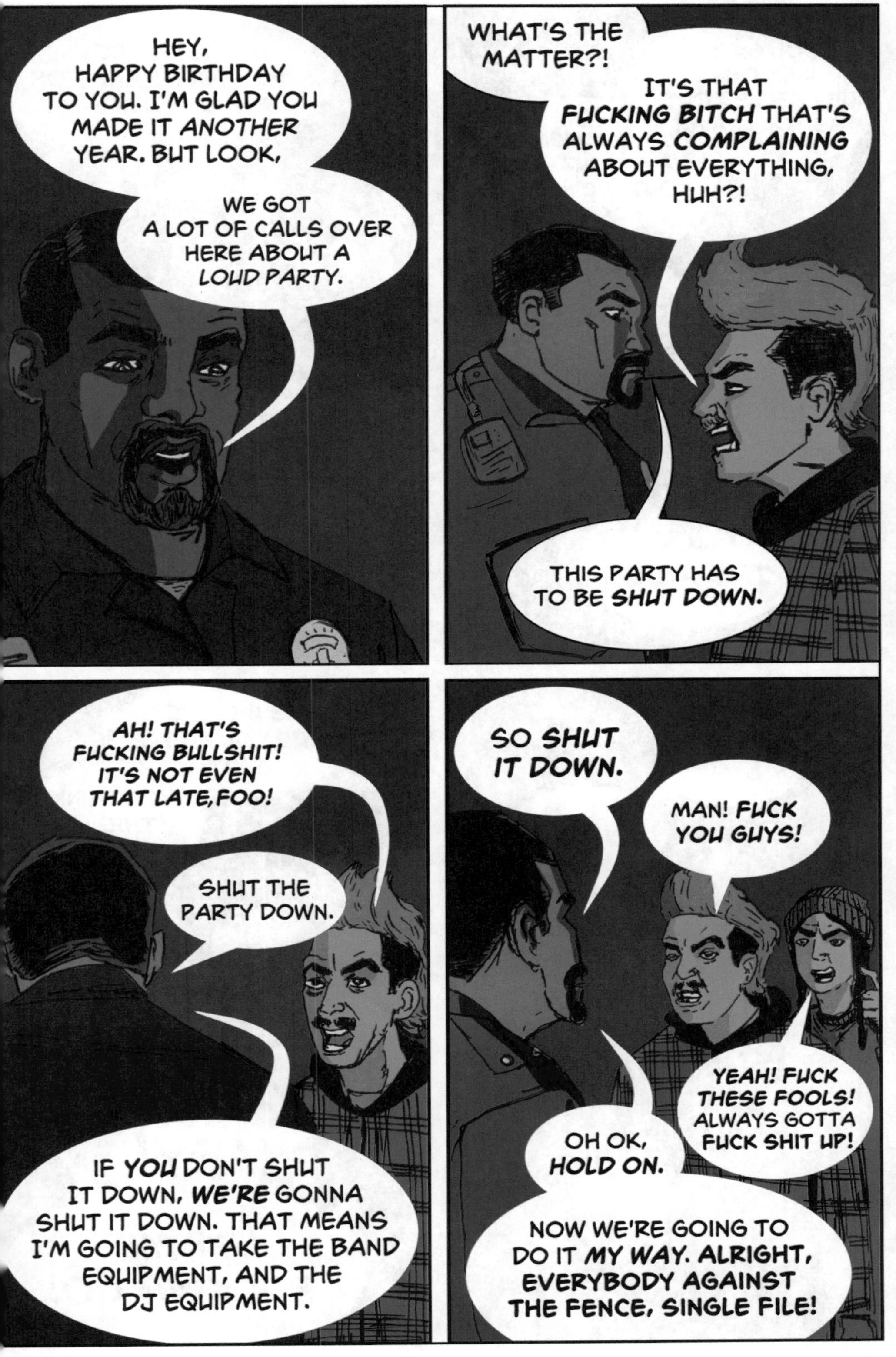
HEY, HAPPY BIRTHDAY TO YOU. I'M GLAD YOU MADE IT ANOTHER YEAR. BUT LOOK,
WE GOT A LOT OF CALLS OVER HERE ABOUT A LOUD PARTY.
WHAT'S THE MATTER?!
IT'S THAT FUCKING BITCH THAT'S ALWAYS COMPLAINING ABOUT EVERYTHING, HUH?!
THIS PARTY HAS TO BE SHUT DOWN.
AH! THAT'S FUCKING BULLSHIT! IT'S NOT EVEN THAT LATE, FOO!
SHUT THE PARTY DOWN.
IF YOU DON'T SHUT IT DOWN, WE'RE GONNA SHUT IT DOWN. THAT MEANS I'M GOING TO TAKE THE BAND EQUIPMENT, AND THE DJ EQUIPMENT.
SO SHUT IT DOWN.
MAN! FUCK YOU GUYS!
YEAH! FUCK THESE FOOLS! ALWAYS GOTTA FUCK SHIT UP!
OH OK, HOLD ON.
NOW WE'RE GOING TO DO IT MY WAY. ALRIGHT, EVERYBODY AGAINST THE FENCE, SINGLE FILE!

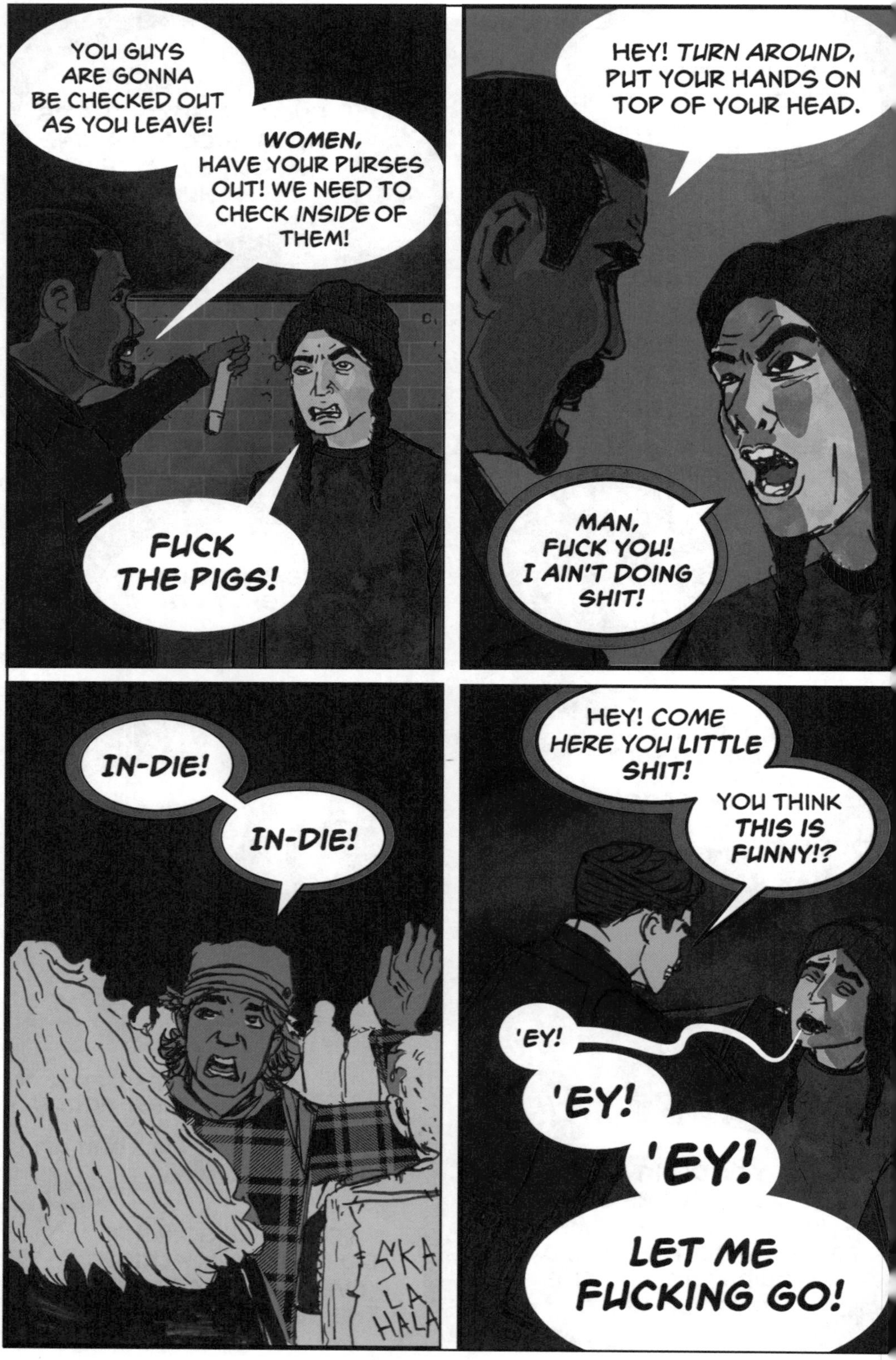
YOU GUYS ARE GONNA BE CHECKED OUT AS YOU LEAVE!
WOMEN, HAVE YOUR PURSES OUT! WE NEED TO CHECK INSIDE OF THEM!
FUCK THE PIGS!
HEY! TURN AROUND, PUT YOUR HANDS ON TOP OF YOUR HEAD.
MAN, FUCK YOU! I AIN'T DOING SHIT!
IN-DIE!
IN-DIE!
SKA LA HALA
HEY! COME HERE YOU LITTLE SHIT!
YOU THINK THIS IS FUNNY!?
'EY!
'EY!
'EY!
LET ME FUCKING GO!

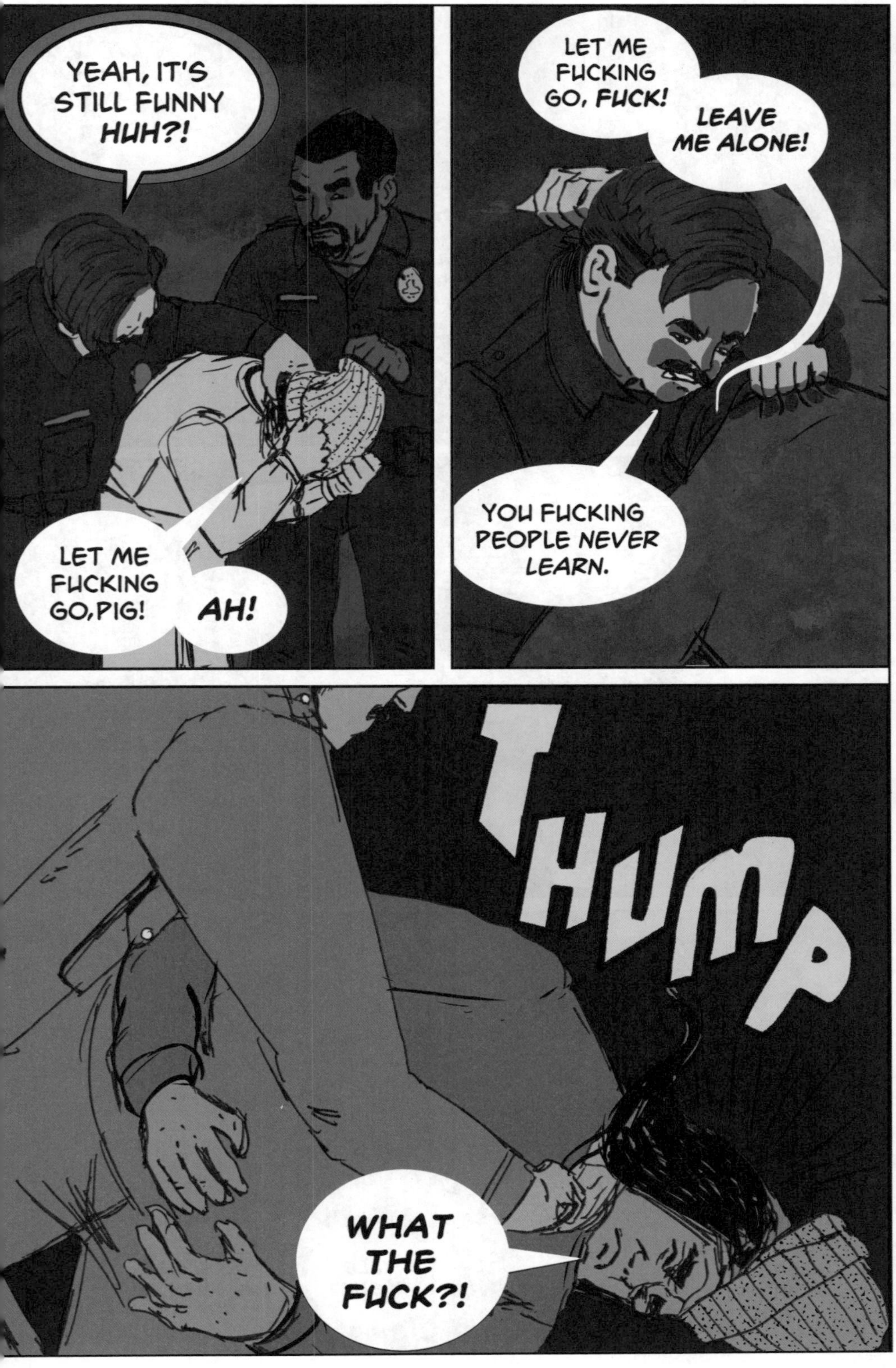
YEAH, IT'S STILL FUNNY HUH?!
LET ME FUCKING GO,PIG!
AH!
LET ME FUCKING GO, FUCK!
LEAVE ME ALONE!
YOU FUCKING PEOPLE NEVER LEARN.
THUMP
WHAT THE FUCK?!

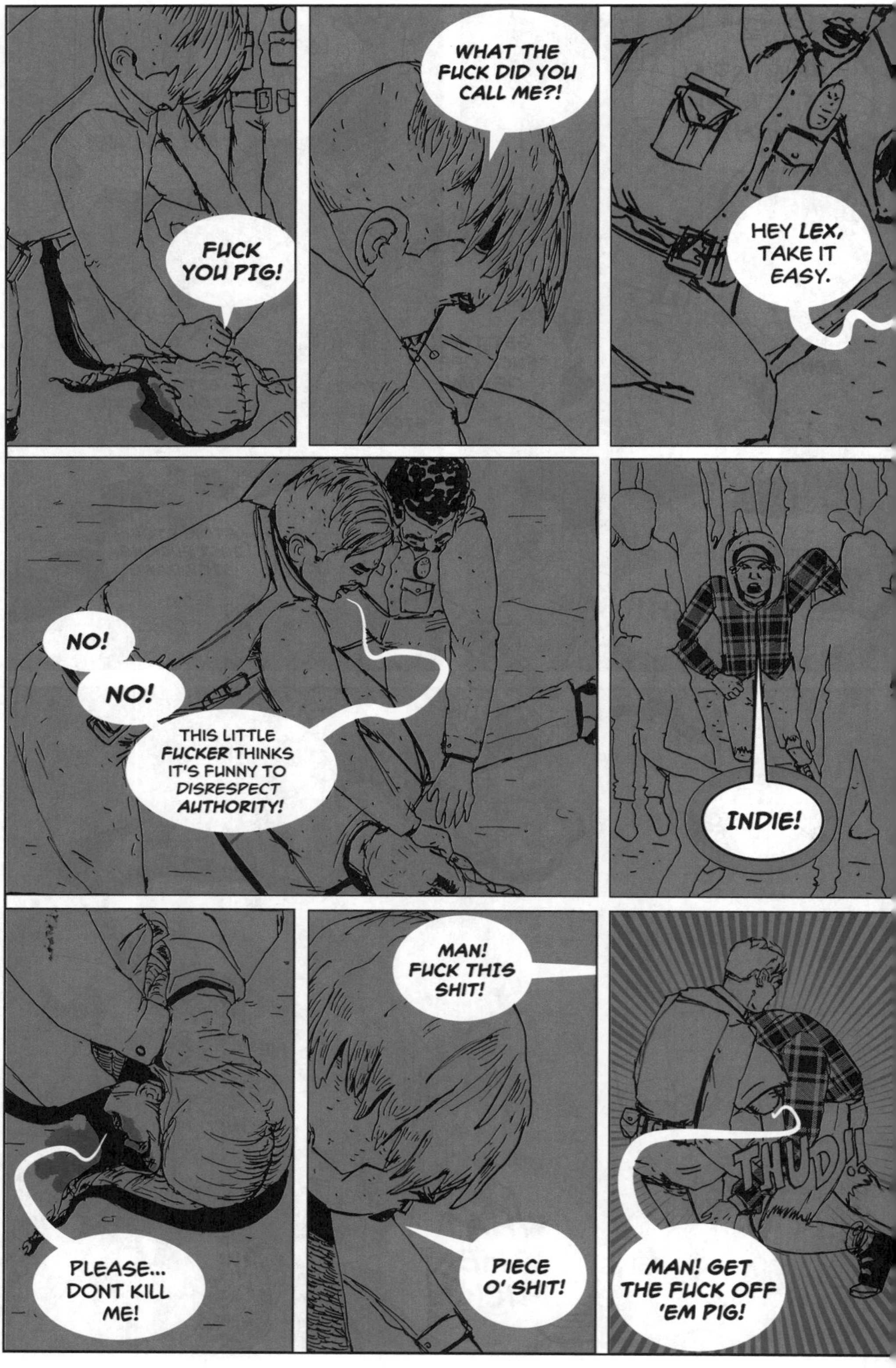
FUCK YOU PIG!
WHAT THE FUCK DID YOU CALL ME?!
HEY LEX, TAKE IT EASY.
NO!
NO!
THIS LITTLE FUCKER THINKS IT'S FUNNY TO DISRESPECT AUTHORITY!
INDIE!
PLEASE... DONT KILL ME!
MAN! FUCK THIS SHIT!
PIECE O' SHIT!
THUD!!
MAN! GET THE FUCK OFF 'EM PIG!

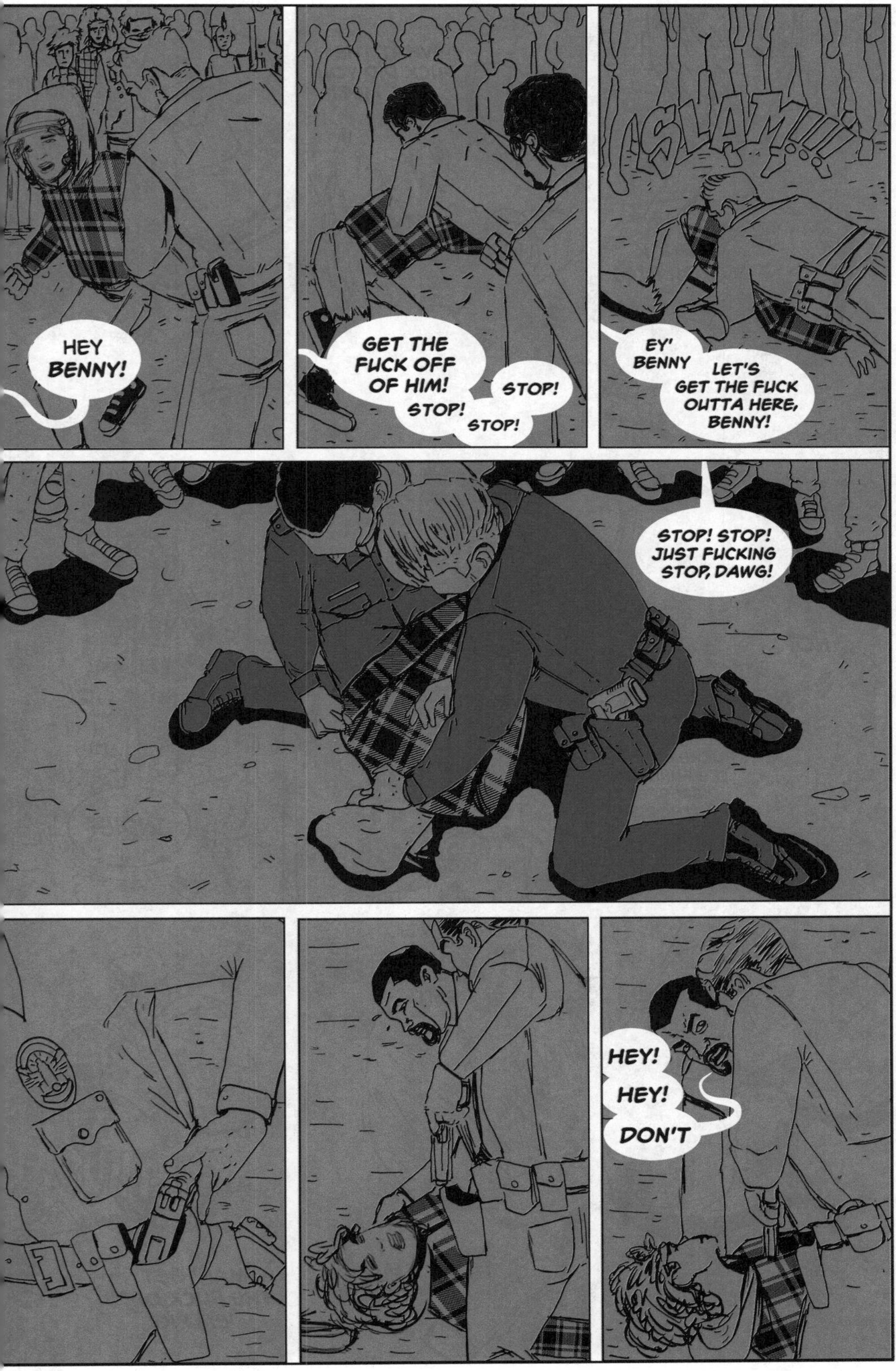
HEY BENNY!
GET THE FUCK OFF OF HIM!
STOP!
STOP!
STOP!
EY' BENNY
LET'S GET THE FUCK OUTTA HERE, BENNY!
STOP! STOP! JUST FUCKING STOP, DAWG!
HEY!
HEY!
DON'T

BLAH!

BLAH!

BLAH!

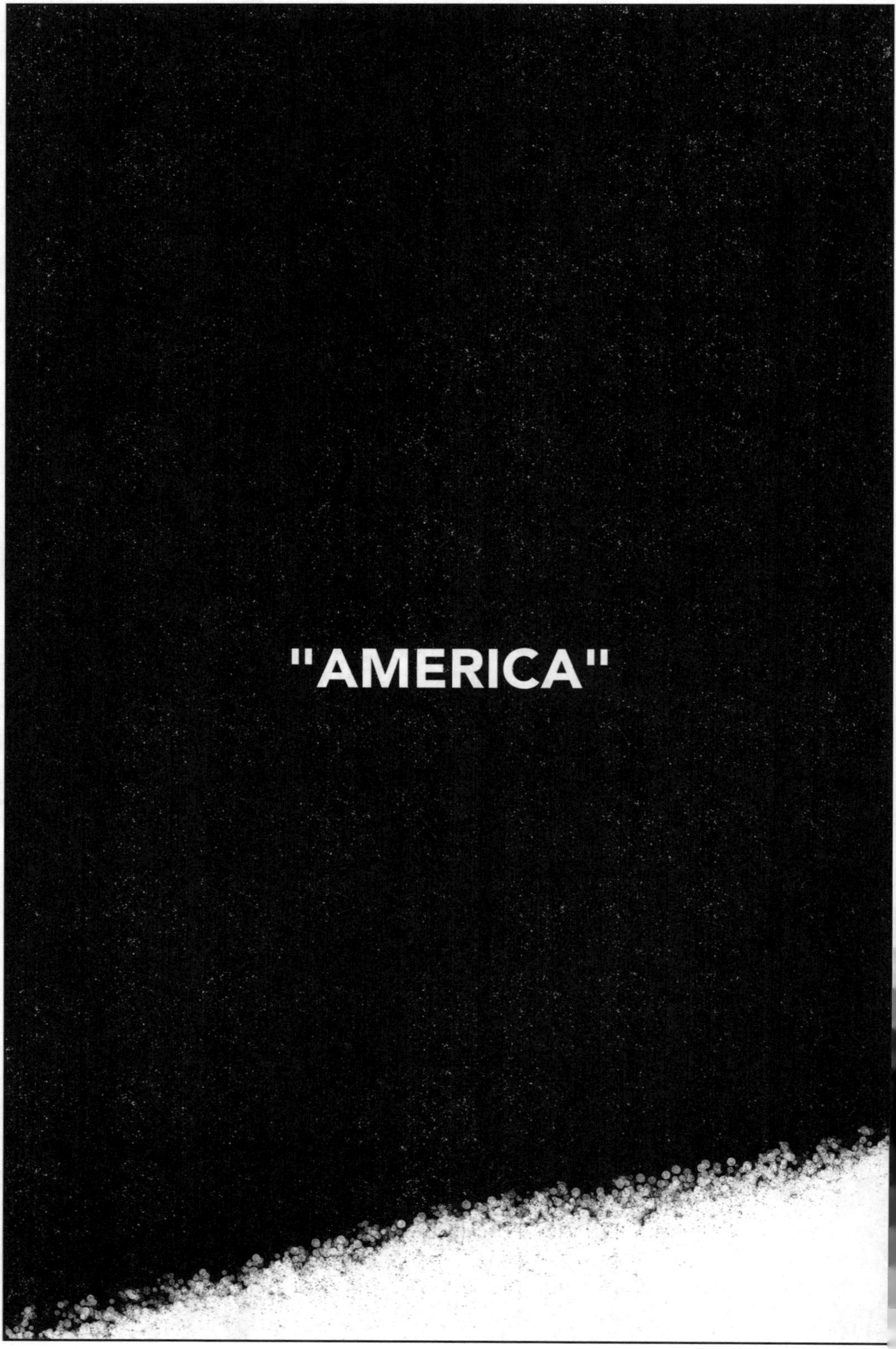
"AMERICA"

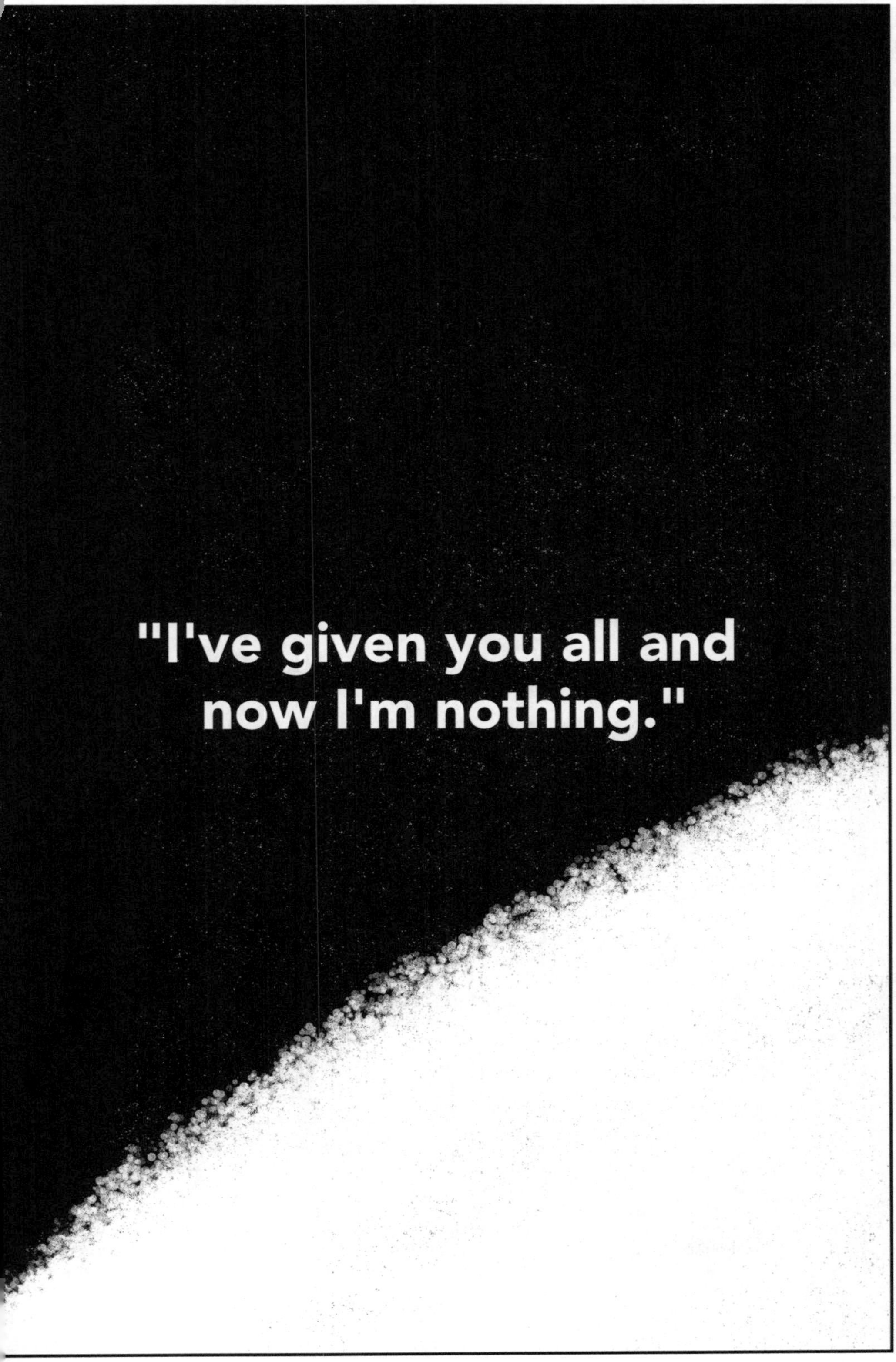
"I've given you all and now I'm nothing."

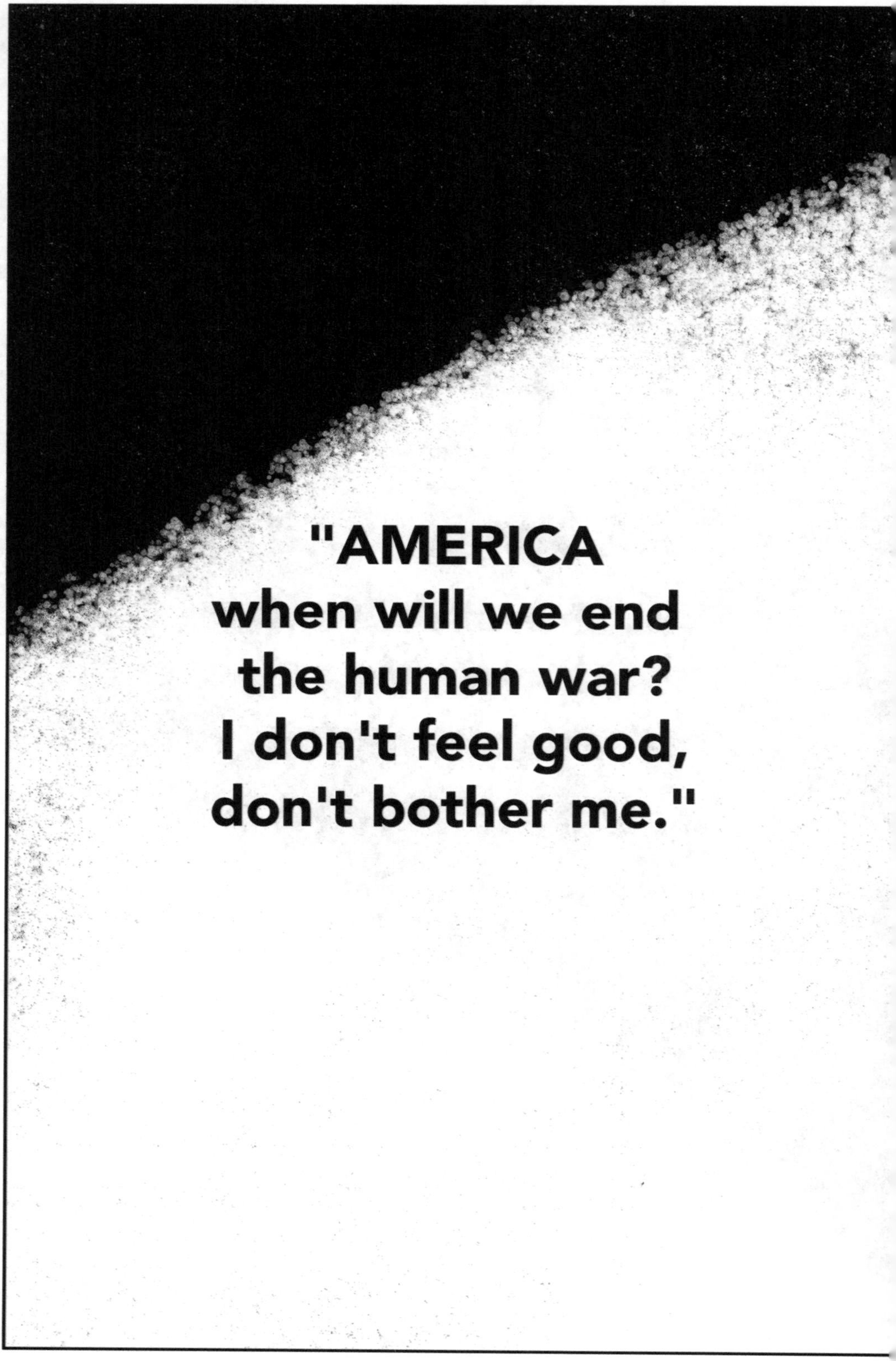
"AMERICA
when will we end
the human war?
I don't feel good,
don't bother me."

"AMERICA
when will you be
angelic?"

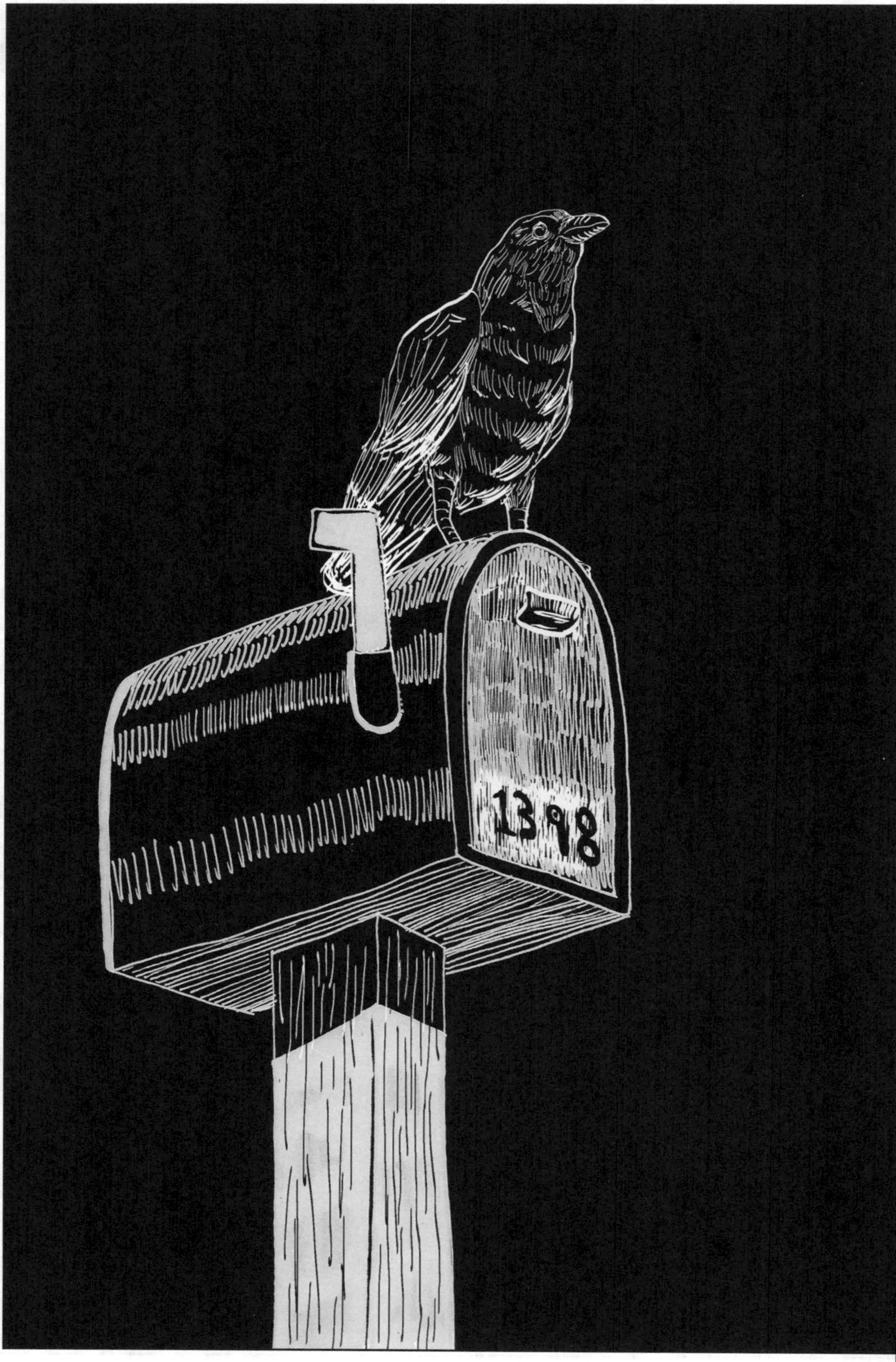
1398

1398 E. 109th Street

WATTS, CALIFORNIA. SATURDAY MORNING
EPILOGUE

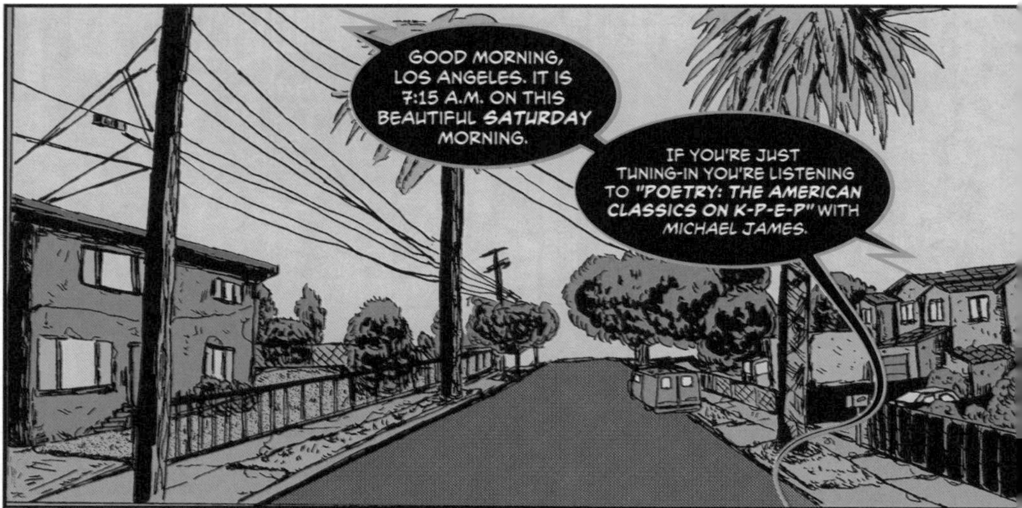
GOOD MORNING, LOS ANGELES. IT IS 7:15 A.M. ON THIS BEAUTIFUL SATURDAY MORNING.
IF YOU'RE JUST TUNING-IN YOU'RE LISTENING TO "POETRY: THE AMERICAN CLASSICS ON K-P-E-P" WITH MICHAEL JAMES.

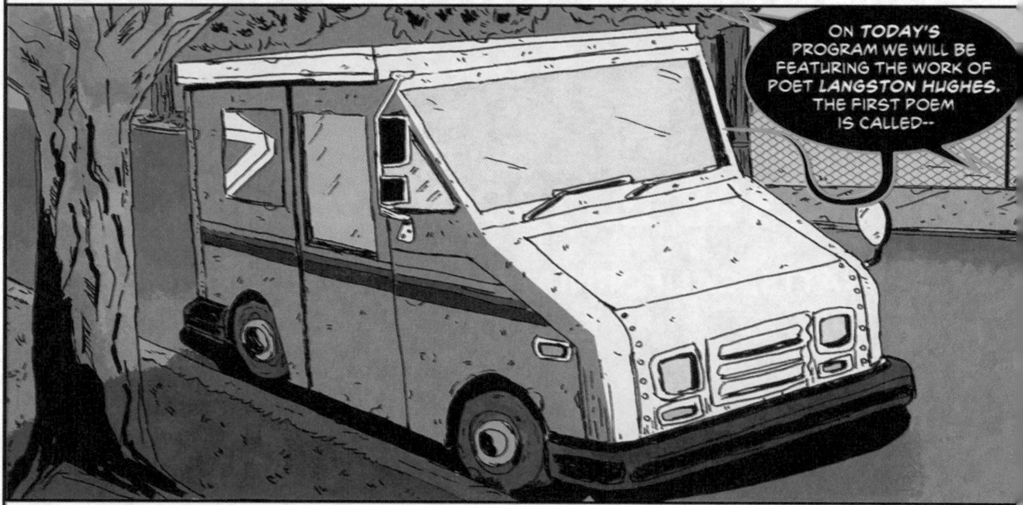
ON TODAY'S PROGRAM WE WILL BE FEATURING THE WORK OF POET LANGSTON HUGHES. THE FIRST POEM IS CALLED--

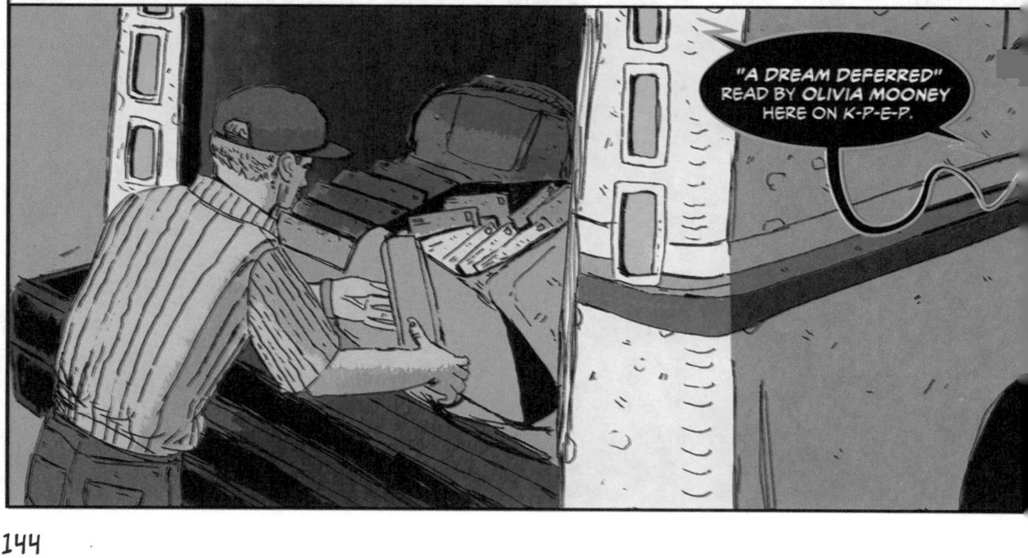
"A DREAM DEFERRED" READ BY OLIVIA MOONEY HERE ON K-P-E-P.

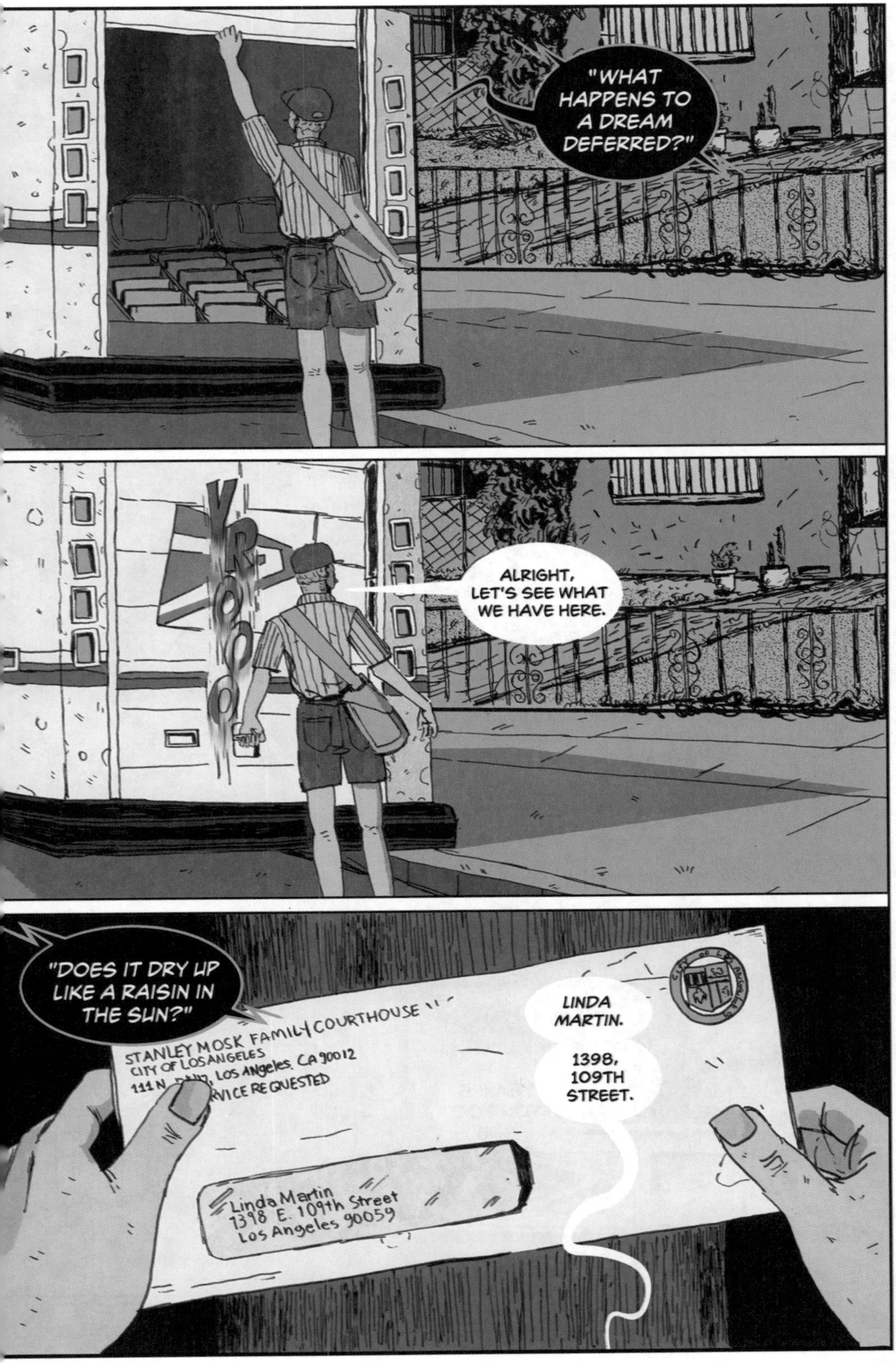

"WHAT HAPPENS TO A DREAM DEFERRED?"
ALRIGHT, LET'S SEE WHAT WE HAVE HERE.
"DOES IT DRY UP LIKE A RAISIN IN THE SUN?"
STANLEY MOSK FAMILY COURTHOUSE
CITY OF LOS ANGELES
LINDA MARTIN.
1398, 109TH STREET.
Linda Martin
1398 E. 109th Street
Los Angeles 90059

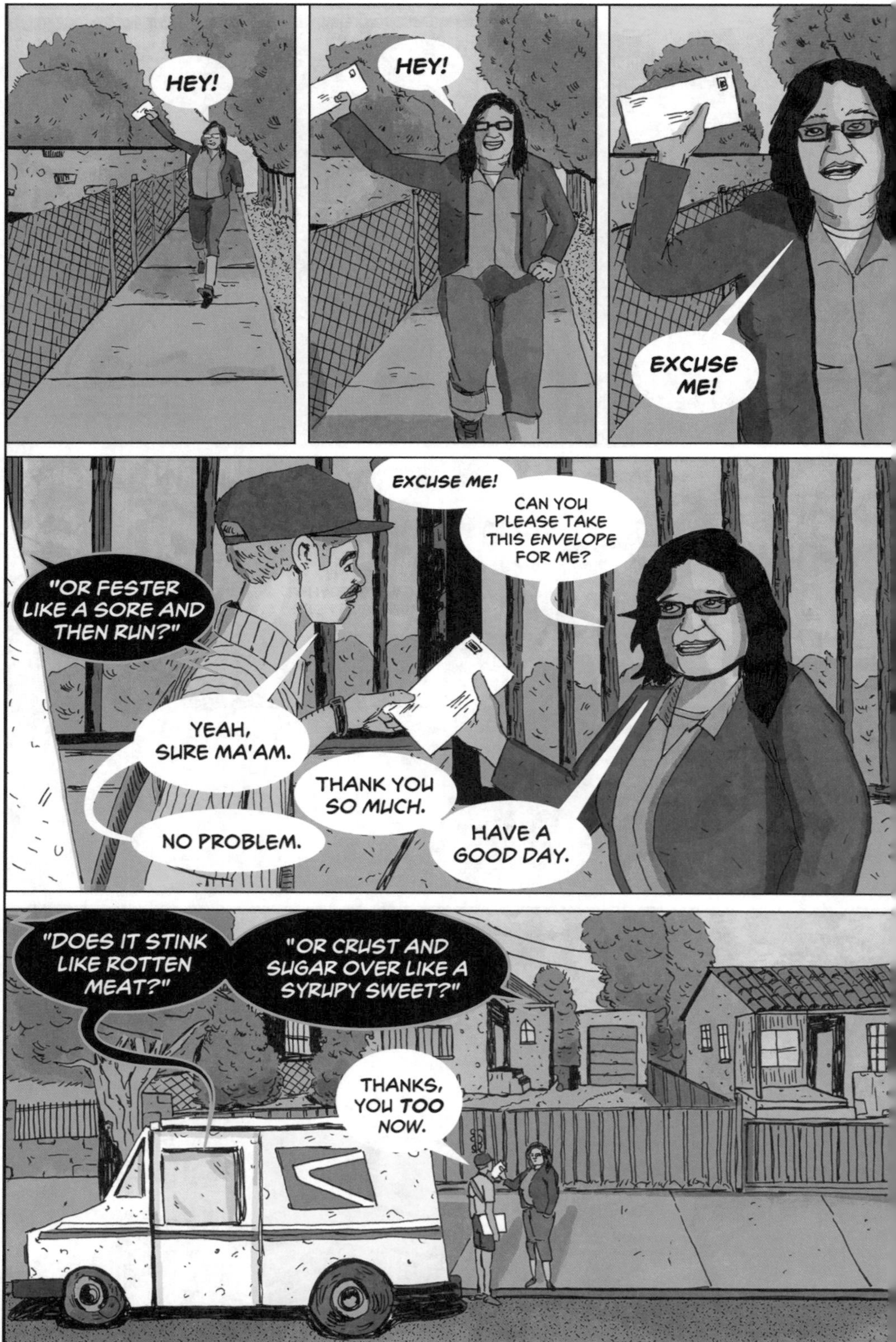
HEY!
HEY!
EXCUSE ME!
EXCUSE ME!
CAN YOU PLEASE TAKE THIS ENVELOPE FOR ME?
"OR FESTER LIKE A SORE AND THEN RUN?"
YEAH, SURE MA'AM.
THANK YOU SO MUCH.
NO PROBLEM.
HAVE A GOOD DAY.
"DOES IT STINK LIKE ROTTEN MEAT?"
"OR CRUST AND SUGAR OVER LIKE A SYRUPY SWEET?"
THANKS, YOU TOO NOW.

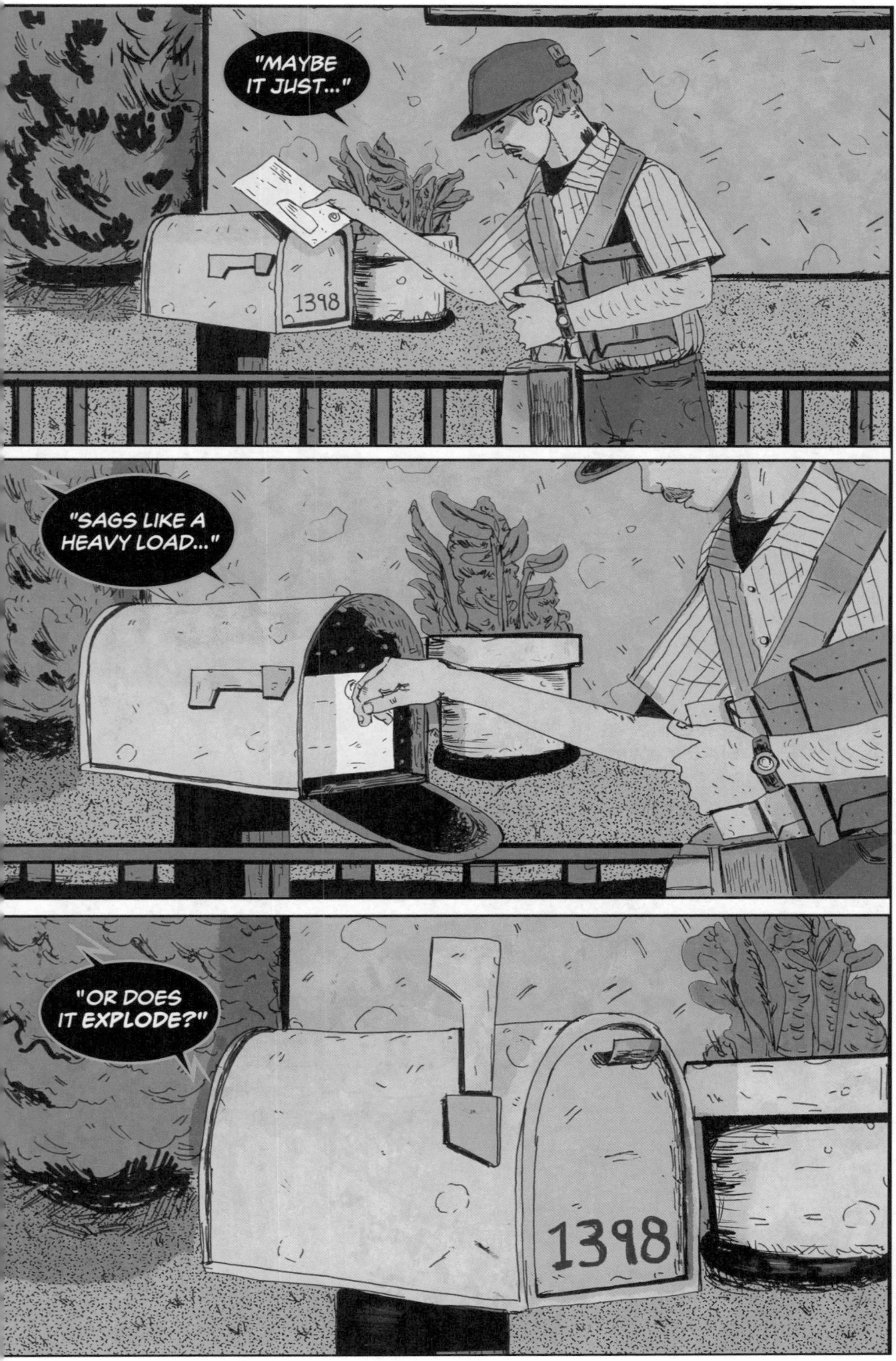
"MAYBE IT JUST..."
1398
"SAGS LIKE A HEAVY LOAD..."
"OR DOES IT EXPLODE?"
1398

WE'RE GONNA
CARRY THAT WEIGHT.

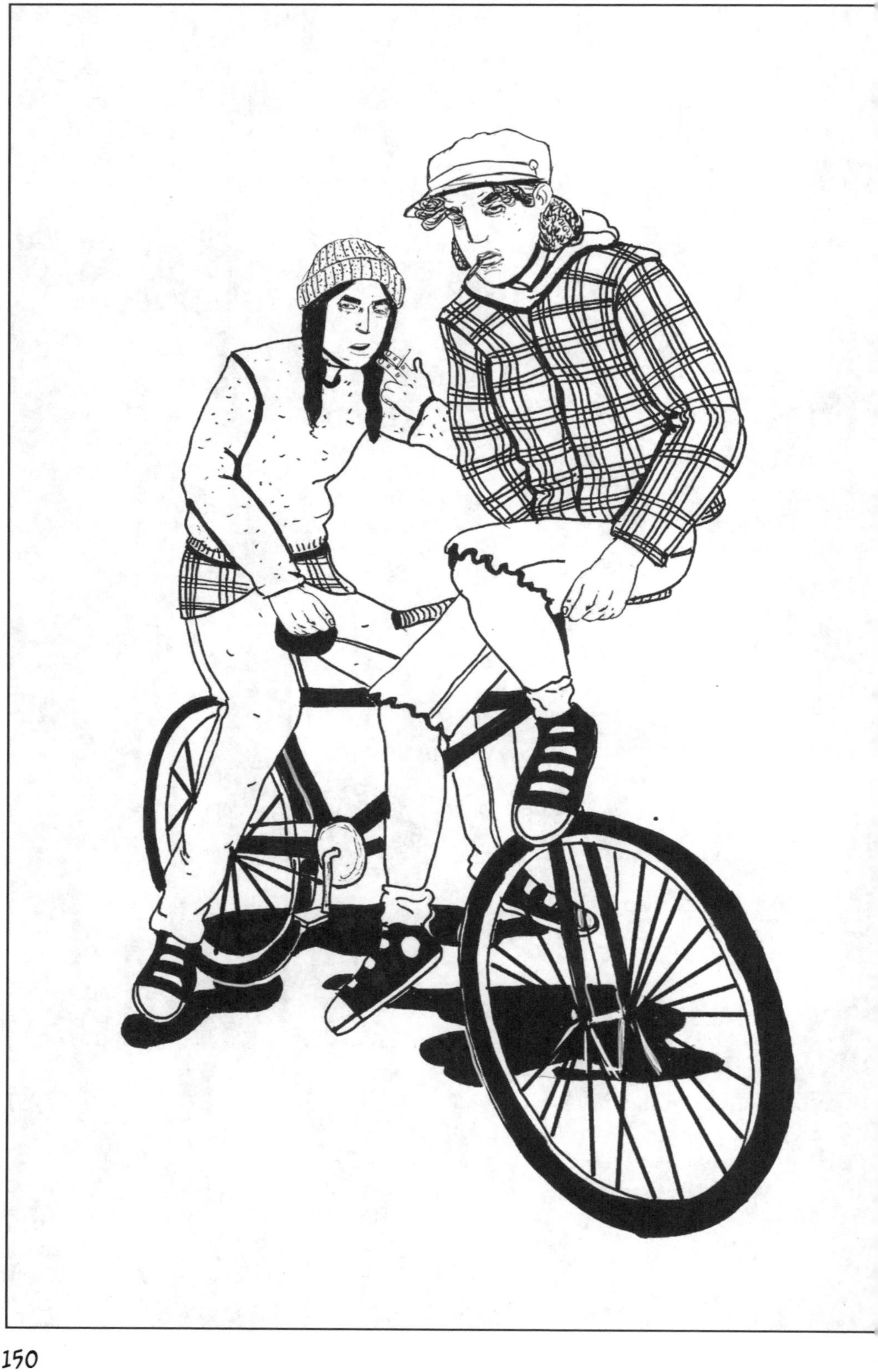

Making this book is a reaction to the death of many young men who die at the hand of law enforcement and proclaimed militias in America---Trayvon Martin's death in particular.

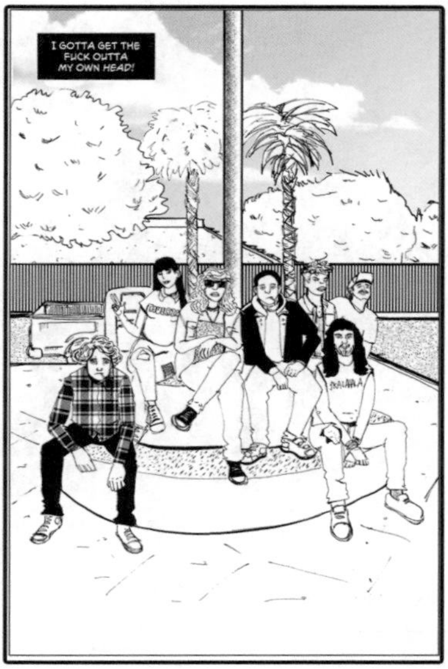
I GOTTA GET THE FUCK OUTTA MY OWN HEAD!

Growing up in Watts in what I call the "crack hangover," I knew the impact that police presence can have in a community where the very people they should be protecting become targets. As a skater in the early 2000s, I had a few encounters with police who loved harassing skaters and reminding us that *they* were the "biggest gang in LA." People like to think that crack cocaine was only an issue at the height of the drug war, but growing up in the time after it, I got to see how it destroyed South Central Los Angeles.

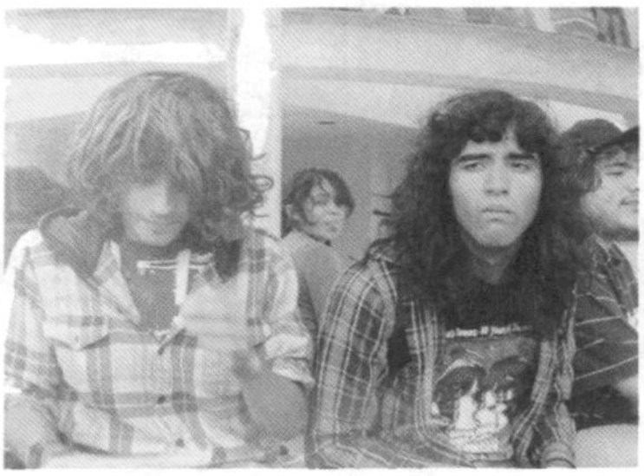

I understood then, on a surface level, that these heavy issues of gang violence and drugs forced cops to measure up to the tough streets of gang infested South Central Los Angeles. They too had been molded by these streets just like everyone else living there. The difference is that they had America on their side.

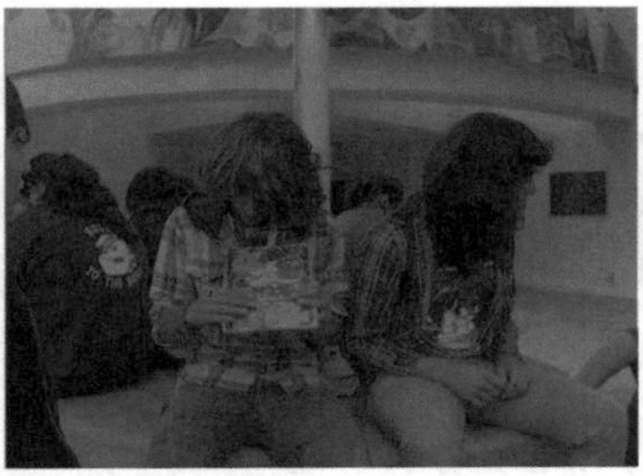

A seventeen-year-old African American teenager named Trayvon Martin was unjustly killed on February 26, 2012 in Sanford, Florida. When Trayvon Martin died, the reaction to his death was a paradigm shift for me. Some say this seventeen-year-old, hoodie-wearing kid deserved to die; "he was a thug, a gangster," they said. Trayvon Martin's death in 2012 was to me what Emmett Till's death was to many Americans in 1955; an affirmation of the unrestrained abuse of power used against people of color.

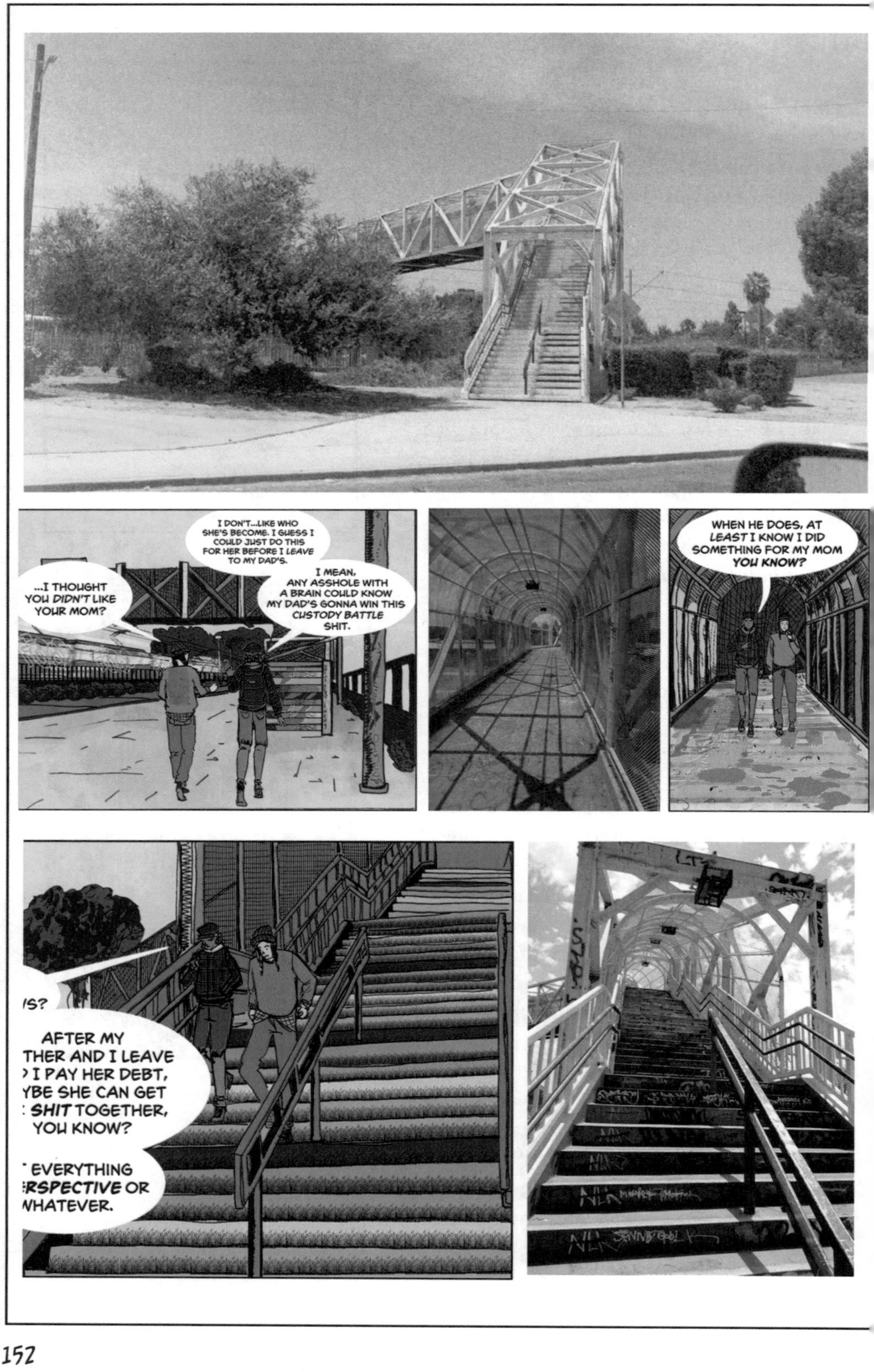
I DON'T...LIKE WHO SHE'S BECOME. I GUESS I COULD JUST DO THIS FOR HER BEFORE I *LEAVE* TO MY DAD'S.
...I THOUGHT YOU *DIDN'T* LIKE YOUR MOM?
I MEAN, ANY ASSHOLE WITH A BRAIN COULD KNOW MY DAD'S GONNA WIN THIS *CUSTODY BATTLE* SHIT.
WHEN HE DOES, AT *LEAST* I KNOW I DID SOMETHING FOR MY MOM ***YOU KNOW?***
IS?
AFTER MY
THER AND I LEAVE
I PAY HER DEBT,
YBE SHE CAN GET
SHIT TOGETHER,
YOU KNOW?
EVERYTHING
ERSPECTIVE OR
WHATEVER.

I was twenty years old and thought I had a pretty good idea of how things worked with cops in this country. Look no further than Los Angeles in 1992 (LA Riots).

However, this was different. The more people decided to spin the situation with Trayvon into an invader-versus-crusader narrative, the more I watched people from my generation speak up against it. This level of unity was the impetus for the Black Lives Matter activist movement that functions as the new vanguard for disenfranchised African Americans.

The not-guilty verdict in the case of George Zimmerman shook me to the floor. It was a clear case in many people's minds that this man was guilty and should face the consequences for killing this young man. George Zimmerman set America up to do the right thing and show us all that it had learned from its bad judgment in the past; it didn't.

It put me in Trayvon's shoes. It made me think I, and especially my close friends from the neighborhood, could suffer the same fate. We, as non-white people have no control of the lens that dominant culture uses to profile us. And historically speaking, whichever one they've chosen is usually used to condemn us. It motivated me to make this book. It moved me to use the love I have for the medium of comics to invite you to view the nuanced realities of growing up in the hood.

It inspired me to use my experience, not in an autobiographical way, but in a textural way to express how an environment can greatly inform life's choices and decisions. My plan with this book was to open a window and show that things aren't as clear-cut and codified as dominant culture has perpetuated in media. It shapes whether Trayvon Martin is seen as the caricature of the "dangerous black hoodlum" or simply a young man walking down the street.

Windows are subtle in the book, but play a huge role for me both metaphorically and in life. They allow the reader to closely observe without interaction. This is problematic when the narrative is shaped by an outsider with bias. When outsiders try to tell our stories, it becomes voyeuristic and affirms the fears of the *other*. I wish this were mere hyperbole. As tour guide of The Watts Towers, it is common place to have guests ask if it's safe to walk outside because they've seen how dangerous Watts can be in movies like "Colors." Representation matters—it certainly matters.

I understand people make bad turns in life. What I'm interested in are *redemption* stories. Countless times I've had the opportunity to shake hands with reformed gang members of my community. Listening to stories of drug abusers turned drug counselors, I got the sense that any life can be altered for the better. This helped me understand that human lives are complicated and nuanced. Trayvon Martin's life was cut short by skewed media stereotypes. There was no redemption narrative available for that stereotype, only violent death or incarceration.

End

Special thanks to:
Harriet Bailey, My Dog Phoebe, Tio Chalio, Tia Guera. Jim Higgins, Pouya Afshar, Patrick Taylor, Daniel Rivera, Sherrie Lofton, Leobardo Rivera, Jerardo Rodriguez, Morgan Smith, Steven Marrero, Allyson Dixon-Duarte, Stefano Valentini and the Staff of the Watts Towers Arts Center Campus.

To my mother Elena Rivera for being the strong woman that she is and always doing her best to a steer a young man in the right direction, away from the temptations of the street.

"PEOPLE GENERALLY SEE WHAT THEY LOOK FOR,
AND HEAR WHAT THEY LISTEN FOR."
- HARPER LEE, TO KILL A MOCKINGBIRD

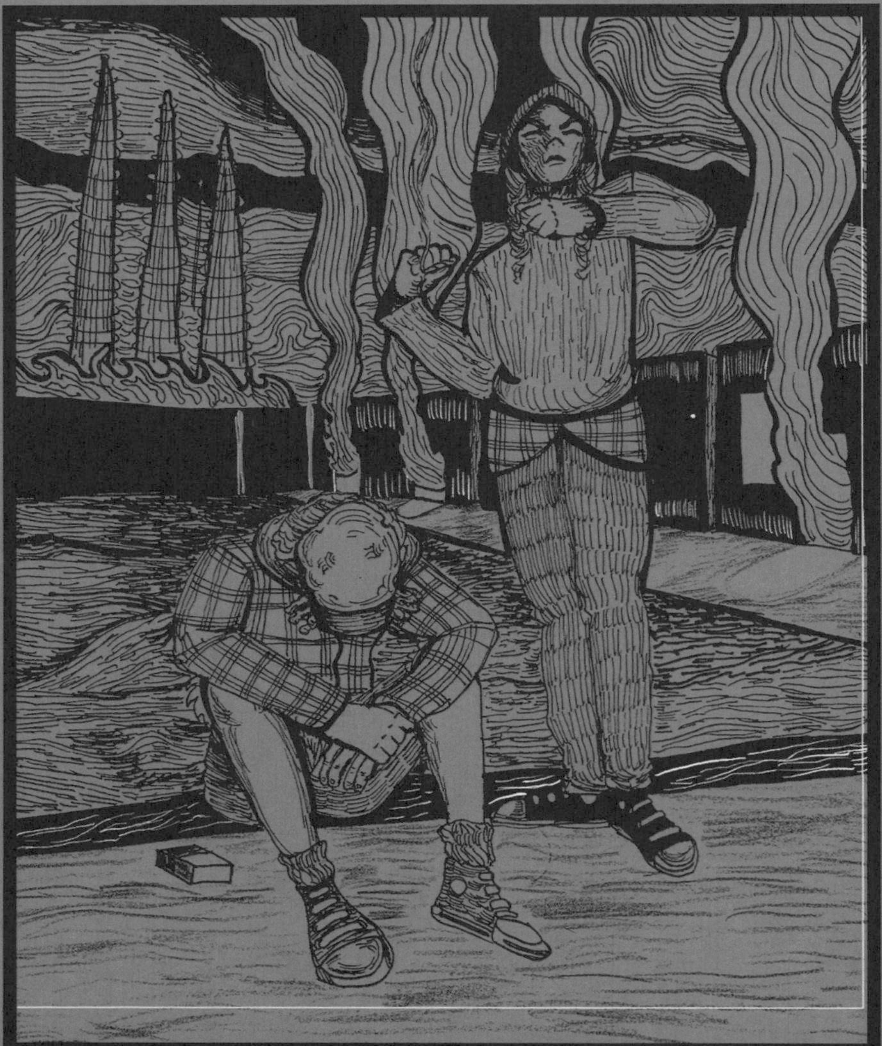

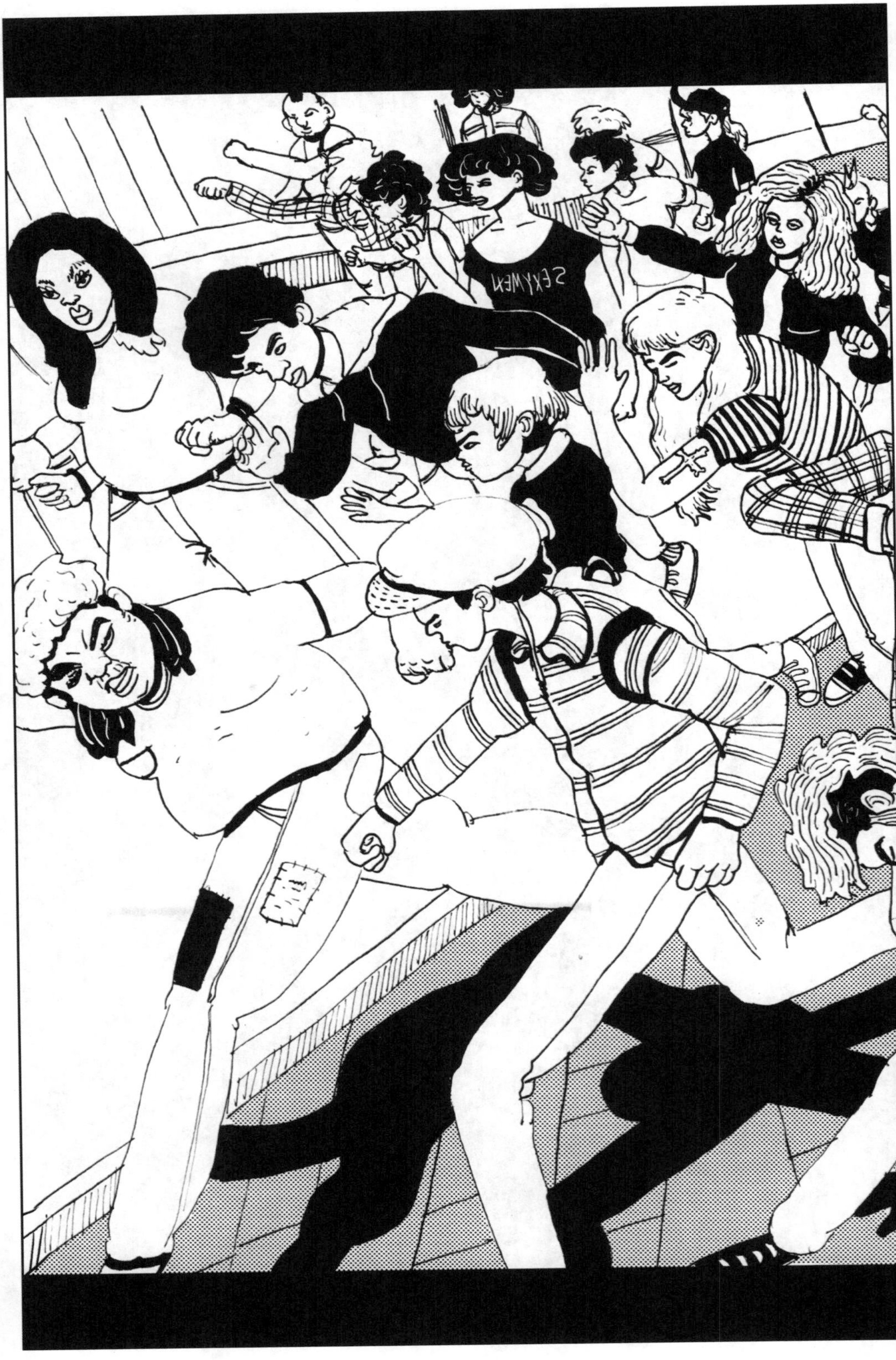
SEXYMEN

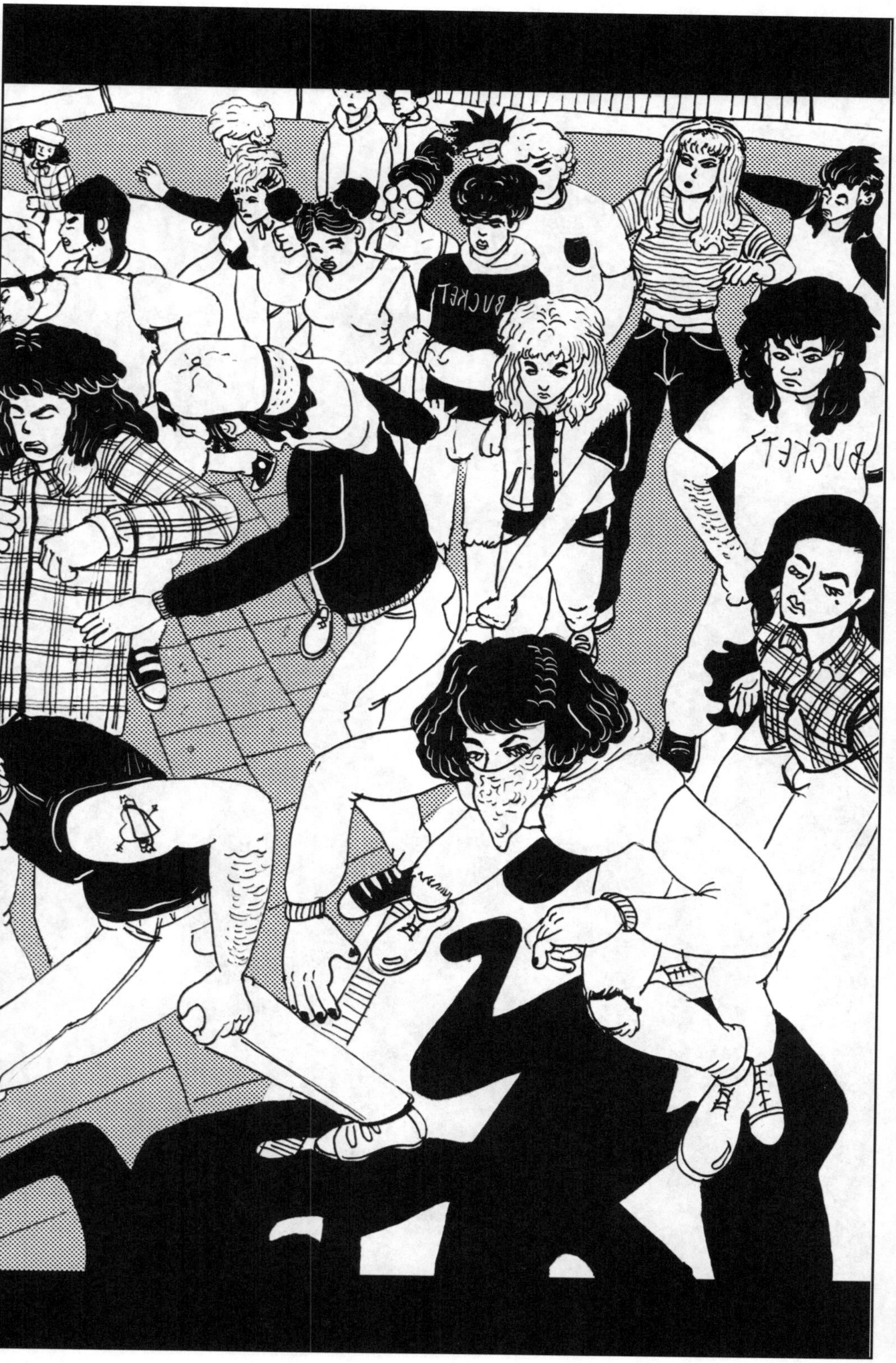